ORKING IN
OST-COMPULSORY
EDUCATION

011

WORKING IN POST-COMPULSORY EDUCATION

*John Lea, Dennis Hayes,
Andy Armitage, Laurie Lomas and
Sharon Markless*

OPEN UNIVERSITY PRESS
Maidenhead · Philadelphia

Open University Press
McGraw-Hill Education
McGraw-Hill House
Shoppenhangers Road
Maidenhead
Berkshire
SL6 2QL

email: enquiries@openup.co.uk
world wide web: www.openup.co.uk

and
325 Chestnut Street
Philadelphia, PA 19106, USA

First published in 2003

A catalogue record of this book is available from the British Library

ISBN 0 335 21105 4 (pbk)

Library of Congress Catagloging-in-Publication Data
CIP data applied for

Typeset by RefineCatch Limited, Bungay, Suffolk
Printed in Great Britain by Bell and Bain Ltd, Glasgow

CONTENTS

PART 1

Post-compulsory education in context

1

Overview: Post-compulsory education in context

John Lea

6 *Accountability and effectiveness in post-compulsory education* 101

Laurie Lomas

PART 3 Conducting research in educational settings 113

7 *Overview: Conducting research in educational settings* 115

John Lea

8 *The case for action research* 146

Sharon Markless

9 *The truths about educational research* 153
Dennis Hayes

PREFACE

This book is intended to be of interest primarily to practitioners in post-compulsory education and training (PCET) who may be undertaking a professional teaching qualification such as the PGCE/Certificate in Education, or a degree or masters qualification in post-compulsory education, or some form of continuous professional development. However, it is also hoped that it will be useful more generally to degree students in the social sciences who are interested in issues that have been raised in debates concerning contemporary post-compulsory education in the UK.

This book is designed to be a natural complement to *Teaching and Training in Post-compulsory Education* with a focus on issues *outside* the immediate classroom context (Armitage *et al.* 2003). It is not the intention that it should read as a comprehensive review of academic literature in the field; rather its aim is to draw readers into the broad nature of the debates which have taken place over the past 25 years. Hopefully this will encourage readers to undertake their own further reading, explore debates as they touch on their own professional practice, and, possibly, contemplate undertaking their own research.

Readers who may already be familiar with the broad nature of the debates might be directed to the more polemical pieces at the end of each part. The aim here is to reflect the contrasting views currently held by commentators and academics in the sector. All the authors have worked on teacher training programmes aimed at PCET practitioners and were asked to contribute to this book precisely because of the contrasting views that they hold on the various topics. Each part ends with a series of exercises and a 'question to think about' aimed at encouraging further engagement with the issues raised in that part.

I would like to thank my colleagues Helen Reynolds and Mandy

Renwick for reading and commenting on early drafts of the parts, and Carol Clewlow and Louise Tonkin for working on the manuscript and the bibliography.

John Lea
June 2002

ABOUT THE CONTRIBUTORS

Andy Armitage is Head of the Department of Post Compulsory Education at Canterbury Christ Church University College. He has previously worked in secondary, further and adult education. He has acted as a consultant on publications in vocational education, was seconded to the Further Education Unit to evaluate pre-vocational courses and has advised the Department of Employment on initial teacher education and advised several local education authorities on staff development. He is the editor of the companion publication *Teaching and Training in Post-Compulsory Education* (2nd edition, 2003).

Dennis Hayes is Coordinator of the Education and Work Research Group in the Centre for Educational Research at Canterbury Christ Church University College. A philosopher by training, his major research interest is the impact of vocationalism on all aspects of education. He is the author of several books and is currently completing *Defending Higher Education: The Crisis of Confidence in the Pursuit of Knowledge* to be published by Kogan Page in 2004.

John Lea is a Principal Lecturer in Education in the Department of Post Compuslory Education at Canterbury Christ Church Univesity College. He is currently the Director for the part-time Certificate in Education (Post Compuslory) programme and has over 20 years of experience of teaching in further, adult, and higher education. His research interests include political correctness in education and youth disaffection and education.

Laurie Lomas is Senior Lecturer in Higher Education at King's College,

London. Previously, he was a senior manager, lecturer and researcher in a business school. He entered higher education after 17 years in primary education, over ten of these as head teacher. His research interests include quality management in higher education and organizational culture.

Sharon Markless currently works as a Lecturer in the Institute of Learning and Teaching, King's College, London, and is also a freelance researcher, consultant and trainer. During her career she has been an education adviser for the Kent, Surrey and Sussex Deanery; a senior research officer at the National Foundation for Educational Research; and a teacher in schools, further education and prisons. Sharon has led several national research and development projects, and her publications include *The Really Effective College Library* (2000) (with David Streatfield) and *Best Value and Better Performance in Libraries* (2002) (with David Streatfield).

ABBREVIATIONS

AE	adult education
ALI	Adult Learning Inspectorate
AP(E)L	Accreditation of Prior (Experiential) Learning
AQA	Assessment and Qualifications Alliance
AVCE	Advanced Vocational Certificate in Education
BERA	British Educational Research Association
BERD	Business Enterprise, Research and Development
BTEC	Business and Technician Education Council
CAST	Center for Applied Special Technology
CAT	Credit Accumulation and Transfer
CBET	competence-based education and training
CPD	continuing professional development
CPVE	Certificate of Pre-vocational Education
CSE	Certificate of Secondary Education
DfEE	Department for Education and Employment
DfES	Department for Education and Skills
EAP	employee assistance programmes
EBR	evidence-based research
EERA	European Educational Research Association
ERA	Education Reform Act 1988
ESRC	Economic and Social Research Council
FE	further education
FEDA	Further Education Development Agency
FEFC	Further Educational Funding Council
FENTO	Further Education National Training Organization
GCE	General Certificate of Education
GCSE	General Certificate of Secondary Education

GNVQ	General National Vocational Qualification
HE	higher education
HEFCE	Higher Education Funding Council for England
HEI	Higher Education Institution
HEQC	Higher Education Quality Council
HND	Higher National Diploma
HRM	human resource management
ICT	information and communications technology
IFL	Institute for Learning (PCET)
ILT	Institute for Learning and Teaching in Higher Education
IQ	intelligence quotient
IT	information technology
LEA	local education authority
LSC	Learning and Skills Council
LSDA	Learning and Skills Development Agency
LSRN	Learning Skills Research Network
MSC	Manpower Services Commission
NATFHE	National Association of Teachers in Further and Higher Education
NCVQ	National Council for Vocational Qualifications
NHS	National Health Service
NIACE	National Institute of National and Continuing Education
NVQ	National Vocational Qualification
OECD	Organization for Economic Cooperation and Development
Ofsted	Office for Standards in Education
PCE	post-compulsory education
PCET	post-compulsory education and training
PGCE	Postgraduate Certificate in Education
QAA	Quality Assurance Agency
QCA	Qualifications and Curriculum Authority
R&D	research and development
RAE	Research Assessment Exercise
SCAA	Schools Curriculum and Assessment Authority
SEU	Social Exclusion Unit
TEC	Training and Enterprise Council/Technician Education Council
TLRP	Teaching and Learning Research Programme
TOPS	Training Opportunities Scheme
TQM	total quality management
TTA	Teacher Training Agency
TVEI	Technical and Vocational Education Initiative
UCAS	Universities and Colleges Admissions Service
UfI	University for Industry
WEA	Workers Educational Association
YOP	Youth Opportunities Programme
YTS	Youth Training Scheme

GENERAL INTRODUCTION

It is common in reviews of recent changes in the post-compulsory sector of education in Britain to take James Callaghan's 1976 Ruskin College speech as a watershed. The reason is obvious: it helped to create the political climate needed to bring about a fundamental reorientation of the purpose of post-compulsory education, indeed, it might be argued, all education. However, the past 25 years have brought about a number of significant changes in the nature of the sector's work. The aim of the first two parts of this book is to review these changes by considering how the issues they have raised have affected both post-compulsory practice in general and the people who work in the sector.

Callaghan's speech in the autumn of 1976 helped to popularize the view that the main aim of education should be instrumental – it should primarily serve the needs of the economy. Putting it simply, how could the British economy hope to compete with Germany and Japan when our children were leaving school and college able (or possibly unable) to translate Chaucer into modern English but with no conception of the requirements for working in a high-tech, high-skilled economy?

Concurrent with this reorientation of the fundamental purpose of education has been the widespread recognition that Britain could no longer justify the elite nature of particularly the higher education sector of PCET. As sociologists were quick to point out it did look very white, very middle class and very male in the 1970s. Indeed, when compared with the US, where 50 per cent of the population were being awarded university degrees, the fact that Britain was awarding only around 10 per cent of the population its degrees did, indeed, seem to indicate that there must be an enormous wastage of talent in the British educational system. Part 1 will consider these issues.

With the election of the Conservative Party to government in May 1979 the vocationalizing of the curriculum took on a much more 'market' oriented front. This was not simply to get educational establishments to recognize what was their market, i.e. who they are (or should be) serving, but also to bring about a more business-like approach to the way they operated. With competition for funding, quality audit trails and mission statements it was hoped that a new sense of efficiency would be brought to these institutions. This is what is often referred to as the new managerialism – the sense that educational establishments need to produce cultures where the management of human resources and accountability are at the forefront of their operations.

Along with this development has been the perceived need for teachers to think less in terms of their own ability to teach, and more in terms of their students' abilities to learn. This was encapsulated in the now (in)famous Rogerian notion that teachers should see themselves as 'facilitators of others' learning' (Rogers 1983). This has important implications for the nature of student accountability. On top of this there have been loud calls for transparent systems of public accountability for PCET practitioners. The issues raised by the establishment of a 'market' philosophy in education, and by the changing nature of professional accountability, are considered in Part 2.

The last 25 years has also seen a burgeoning of the notion that educational practitioners should consider themselves as researchers and the ways in which this might be achieved. Part 3, therefore, considers the various ways in which research might be conducted in educational establishments. Alongside a general consideration of the nature of educational research knowledge we consider the means by which practitioners within PCET organizations might conduct their own research. It is hoped that the way in which the issues have been discussed in the previous two parts will prompt practitioners seriously to consider undertaking some form of research.

PART 1

POST-COMPULSORY EDUCATION IN CONTEXT

OVERVIEW: POST-COMPULSORY EDUCATION IN CONTEXT

John Lea

Introduction

It is often argued in philosophical circles that everything is a footnote to Plato. In his most famous text *The Republic*, Plato invites us to consider the nature of a just society. Not surprisingly (for it was a commonly held view at the time), he connects the notion of a just individual with a just state, i.e. if we consider what it means to be a just individual it will provide a clue as to the nature of a just society. Plato invites us to consider the very simple notion that if each individual performs tasks which are in keeping with their own unique talents this will ultimately be to the benefit of all. This *organic* conception of the nature of the social order, as it is often called, has been recycled on many occasions. It is at the heart of the functionalist school of sociology and could be said to be the foundation of the tripartite education system founded during the Second World War in Britain. The idea that the education system should fundamentally serve the purpose of allocating individuals to future jobs which are in keeping with their 'natural' talents, has a compelling logic and, indeed, might be argued to be the most important footnote to Plato that British education reform has written.

Perhaps the most intriguing section in *The Republic* is where Socrates (or more accurately the Platonic Socrates) outlines the *noblesse oblige*, which will function to help people understand the nature of justice. It is worth quoting this allegory in full:

> You are, all of you in this community, brothers. But when god fashioned you, he added gold in the composition of those of you who are qualified to be Rulers (which is why their prestige is greatest); he put silver in the Auxiliaries, and iron and bronze in the farmers and

other workers. Now since you are all of the same stock, though your children will commonly resemble their parents, occasionally a silver child will be born of golden parents, or a golden child of silver parents, and so on. Therefore the first and most important of god's commandments to the Rulers is that in the exercise of their function as Guardians their principal care must be to watch the mixture of metals in the characters of their children. If one of their own children has traces of bronze or iron in its make-up, they must harden their hearts, assign it its proper value, and degrade it to the ranks of the industrial and agricultural class where it properly belongs: similarly, if a child of this class is born with gold or silver in its nature, they will promote it appropriately to be a Guardian or an Auxiliary. And this they must do because there is a prophecy that the state will be ruined when it has Guardians of silver or bronze.

(Plato, Penguin Classics: 182 Stephanus 415)

> **Discussion point**
>
> To what extent would you say that this allegory has served the British education system well? Would you say it still does?

Let us use Plato's *Republic* as the backdrop to the issues we will discuss in this chapter. We will consider these issues under two (interrelated) headings: the rise of the new vocationalism and the widening participation agenda. What we need to keep in mind here is what we feel the fundamental purpose of education should be, and, what we want the notion of 'education for all' to imply?

The new vocationalism

Background

Throughout the 1980s a series of educational initiatives were implemented by central government in an attempt to 'tighten the bond' between education and the immediate needs of industry. This was combined with an extension of the 'market' philosophy to education, in effect reducing the power of local education authorities and establishing new forms of professional accountability (see Part 2).

There seem to have been several important contributory factors at work here:

- The Callaghan 'Ruskin' speech in 1976, which emphasized the role of education as a preparation for work; that Britain needed a 'core' curriculum; that education needs to become more accountable to employers and parents rather than teachers. For some this was seen as an endorsement of the right-wing backlash against so-called progressive education (Cox and Boyson 1977).

- Local authorities had come under increasing attack in the early 1980s for being politically motivated institutions, controlling schools and local services with provision in opposition to central government concerns, for example, focusing on race and gender issues at the expense of the '3Rs'; encouraging multicultural curricula at the expense of British history; promoting minority rights (for example, of homosexuals) at the expense of the moral majority. The extent to which this was a reality or simply an agenda set by a politically motivated right-wing press is, however, debatable (see for example Curran *et al.* 1988).
- It was seen as desirable that public services such as health and education should be made more accountable in market terms, i.e. competition between institutions should become the guardian of quality and efficiency and direct central government funding would make such institutions more directly cost aware. This would have the effect of giving more power to parents and governors, and not local councils. We might also add that the general aim of right-wing thinking in the 1980s was to reduce direct taxation and public provision in favour of direct consumer power (Friedman and Friedman 1979).

Discussion point

To what extent do you think it is necessary to place education in this wider political context to understand reform?

These debates culminated in the Education Reform Act 1988. Some of the main features of the Act were (see McClure 1988):

- *A National Curriculum* of core subjects which all students must study until the age of 16.
- *Standardized testing* at the ages of 7, 11 and 14, with publication of results.
- *Opting out* – all schools, through a ballot of parents, could decide to opt out of local authority control, by voting to be funded directly by government.

Although these reforms were aimed at compulsory education; it is important to consider how the political agenda that drove the reforms might eventually feed into the post-compulsory sector. Of course, on the last matter, further education colleges were in effect opted-out by the incorporation legislation of 1992 and the establishment of the Further Education Funding Council (FEFC).

Discussion point

To what extent do you feel that the Education Reform Act 1988 has acted as the background agenda for reforms which subsequently took place in PCET?

Vocational initiatives in PCET (1977–1992)

Throughout the 1980s various attempts were made to bridge the gap between vocational and academic education (indeed, this is still happening). This seems to have had two main assumptions. First, British curricula (in general) were centred on academic concerns, but the majority of the population did not succeed in, or need, such an education, with the result that the curriculum was perceived as being out of touch with the needs of individuals and industry. Second, academic education was itself seen as too narrowly focused, with students concentrating very quickly on only a few subjects, and the knowledge itself rarely being of an applied nature.

For readers unfamiliar with some of the earlier curricula reforms here is a brief summary:

• The *Youth Training Schemes (YTSs)* – derived from the Manpower Services Commission (MSC), which was established in 1973 to promote an easier transition from school to work for 16-year-olds (work experience, etc.) In 1978 YTSs became the Youth Opportunities Programmes (YOPs), with 'day-release' provision for young people. In 1983 YOPs became the One Year YTSs, with the government increasing provision by financing the employment of young people as trainees with local firms. In 1986 the One Year YTSs became Two Year schemes. The schemes were subsumed under the Training and Enterprise Councils (TECs) in 1990.

• In 1982 the government began the *Technical and Vocational Educational Initiative (TVEI)* which attempted to promote the introduction of elements of vocationalism across all curricula. In effect, it was used by many colleges to establish a greater awareness of work experience schemes; promoted the use of records of achievement where students, teachers and employers could monitor the building up of a range of competences amongst students; and it encouraged a more widely spread provision of information technology.

• In 1983 the *Business and Technician Education Council (BTEC)* was formed, and by 1986 it had established the basis for provision of a range of courses aimed at providing qualifications for entry into a number of professional vocations which would have academic rigour, but would emphasize more practical vocational competence, when compared with GCSE (then O level) and A level qualifications. (BTEC Firsts would be equivalent to five GCSEs; BTEC National Diplomas would be equivalent to two or three A levels).

• In 1984 a *Certificate of Pre-vocational Education (CPVE)* was established as a qualification rather than an initiative or scheme. This was intended to be taught, more like a traditional course, but with an emphasis on competence and skill in a range of areas directly relevant to the world of work, and aimed at those students who were in danger of leaving school or college with no formal qualifications.

• In 1986 a government sponsored committee recommended the establishment of a *National Council for Vocational Qualifications (NCVQ)*, which would seek to bring *all* the vocational qualifications under one umbrella, establishing a national framework of levels of achievement. This would mirror the traditional academic ladder, with five levels – from 1 to 5 (this notion will be discussed later). The NCVQ would not establish new courses but accredit existing courses and work-based experience by establishing practically based Competence and Performance Criteria, which they should incorporate. Indeed, NCVQ became largely responsible for introducing into Britain what is often referred to as competence-based education and training (CBET) (Jessup 1991).

- In 1992 *GNVQs* (G for general) were introduced as distinct courses and qualifications. In part this was because, in effect, many NVQs were being taught and awarded through simulated work experiences in colleges and training centres and also because it was felt that the time was right to establish a new taught-based vocationally oriented alternative to the GCSE/A level which were still (by far) the most popular courses for students to take.

Discussion point

From your knowledge and understanding of these curricular initiatives and reforms, how far would you say that they bridged or widened the academic/vocational divide in PCET?

Against the new vocationalism

Although further reforms continued throughout the 1990s and into the new century, for example, Modern Apprenticeships, University for Industry (UfI) (see later), it could be argued that the dual establishment of the NVQ ladder and the GNVQ equivalence to the traditional academic structure were the key foundational elements in the new vocationalism. However, it would not be an exaggeration to say that the debates that surrounded the introduction of these reforms have been bitterly fought. The most controversial issue has perhaps been the very notion that Britain should move towards competence-based curricula provision. However, concurrent with this has been a social and political commentary concerning hidden agendas and a reopening of debate concerning the purpose of education.

Several academics (for example Bailey 1984; Abbs 1994; Hyland 1994a) felt very strongly that they needed to defend traditional academic education from this new vocational onslaught.

> It is a gross mutation of the aims of education to suggest either that knowledge is only important to the extent that it reveals itself in the performance of certain tasks or that the only understanding worth having is that which contributes to vocational competence.
>
> (Hyland 1990)

The implication here is that the humanistic and cognitive aims for (particularly) adult education are being sacrificed in favour of a narrow agenda set by the needs of industry. Abbs went further in suggesting that this also serves the purpose of a state operating with:

> the crippling assumption that the first task of teachers is to serve the economy, to turn out skilled robots and uncritical consumers for the hi-tec age.
>
> (Abbs 1986)

This, he claims, has had the effect of undermining the Socratic tradition in teaching, which sees education as an attitude of mind:

> Education is not an object (a mass of knowledge or information or skills) which can be unambiguously handed from the teacher to the student. Education is rather an activity of mind, a particular emotional and critical orientation towards experience.
>
> (Abbs 1994: 17)

Hyland's essentially philosophical critique centred on how vocational qualifications (largely NVQs) were founded on what he considered to be a flawed theory of behaviourist learning, i.e. that learning is defined as measuring changes of behaviour. This completely ignored both cognitivist and humanist traditions – the latter being widely accepted as the foundation for good practice in the teaching of adults (Jarvis 1995).

Discussion point

From your knowledge and understanding of the humanistic tradition in the teaching of adults, to what extent could it be argued that we can no longer afford such an approach to education?

A *liberal* approach to education requires us to consider two aims in education: the need to establish a meritocracy, and the need for a broad curriculum valued for its own sake. All students, regardless of background, should be able to aspire to the increasing opportunities that have emerged due to the growth of middle-class occupations throughout the twentieth century (a 'more room at the top' thesis). However, for such aspirations to be meaningful the education received by all students needs to be as broad as possible, not only because a broad education is necessary to produce the kind of cultural awareness previously only afforded the well to do, but also because if students receive different types of education (and subsequent qualifications) this will enable forms of social closure to be established around the possession of the (different) qualifications.

Defenders of the liberal creed, such as Charles Bailey, have also argued that the key concern in education should be to enable students to look beyond the 'present and the particular'. Vocational qualifications have the effect of locating people *within* the present and particular because of their narrow focus on the existing work and employment structure (Bailey 1984). Indeed, it might be argued in this context that forms of vocationalism should not be called education at all – rather there should be a dichotomy between education, on the one hand, and training on the other. Also, liberal theorists are often quick to point out that when employers are asked what they want from young people in terms of skills they often respond with precisely the sorts of aptitude that one would associate with liberal education.

Discussion point

To what extent do you think that it is inevitable that there will always be a social hierarchy of qualifications, benefiting some to the detriment of others?

Some commentators attempted to identify a much more overtly political agenda behind the various vocational reforms (see Haralambos 1995 for an excellent discussion of these critics, from which the following is a short summary). Many of these criticisms have focused on the various YTSs and the low-level NVQs. Indeed, some have argued that the YTSs were not even training, but served a political purpose of removing large numbers of young people from the growing unemployment statistics and enabled employers to recruit a new source of cheap labour, which might have the added benefit of lowering young people's expectations of high wages and secure employment (Finn 1987). It was also argued that the schemes offered employers more flexible employment arrangements, where these young workers could easily be replaced by new recruits without concern for redundancy payments (Clarke and Willis 1984).

Finally, it was argued that the hidden curriculum of many vocational courses was to fashion attitudes in young people, disguised as transferable skills, which would foster the view that unemployment is a personal problem of not working hard enough to secure a job, rather than a structural problem in the economy – that there simply are not enough jobs (Cohen 1984). In this respect, all that vocational courses do is help reproduce existing social and economic inequalities and fashion a set of attitudes in working-class youth to prepare them for the prospect of low-paid, low-status work and possibly unemployment (Clarke and Willis 1984)

All of these, essentially Marxist, perspectives emphasized how many of the early initiatives in the new vocationalism represented nothing more than a political solution to an economic problem – the precarious nature of employment in the late twentieth century. It might be considered ironic that societies like Britain only concentrate on training for jobs when there are not enough to go around.

Discussion point

To what extent would you say that these Marxist critiques of the early vocational initiatives have largely evaporated due to an increasing perception of the educational value in vocational alternatives to academic education?

Defending the new vocational creed

In his book *Outcomes*, Jessup (1991) took on the job of defending CBET from the above criticisms by arguing that it is all too easy to forget how out of touch education had become throughout most of the post-war period. Education was largely academic, being both beyond the capabilities of most students, and largely irrelevant to most people's lives. It was extremely teacher-centred, in that individual teachers had enormous powers to produce ill-defined broad aims and woolly assessment criteria and leave students as passive recipients. And, we might add, what is wrong with education meeting the needs of the economy? Without a wealthy economy there would not be any feasible way of providing any form of mass education.

In conclusion, it could be argued that the 1980s was a period in education provision where the dual concerns of 'tightening the bond' between school and work and the desire to bring market forces to education helped to create a political climate in which:

- progressive education was seen as undermining the traditional teaching of the 3Rs;
- local education authorities were seen as politically motivated institutions undermining the wishes of other stakeholders in education;
- students were leaving school and college ill-prepared for the needs of industry, and we were thus losing out to our international competitors, and unnecessarily swelling the ranks of the unemployed.

Given the general thrust of right-wing economic policies, such as low direct tax and reductions in public expenditure, it was clear that the type of state-funded education established in the 1960s was likely to be changed. On the positive side, it could be said that all education in Britain in the mid-1970s had become too academic (particularly given that only around 13 per cent of students were going on to higher education), and it was important that British industry should begin to compete more equally with countries like Germany.

On the negative side, it could be said that the new vocationalism narrowed the aims of education – fostering not a Socratic attitude of mind in young people, but a set of attitudes consonant with the realities of low-paid, low-status, scarce work. Furthermore, this type of realism could not offer a challenge to the existing social and economic inequalities, but could only foster an acceptance of their inevitability, where young people compete to market themselves for what work is available, with what vocational qualifications they can acquire.

The present vocational context (1992–2002)

Vocational reforms continued throughout the 1990s. Many of these were prompted by the scrutiny that ensued from the above controversies. NVQs have been subject to a wide-ranging review (see particularly Smithers 1993) and GNVQs have been constantly monitored (see particularly Bates *et al.* 1998). Others have been prompted by the change of government in 1997 and might be viewed as part of the New Labour philosophy, the Third Way. Most important in this context have been the New Deal and the University for Industry. Both reforms are clearly vocational in that the former is aimed at getting people into work and the latter is aimed at providing educational opportunities for those wishing to update their skills and qualifications. The Third Way philosophy is looked at in more detail in Part 2, suffice it to say here that the broad aim is to be seen to be helping people to help themselves, i.e. it is a deliberate policy shift away from both a welfare model of assistance and a market-oriented model of atomistic individualism. In this context the government will put into place the infra-structure to enable people to take responsibility for themselves (Hodgson and Spours 1999).

Discussion point

Do you think that the vocational reforms since 1997 (such as New Deal and UfI) demonstrate a significant change in social policy? How would you describe the effects?

Alongside these curriculum and government reforms have been more academic discussions of the way forward. For example, Ainley (1993) produced a wide-ranging discussion of the notion of skill, emphasizing how new technologies could help produce a multiskilled workforce, whilst Pring (1995) put forward a broad strategy to integrate the academic with the vocational. Although both were critical of the current vocational context, they were also keen to outline the possibilities it presents.

NVQ reformers have made concerted efforts to address the problem of an outcomes-led approach which had been accused of ignoring both under-pinning knowledge and the notion of reliability in assessment procedures (see particularly Wolf (1995) and Tarrant (2000) for interesting discussions of assessment and competence). GNVQ reformers have made concerted efforts to address the assessment burden and prevent the qualification from being led by its assessment mode. There has also been a wide-ranging discussion of the way that GNVQs have tried to incorporate elements of progressivism in the curriculum and concentrate on student-centred self-development, and how this is often constrained by its inherited legacy of

CBET (Hodkinson 1998). In all of this, the A level 'gold standard' has survived relatively unscathed by vocational discussions. However, there have been numerous calls for A levels to become more like French-style baccalaureates and to integrate key skills elements into the subject specifications. Curriculum 2000 addressed both of these issues, but the former seems only to have produced a call for A level students to take a larger number of AS qualifications in their first year of study and the latter seems to have been overshadowed by the need for students to be seen to be taking 'discrete' key skills qualifications.

It might be argued that these developments have helped to move us towards attempts to design curricula which, on the one hand, meet the needs of a wide range of learners and, on the other, are both relevant and intellectually challenging, and, in the process, help move us away from the PCET curriculum being focused too narrowly on a 'preparedness for jobs' agenda. However, it could equally be argued that the legacy of the new vocationalism hangs over the current reforms and this has enabled entrenched attitudes to persist and be used in judgement against them. Dearing's report (Dearing 1996) on the PCET curriculum was precisely aimed at taking a hard look at the state of play in the mid-1990s and it culminated in the PCET reforms usually referred to as Curriculum 2000 (DfEE 1997)

> **Discussion point**
>
> Review Dearing's original report of 1996 and ask yourself to what extent it was inevitable that his proposed reforms would be undermined by entrenched attitudes.

The aftermath to the Dearing report seemed to produce the following options for further progress in searching for the ideal PCET curriculum:

- Accept that there is an academic/vocational divide rather than seeking to bridge it.
- Encourage students to cross the divide whenever they can.
- Rewrite the PCET curriculum as a new, unified set of qualifications, possibly with one graduating diploma.

The Curriculum 2000 reforms

Curriculum 2000 fits neatly into the thinking behind the second of the above options. By establishing a tariff of learning blocks, all students will be able quickly to see what is equivalent to what and how much credit they will need to achieve their aims. An example is shown in Figure 1.1.

The drive towards increased relevance and vocational preparation can still be seen in the much-vaunted introduction of Key Skills across the curriculum and the subsequent debates on their desirability. Apart from asking the somewhat obvious question about why compulsory schooling is

Figure 1.1

UCAS points	Single units		Vocational and GCE A and AS levels		
	Main key skills	1 unit award	3 unit award	6 unit award	12 unit award
240					A
200					B
160					C
120				A	D
100				B	
80				C	E
60			A	D	
50			B		
40			C	E	
30	Level 4		D		
20	Level 3	A	E		

Source: www.UCAS.co.uk

not able to deliver students to PCET with 'key skills', there are clearly several other questions that need to be asked in this context. For instance, when taught discretely, do they simply act as a distraction for students and staff alike from what is seen as the main purpose of their PCET presence? However, when they are integrated into mainstream qualifications, do they simply distract, once again, this time from the core skills and knowledge contained in the original qualifications? Finally, if some students realize (quite quickly) that they can achieve their aims (say a university place) without any Key Skills qualifications, does this leave us contemplating, yet again, whether we have created a new round of second-class qualifications?

Discussion point

What evidence do you have from your own PCET practice that key skills are either becoming an integral part of the PCET curriculum or being relegated as an unnecessary bolt-on?

It is for reasons such as these that it is becoming popular to believe that the only way out of this malaise is to start again. Using the university sector as a model where each student (or, perhaps better, the vast majority) graduate with one qualification, the degree, graded to reflect personal achievement, surely it is not beyond us to contemplate a similar graduating certificate (for example, diploma in further education), similarly graded to reflect personal achievement? Indeed, this is a clear proposal in the Green Paper *14–19: Extending Opportunities, Raising Standards* where there is discussion of a matriculation diploma for 19-year-olds (DfES 2002: 12).

As it stands, the new vocationalism in PCET seems to have delivered the following ladders of opportunity for students:

Traditional academic	New vocational	NVQ
University degree	Professional institute exam	5
Diploma in HE	HND	4
2–3 A levels	AVCE or GNVQ adv	3
5 GCSEs (C+)	GNVQ intermediate	2
5 GCSEs (D–G)	GNVQ foundation	1

The beauty of this model lies not just in the progression, which is built into each ladder, but the equivalence it establishes between the rungs on each ladder. Furthermore, the introduction of Curriculum 2000, particularly in colleges working hard to timetable opportunities for people to 'mix and match', establishes opportunities for students to collect the appropriate credit from *across all three* rungs of the ladders at the same time and feel confident in moving up to the next rung(s) on *any* of the ladders.

There are clearly opportunities for research (see Part 3) into student movements on these ladders and discussion of the accompanying issues. For instance, in reality, do students move sideways; is there evidence of 'pick and mix'; what is a mix of academic and vocational elements within each ladder; how many students move all the way up the NVQ ladder; is there still an A level gold standard/academic snobbery; and, finally, are GNVQ students simply failed A level students? (See particularly Avis (1996) on the last issue.) There are important issues to be addressed here, many of which could be the focus for evidence-based practitioner research (see Part 3).

There is a long tradition in British education that education should suit the abilities of students, and that there will always be three classes of abilities: intellectual, technical and practical. Could it be argued that the metaphorical search for gold, silver and bronze in the souls of students is what gave us the tripartite secondary education of the post-war period and that the introduction of the new vocationalism in the 1980s is simply another chapter in this search? In this model we would have: A levels = intellectual, GNVQ/AVCE = technical, and NVQ = practical.

In this respect the previous table should now be reproduced on its side, indicating that any student on any rung of the now horizontal ladders will be perceived as being of higher educational value if they have a footing on the intellectual ladder as opposed to the technical or the practical.

5 GCSEs (D–G)	5 GCSEs (C+)	2–3 A levels	Diploma in HE	University degree
GNVQ foundation	GNVQ intermediate	AVCE or GNVQ advanced	HND	Professional institute exam
NVQ 1	NVQ 2	NVQ 3	NVQ 4	NVQ 5

There are extremely important issues at stake here. Do we want to accept the argument that it is inevitable that an unequal society will always reproduce an unequal education system, or do we want to pride ourselves that new curricular initiatives are bringing a wider range of students into the educational fold? This brings us to the whole question of widening participation in PCET.

The widening participation agenda

Background

The idea that post-compulsory education in the 1970s was very white, very middle class and very male might have served as a convenient derogatory way of describing a typical university in Britain but it could hardly have meant much in the context of the sector in general. Indeed, it could be argued that many courses, indeed, whole departments in some further education colleges, have had predominantly female and working-class students (Skeggs 1988). However, this may be part of the problem itself and simply highlights the extent to which various social groups have been both over- and under-represented in the various departments of the various post-compulsory institutions.

Equality is variously defined in discussions of widening opportunities. In some cases the term refers to *equal treatment* and is aimed at anti-discriminatory practice with the focus on attitudes and behaviour within a college. Sometimes the term is used in discussions of *widening access* to education and this is often what is understood by the term *equal opportunities*. However, the term is also used by egalitarians who have a more radical agenda and understand equality to mean *equal shares*. Policies framed under this definition are aimed at inequality in society at large, where schools and colleges are asked to help pursue a wider social policy of equalizing the ratio between a social group's presence in a community and its share of resources in that community. For example, if a London borough has an 11 per cent West Indian population then there could only be said to be equality in that community when 11 per cent of the local college community and 11 per cent of local employment is being undertaken by West Indians.

Some colleges now effectively outlaw certain expressions and behaviour and monitor all college documents and prospectuses with a view to promoting a positive image of that college's work with respect to all individuals and social groups. Certain courses have been developed specifically aimed at social groups whom it was felt may have suffered from the 'taken for granted' world of schooling in the past. For example, the original Access courses were specifically for ethnic minority groups in Inner London in the late 1970s.

Equal opportunities and PCET

To some equal opportunities has become the most important means by which disadvantaged groups in society might become stakeholders; however, to others it is nothing more than 'political correctness gone mad'. Some of the more controversial matters might be considered under the following headings: education compensating for society; assessment as a barrier to success; and the need to politicize the curriculum. The following examples are aimed at exploring these notions.

Let us take the example of the lone parent who enrols on an Access course knowing that one of the degree courses that he or she could aspire to is an American studies programme, which requires a year's study in the US. Clearly, the Access course is giving the student access opportunities to the degree, but at what point should a discussion concerning the implications of a year's study abroad be entertained? Or, perhaps, more importantly, should such a discussion be entertained? Surely the implications behind a year's study abroad, which would include schooling for the children, should be the parent's own? However, could it not be argued, particularly in cases where the parent is poor, that an educational opportunity is in danger of being denied if some compensatory package is not put in place? Furthermore, should not the HE provider seriously consider whether a year abroad ought to be an obligatory requirement when it is known that it causes difficulties for several students each year?

Discussion point

How far would you go in accepting that it is the PCET provider's duty to provide extra-curricular assistance for students to achieve their learning goals?

Let us now take the example of a student who is deaf who enrols on a degree course knowing that they must undertake a 2500-word written assignment for each of the units on the degree. However, when it comes to handing the first one in, the student questions why this has to be in written form. The student suggests that a signed version on video assessed by a qualified signer would more readily suit them as a method of assessment.

Discussion point

You work at the university where the deaf student is registered and are asked for your opinion on the student's request. What is your response?

Of course, the simple solution to this dilemma is to take a look at the university's equal opportunities document to see what it says. Let us imagine that the only statement that clearly addresses this issue is one stating that 'the university will do everything in its power to ensure that all types of learner are able to achieve their learning goals'. Could the student not claim that the university is in breach of this if it does not accommodate their request?

Finally, let us consider the GCSE English class where students are discussing Graham Greene's *Brighton Rock* and the following passage is referred to:

In Seven Dials the negroes (sic) were hanging round the public house doors in tight natty suiting and old school ties and Ida recognised one of them and passed the time of the day . . . the great white teeth went on like a row of lights in the darkness above the bright stripped shirt.

(quoted by Kiwi 1989)

The novel is well known as an exploration of Catholicism, but this passage seems to raise the issue of racism. If there has never been a question in the exam that invites a discussion of racism, to what extent should the teacher now invite this discussion? Perhaps more importantly, how should the discussion proceed? Is this an example of writing from its time (several editions of the novel interchange negro with nigger)? Should the class discussion document student testimonies on their reaction to the paragraph? Should teachers lobby exam boards to have such texts removed or balanced by others with more positive images, and who should decide what causes offence?

Discussion point

How would you conduct the above GCSE class discussion if the above paragraph was referred to in the class?

These examples raise important questions concerning the responsibilities of PCET practitioners in operating with the principle of providing equal opportunities. First, it also raises the question of the extent to which it is possible for PCET institutions to effectively compensate for society. If society produces social inequality, and it is brought to the classroom, surely the search for solutions should be centred not on the classroom but on society? Second, to what extent should we, as teachers, accept that assessment techniques are prone to create unnecessary hurdles for students in demonstrating their learning and, thus, that we should open up these techniques for critical scrutiny, and allow students to choose from a wider range of assessment options? Or is this simply a recipe for absurdity, encouraging students who once might have handed in their assignment on 'recent reforms in PCET' as a traditional essay, to do so now in the form of a poem, or video dance routine with their peers?

Equal opportunities and curriculum reform

Curriculum reforming groups such as the Center for Applied Special Technology (CAST) in the US have been working for some time to encourage teachers to consider these issues as a routine part of curriculum design and provision (CAST 2002). Utilizing the architectural principle of universal design, i.e. that buildings should be designed on the principle of multiple usage and users, CAST suggests that teachers should design curricular resources and assessment methods in the same way. More practically, teachers should design with the following in mind:

* multiple representations of content;
* multiple options for expression and control;
* multiple options for engagement.

In other words we all need to consider not just the forms through which we communicate information, but also the different means by which students might engage with educational material, and also how they might exercise more control over the ways in which they are assessed. If we are to be serious about what has been learnt about the way that the brain processes information and different representational systems (O'Conner and Seymour 1990); different learning styles (Honey and Mumford 1992) and multiple and emotional intelligences (Gardner 1993; Goleman 1995) we must translate this knowledge practically in curricula reform.

Finally, to what extent do we all have a responsibility to change, not just access opportunities to curriculum and assessment techniques, but also the actual content of the curriculum? If Shakespeare and Chaucer are boring to 16-year-olds, could they be removed? Could history classes be framed around the concerns of the actual students about to embark on the course? This list of questions is endless and would take us into the history of multiculturalism both in the US and in the UK. What is at stake is the extent to which the curriculum should be seen to be serving different purposes. It has long been believed in the US that the disaffection of minority groups in education can be challenged through curricula which reflect their interests, cultures and languages and that this could be achieved when the curriculum is used as a critical means of self-understanding (Giroux 1983).

Discussion point

How often do you entertain educational aims that are not strictly within the scope of the immediate specifications or syllabus?

Readers who are familiar with the radical agenda in adult education might be dismayed at this point to have to hear talk of reorienting the curriculum towards specific learners' needs when there is a long tradition of this in adult education centres throughout the UK. Indeed, rising to the 'basic skills' agenda has often been accomplished precisely through a more liberatory and contextualized curriculum model:

> Reading not only helps define the individual's relationship to society but provides a mechanism for understanding and developing the self and constructing an identity.
> (Kean 1995, quoted in Mayo and Thompson 1995: 58)

In this context the relevance of the curriculum is defined not in strict instrumental terms, i.e. as a preparation for work, but in terms of its relevance to one's life, social context and individual self-development. Equal opportunities, in this context, might be defined as designing curricula for particular groups of individuals who have been traditionally under-represented in PCET. It is not about giving access to a nationally prescribed curriculum, or about achieving national targets for numeracy and literacy (important as this might be), but about working innovatively and imaginatively with local individuals and social groups, be they female returners, redundant manual workers or various ethnic minorities, to choose some obvious examples.

On the one hand, it could be considered ironic that, in the desire to widen participation in PCET in general, the various sectors within it – higher education, further education, adult and community education – have become blurred as they all chase all types of learner and try to meet a range of learners' needs, thereby risking losing the distinctiveness of the traditions that had grown up within them. In this respect 'the really useful knowledge' tradition of adult education, which has made enormous contributions to the opening up of opportunities to students has now got somewhat lost as higher education and further education seek to cater for all needs (Hughes, in Mayo and Thompson 1995). On the other hand, we might argue that this has far more to do with the state taking control of mainstream education, indeed, defining what mainstream education is, and the inevitability of innovative practice losing out in the ensuing funding battles. In this context, what central government has been able to do is define what useful knowledge is, i.e. useful knowledge is now narrowly defined as vocational relevance rather than individual self-development. This is clearly the point where the new vocationalism meets the widening participation agenda. We might say that there are now more widely available educational opportunities but they are also more narrowly defined in scope.

Discussion point

How far would you say that it is PCET reform itself that has limited students' opportunities to experience 'useful' education?

Social exclusion and disaffection

Since 1997, 'targeting' the under-represented in PCET has been largely focused around debates concerning social exclusion. It could be argued that this is clearly an area where adult education has a large amount of accumulated expertise. However, it seems to be further education that is receiving the bulk of funding. This could largely be to do with the different ways in which exclusion might be conceived. It is often taken to refer to the increasing number of school students who are permanently excluded from their schools and the number of 'units' now in existence in further education colleges who are accommodating them (and this, of course, raises the question of what exactly the term 'post-compulsory' education now means). This might be referred to as a narrow focus, not because of its scope, but because it acts on young people who have been labelled 'excluded'. The wider focus includes all the initiatives aimed at more general social problems:

> Social exclusion is a shorthand label for what can happen when individuals or areas suffer from a combination of linked problems, such as unemployment, poor skills, low incomes, poor housing, high crime environments, bad health and family breakdown.
> (SEU 1999, quoted in Hayton 1999: 2)

It could be argued that as these are social problems we might simply end up using education as the scapegoat for a lack of social policy. However, to a large extent, education is part of social policy and it can obviously play an important role particularly if it acts on the 'disaffection' which is often associated with the social problems mentioned above. Most starkly if we consider that young offenders are currently in a position to apply for only four jobs in every one hundred, it is hardly surprising that the 'basic skills' agenda currently has a high profile:

> 30 per cent of prisoners were regular truants while at school. 85 per cent of short-sentenced male prisoners involved in drug misuse had truanted; 49 per cent of male sentenced prisoners were excluded from school; 52 per cent of male and 71 per cent of female adult prisoners

have no qualifications at all; half of all prisoners are at or below level 1 (the level expected of an 11 year old) in reading; two thirds in numeracy; and four fifths in writing. These are the skills required for 96 per cent of all jobs.

(SEU 2002: 44)

Furthermore, if we know that these young offenders are leaving compulsory schooling largely without any formal qualifications we might want to question the nature of the curriculum experiences they might have had and how we might (re)engage them in their studies. Unfortunately, it is a difficult tightrope for some radical adult and community educators to walk if their funding is tied to meeting nationally agreed 'basic skills' targets when their experience suggests that it would be more fruitful to experiment with more radical curricular initiatives.

Of course, in general, this raises the whole question not just of the skills and attributes we would expect PCET practitioners to have, but also, once again, of the teaching methods which would be appropriate, as well as the curriculum content. If students have severe behavioural problems, clearly the traditional teaching skills of group management will need to be enhanced through some specialist training. Indeed, practitioners may increasingly find themselves needing to work in small groups and even on a one-to-one basis with individual learning plans. However, we might also find ourselves revisiting pedagogical practice and possibly utilizing the knowledge gained from discussions of andragogy (as opposed to pedagogy) as being more appropriate not just for adult learners but for a whole range of disengaged learners.

This itself raises the whole question of whether alternative teaching methods and alternative curricula are simply the means by which disaffected students might re-enter more mainstream PCET education or whether we might see this as a challenge to the mainstream itself. It is perhaps ironic that at a time when PCET practitioners are being asked to see themselves less as teachers and more as 'facilitators of others' learning' that we are still talking about the difficulty that many students have in aligning themselves to the authority structure of the mainstream classroom.

Discussion point

From your own experience what would you say is the balance between disaffection being caused by a student's own behavioural problems and the teaching methods and curriculum that they are subjected to?

This brings us to what is perhaps the most far-reaching dimension to the debates concerning equal opportunities, that is, the extent to which we would want to embrace the view, often put forward by sociologists, that it is teachers, educational establishments and the curriculum itself, and not students and their own deficiencies, which fail them. If it is the latter we can either conclude that we should help students with difficulties or, in extreme cases, accept that some will never be able to 'make the grade'; if it is the former, we must entertain the idea that it is our own practices as PCET practitioners that produce not just 'failures' but what constitutes the very meaning of the word 'failure' (this conceptual issue is returned to in Part 3).

At this point it might be wise to reflect on the term 'disaffection'. This is a relatively new term in social scientific literature. Indeed, it might be suggested that 20 years ago we would probably have used the term 'disadvantaged' when discussing the kinds of social problems listed in the quote from Hayton above. Perhaps this reflects a changing political climate which has seen us move away from a socio-structural explanation for social inequality which looked at how individuals and social groups are shaped by their social circumstances, and move towards a more cultural approach emphasizing how individuals and social groups shape their own social circumstances. This distinction could be most clearly seen in the debates concerning the presence of 'the underclass' in the US and Britain (R. MacDonald 1997). This would indicate that the term 'disaffection' is politically loaded, aimed at asking us to see social problems revolving around the need for individuals to reorient themselves. In this respect it is not 'disadvantage' that causes social problems but an individual's own 'disaffection' – society is not the problem, just an individual's relationship with it.

A complicating factor in this political debate has been the more recent discussions prompted by the publication of the Tomlinson report (Tomlinson 1996). Indeed, it might be argued that the discussion that ensued has moved us beyond equal opportunities as an operating notion to the notion of inclusion and the gradual acceptance of a more sociological understanding of 'learner identity'.

Disability and disabling environments

One of the recent trends in social science literature has been to challenge the notion that disability, or 'being disabled', is, on the one hand, a person's own physiological or neurological problem and, on the other, an essential and all-encompassing component of one's being (Barton 1996). As strange as it might initially sound, disability is increasingly being understood as a social relation. A straightforward example might illustrate the point. Imagine that I, as a sighted person, am having difficulty locating a book for a degree course, but when I discover that there is a library in London that has it I rush to catch the train armed only with the library's address. Imagine further my surprise upon arrival to find that all the books in the library's stock are held in Braille versions only. I might complicate the scenario by adding that all the instructions to enter the library are only in Braille as well. Would it be possible to argue that the environment in which I find myself now disables me?

These notions of 'abling' and 'disabling' environments are a common theme in recent literature on disability (Barton 1996). The language of disability is complicated by the rapidity of change in the terms being used. For some this signifies important developments in the treatment of people. However, for others it signifies little more than forms of political correctness, to be derided. For example, in 1980, the World Health Organization (quoted in Trowler 1995: 228) used the following definitions:

- *Impairment* – any loss or abnormality of psychological, physiological or anatomical structure or function.
- *Disability* – any restriction or lack (resulting from an impairment) of ability to perform an activity in a manner or within the range considered normal for a human being.
- *Handicap* – any disadvantage for a given individual, resulting from an impairment or disability, that limits or prevents the fulfilment of a role that is normal depending on age, sex, social and cultural factors for that individual.

All three definitions rested on assumptions that a social relations approach might want to challenge. For example, to what extent was the word 'normal' taken to be a reference to a physical being or an ideal image? And, to what extent was an impairment a physiological or neurological fact or simply a particular imposition of meaning?

Discussion point

To what extent would you agree with the idea that disabilities are problems only because of other people's prejudices?

Compare the following two statements, which might be said to a prospective college student:

- Lecturer 1: 'Because you are disabled I should warn you that you may have trouble completing the course you have chosen.'
- Lecturer 2: 'I should you warn you that this college is in many respects a disabling environment and this may cause you to experience some difficulties in completing the course you have chosen.'

This change in language mirrors the changes that have occurred in theories of disability:

> The most fundamental issue in the sociology of disability is a conceptual one. The traditional approach, often referred to as the medical model, locates the source of disability in the individual's deficiency and her or his personal incapacities. In contrast to this, the social model sees disability as resulting from society's failure to adapt to the needs of impaired people.
>
> (Abberley, in Barton 1996: 61)

The contrast between the two approaches can be seen most starkly by asking the question: 'Whose problem is disability?' Whereas the deficiency theory would argue that the problem lies with the individual, a social relations approach would argue that the problem is clearly social. However, there are theoretical differences in how the word 'social' is used. Labelling or interactionist theorists argue that in order for impairments to become 'problems' a social interaction needs to take place where the problem is the result of the attachment of a negative label by other individuals or whole social groups. More radical theorists, however, would emphasize that it is not labels that cause problems but the material circumstances, in which people live, which cause impairments to become problems. This argument is similar to a Marxist approach emphasizing the nature of the mode of production of material wealth, and how individuals are shaped to fit its needs, often marginalizing those whom it is difficult to shape:

> those working within a materialist perspective maintain that the oppression of disabled people is not reducible simply to problems within the individual or within the attitudes of others, but is rooted within economic structures.
>
> (Riddell, in Barton 1996: 86)

There is perhaps a sense here that if we could picture life as a game, the deficiency model appears to be saying to those with disabilities that you will have difficulty playing, but we will help you (for many, this is what keeps people in a dependent state); the labelling perspective seems to be saying it *is* possible to play, but we must first stop the existing players from using excluding tactics; the materialists, however, might be said to be arguing that it is about time we thought about what game we are playing and whether we could invent new ones.

There is an appealing logic in interactionist approaches that suggests that if only we stopped labelling people, particularly negatively, then any problem associated with the behaviour so labelled would disappear. For example, if only psychiatrists would stop calling the mentally ill 'the mentally ill' then mental illness would simply evaporate. If only teachers would stop calling certain students 'disruptive' then classrooms could become seas of tranquillity. Presumably when the famous interactionist Howard Becker wrote that 'deviance is behaviour which has been so labelled' (Becker 1963), he was referring, at least in part, to the way that certain forms of human behaviour have come to be understood, i.e. it is not that the behaviour would disappear if the label was removed, but the *association* of the behaviour with bad, wrong, or unnatural.

Thus, if we return to the case of disability, when we say that people 'suffer' from disabilities we need to consider the extent to which the social environment caused the suffering, be it through negative labels, or disabling environments, as well as to consider how one understands *one's own* situation. If we remember my (imaginary) trip to the library, I might have to suffer prejudicial statements made by unhelpful librarians working in the library, as well as suffering from the inability to read my book.

However, depending on the nature of my disability I might also suffer from my own mental anguish.

One of the clear messages that emerge from sociological literature on disability is the extent to which we are all involved in the social construction of disability. As educators we need to ask ourselves the extent to which we contribute to educational encounters which either produce (or reproduce) relations of dependence, and/or prejudice, or which seek to empower individuals in their social lives:

> Disabled people are . . . involved . . . in struggle to capture the power of naming difference itself. An emancipatory meaning of difference is one of the goals of social justice. This entails challenging definitions which isolate and marginalise and replacing them with those which engender solidarity and dignity.
>
> (Barton 1996: 10)

We need to ask ourselves about the ways in which our everyday practice uses a language which frames the ways in which people can experience their lives – for example, 'failure', 'special needs', etc. We need to consider the extent to which our language reflects and reproduces power relations in an organization and in society at large. In this context consider the way that the American rap group NWA (Niggas With Attitude) sought to take back the language of oppression to make it their own, and how some people in the gay community now celebrate the use of the word 'queer', such that it loses its discriminatory, negative, meaning.

As in the cases of racism and sexism, we need to enable people to escape from the blanket use of 'disabled' as a summary of the entire being of a person. Even if the intention is well-meaning the effect may not be without harm, as in the case of people leaning over wheelchair users, speaking loudly and slowly, indicating that they must have hearing and cognitive difficulties if they are using a wheelchair.

> The reality of most current provision in FE colleges is that of inaccessible buildings and ill-resourced, low status special needs departments
>
> (Corbett and Barton 1992: 85)

> being treated as an equal is very much on the surface. Scratch this surface and you will find the fear and contempt which underlies much of the discrimination against people who don't measure up to what we consider to be 'normal'.
>
> (Morris 1987, quoted in Corbett and Barton 1992: 86)

Discussion point

Ten years on from these statements, how successful would you say that PCET institutions have been in changing their learning environments and cultures?

Educational inclusion

It is surely against this backdrop that the following quotation from the Tomlinson report should be read and understood:

> Put simply, we want to avoid a viewpoint which locates the difficulty or deficit with the student and focuses instead on the capacity of the educational institution to understand and respond to the individual learner's requirement. This means we must move away from labelling the student and towards creating an appropriate educational environment; concentrate on understanding better how people learn so that they can be better helped to learn; and see people with disabilities and/or learning difficulties first and foremost as learners.
>
> (Tomlinson 1996: 2)

Educationalists were quick to realize the implications of these statements and to lay out the challenge to PCET practitioners:

> The redesigned provision called for in the Report [Tomlinson] would match the requirements of the subject matter, materials and teaching methods to students' predispositions and developmental levels.
>
> (Florian 1997)

No longer would students be expected to adapt to the requirements of the currently constructed PCET institutions. PCET institutions would have to adapt to the needs of the learners coming through their doors. Perhaps the most important lesson to be learnt from the sociological analysis of disability is the extent to which PCET institutions either contribute to the reinforcement of disabling aspects of self-identity or contribute to the empowerment of individuals to enrich their lives. In general, we might say that widening participation is clearly about opening up access to education and training opportunities but it is equally about how students experience that education and training. To do this has required a thorough questioning not just of the attitudes and attributes required of PCET practitioners but also of the nature of the student's engagement with the curriculum and, to some extent, the very content of the curriculum.

Conclusion

Two of the main concerns in PCET in the past 25 years have been those of relevance and participation, i.e. addressing the questions of what it is that people should be learning and why people are not queuing up to do it. Obviously the questions are not unrelated. For example, if we take the case of a student with 'learning difficulties', it is one thing to encourage them to have more access to the PCET curriculum but it is another to ask whether the curriculum on offer is itself of value. One of the main aims behind vocationalizing the PCET curriculum was to make it more relevant both to the needs of the economy and to the needs of a wider population of students. In this respect this was a widening participation agenda itself. However, more recent attempts to widen participation have, once again, opened up the question of what students are being given access to:

> It [learning] is a weapon against poverty. It is the route to participation and active citizenship.
>
> (Kennedy 1997: 4)

Presumably this provocative statement indicates the extent to which education is seen as a key to unlock the door to success in life in general. Laudable as this might be, we surely need to place this statement into the social context of Britain in the early twenty-first century. There is little doubt that formal education is able to generate knowledge and understanding for people about a whole range of subjects; to give people the qualifications, which will enable them to enter worthwhile jobs and careers; and to engender a self-confidence about shaping their own self-identity. However, education, in and of itself, is not able to create jobs nor is it able to spirit away disagreeable jobs. Furthermore, as Weberian sociologists would say, whenever there is competition for scarce resources – be it jobs, housing or social status in general – there will be modes of social closure to ensure that some remain more equal than others.

One of most intriguing recent suggestions (Kennedy 1997) is the targeting of the most disadvantaged in society through a 'postcode carrot', i.e. colleges would be rewarded more highly for recruiting students from 'deprived wards' within their catchment areas. To paraphrase the comedian Alexei Sayle, it conjures up images of working-class youth, returning from their evening classes, standing around on windswept housing estate concrete piazzas discussing Chekov. But also it suggests that the qualifications that they will attain will grant them access to more rewarding jobs. This is a mighty task to set the PCET institutions. We might suggest that it is a task which cannot even begin to be addressed if education is not placed within a wider social context.

It is common these days to refer to all curricular reforms as moving us towards a 'learning society'. Clearly, in an increasingly post-industrial (and some would say post-Fordist) society, people will have to get used to the idea that there are no longer 'jobs for life'. Employment is increasingly being experienced as insecure and transient, requiring the constant updating of, often, the 'softer' communication skills. In this context we could argue that we cannot but create a 'learning society', i.e. people will need access to educational opportunities on a regular basis, throughout their lives, if they are to survive this transformation of the social order. Hopefully, this book will cause you to reflect on what exactly is the nature of the 'learning' that this society is giving people access to.

One of the demands of rising to a more postmodern existence is not just to accept the transient nature of the knowledge and skills we might currently own but also to accept the corollary to this, that the curriculum will increasingly receive calls to accommodate 'the distant voices' of the previously unrepresented. Access to the curriculum in this context is thus also about the nature of its content and the political purposes it might serve its recipients. Opening up the curriculum in this way could be conceived as being both liberatory and also as an inevitable consequence of the post-modern sensibility. However, if the curriculum is increasingly perceived as being directed at providing narrowly defined and prescriptive work-based and work-oriented learning opportunities, it could equally be construed as being an attempt by the state to *contain* the nature of 'learning' and the definition of what constitutes 'society'. We might say that we find ourselves increasingly being innovative in meeting the widening participation agenda, but at the same time often feeling restricted by the more narrow curriculum aims of the new vocationalism.

Over the past 25 years we have heard many rallying cries which would support many of the reforms seen in PCET: 'Post-compulsory education is elitist and encourages wastage of talent', 'We need a skilled workforce', 'There's too much social disaffection'. PCET institutions have risen to these challenges but they have done so within a wider social, economic and political context where social inequality persists on a large scale, where secure employment is more scarce, and where entrenched social attitudes are pervasive. Furthermore we might come to see a legacy of the last 25 years as being one where, despite numerous educational reforms, increasing participation in PCET was far more successful than widening participation, where those who benefited most from PCET in the past were simply given more opportunities to benefit further.

The new vocationalism has clearly reawakened our interest in the relevance of the curricula and whom and what they should be serving. This has been a challenge to all parts of the sector – higher education with its traditional concentration of the cognitive and the academic; further education with its traditional combination of liberal education and apprenticeships; and adult education with its traditional ethos of education as being intrinsically and personally fulfilling. However, in our desire to widen educational opportunities we find ourselves not just blurring the boundaries between these once somewhat distinctive institutional settings, but also offering those opportunities within a state agenda which has overseen the introduction of prescriptive curricula, national targets and funding carrots. This has largely been the result of the state wishing to produce a new sense of professional accountability in PCET and this is the subject of Part 2.

Further reading

Ainley, P. and Bailey, B. (1997) *The Business of Learning*. London: Cassell.
Armitage, A., Bryant, R., Dunnill, R. *et al.* (2003) *Teaching and Training in Post-Compulsory Education* (2nd edition). Buckingham: Open University Press.
Barton, L. (ed.) (1996) *Disability and Society*. London: Longman.
Gray, D.E. and Griffin, C. (eds) (2000) *Post Compulsory Education and the New Millennium*. London: Jessica Kingsley.
Hayton, A. (ed.) (1999) *Tackling Disaffection and Social Exclusion*. London: Kogan Page.
Hyland, T. (1994) *Competence, Education and NVQs: Dissenting Voices*. London: Cassell.
Jessup, G. (1991) *Outcomes*. London: Falmer Press.

Mayo, M. and Thompson, J. (eds) (1995) *Adult Learning, Critical Intelligence and Social Change*. Leicester: NIACE.

Pring, R. (1995) *Closing the Gap*. London: Hodder & Stoughton.

Raggatt, P., Edwards, R. and Small, N. (eds) (1996) *The Learning Society: Challenges and Trends*. Buckingham: Open University Press.

Smithers, A. and Robinson, P. (eds) (2000) *Further Education Reformed*. London: Falmer Press.

Thomas, L. (2001) *Widening Access and Participation in Post Compulsory Education*. London: Continuum.

Part I exercises

I The book synopsis

Choose five to ten books, written in the past ten years, which discuss reforms in PCET (use the Further reading as a guide). Produce a one page synopsis of each book using the following headings:

(a) A Harvard-style reference,
(b) Chapter headings,
(c) Summary of the main argument of the book,
(d) Choice, short, quotations.

If you undertake this exercise within a group context, and you exchange synopses, you could end up with ten synopses but only having read one book.

2 Critical review

Write a critical review of a recent PCET reform focusing on its strengths and weakness in terms of your own knowledge gained from professional practice and your knowledge and understanding of other academic work. Use the following list of official reports as a starting point for your focus:

Dearing, R. (1996) *Review of Qualifications for 16–19 Year Olds*. Hayes: SCAA.

DfEE (1997) *Qualifying for Success*. London: DfEE.

DfEE (1998) *The Learning Age*. London: HMSO.

DfEE (1999) *Learning to Succeed: A New Framework for Post-16 Learning*. London: DfEE.

Fryer, R. (1997) *Learning for the 21st Century*. London: NAGCELL.

Fryer, R. (1999) *Creating Learning Cultures*. London: DfEE.

Kennedy, H. (1997) *Learning Works: Widening Participation in FE*. Coventry: FEFC.

Tomlinson, J. (1996) *Inclusive Learning: Report of the Learning Difficulties and/or Disabilities Committee*. Coventry: FEFC.

In the first of the following two polemical pieces, Andy Armitage attempts a celebration of vocationalism by aligning it with progressivist forms of curriculum design, rather than the narrowly defined behaviourist model with which it is more often associated. Furthermore, if we are to be serious about widening participation, rather than just increasing participation, he invites us to consider the urgent need to move away completely from the traditional academic forms of assessment that still pervade PCET. By contrast, in the second of the two pieces, Dennis Hayes revisits the interface between education and work, i.e. the nature of the relationship, which permits us to talk of forms of vocationalism. In a broad-ranging discussion he analyses what it means to create a 'knowledge economy', and more specifically, what sort of knowledge is deemed to be required to furnish workers for the contemporary job market.

QUESTION TO THINK ABOUT

When you have read the two polemical pieces, consider to what extent you would want to argue that PCET reform in the past 25 years has 'dumbed down' education.

Chapter 2

IN DEFENCE OF
VOCATIONALISM

Andy Armitage

There is an important sense in which the debate about vocationalism in education is historical. The reforms of Curriculum 2000, in spite of initial problems of implementation (see Hodgson and Spours 2001; QCA 2001a,b), are producing a 14–19 curriculum framework in which both the academic and vocational are intended to achieve parity: indeed, so determined are policy makers that they should do so, that the word 'vocational' is to be removed from qualifications altogether (DfES 2002). 'Inclusion' has now followed 'lifelong learning' as a focus for public, political and educational debate and those voices raised against it come, in the main, from the same quarter as those which decried vocationalism for its instrumentalism, its denial of education for its own sake and its undermining of the importance of knowledge and understanding. Inclusion, it is argued, will, particularly in post-16 education, depress standards, lead to ever-increasing credentialism and uniformity in experience for students resulting in an emphasis on the product and outcome of education rather than its intrinsic value. Although both debates have arguably been resolved in terms of policy formation and implementation, it is important to clarify why vocationalism and inclusion have been embraced by those who have seen in them the opportunity to challenge the disenfranchisement of so many for so long. Usher and Edwards (1994) note, in terms which indicate what they clearly regard as a conspiracy, how

> The NCVQ, government departments ... articulate competence not simply through a discourse of vocationalism [but] ... as a 'progressive' form of educational and training practice. This has happened through its articulation in humanistic language and practices of meeting

individual need, providing equal opportunities for access and progression, etc.

(Usher and Edwards 1994: 107)

The reason for this sheep's clothing?

The assessment of performance through competences, articulated within the dominant liberal humanist discourse is powerful in sustaining a regime of truth and in itemising and normalising the behaviour of people in the workplace. Discipline and governance are exerted as the ever more 'humane exercise of power'.

(1994: 108)

Usher and Edwards are right to identify liberal humanism as being at the heart of vocationalism, wrong to dismiss this as an appropriation of discourse by the competence movement in search of educational respectability – an exercise in spin. This is because, as I intend to argue, it was no accident that vocationalism became the arena for radical innovation, for the introduction of progressive, humanistic practices such as active, experiential learning, student-centredness, criterion-referenced assessment into mainstream educational orthodoxy resulting in the post-16 framework now taking shape.

Those who defend the early Hirst (1974) 'forms of knowledge' academic curriculum, traditionally appeal to eighteenth-century Enlightenment thinkers as well as further back to Socrates in their belief in the objectivity of knowledge and the supremacy of reason and the scientific process. Their defence is usually framed in the context of an epistemological challenge by various more contemporary groups: post-structuralists who call into question the notion of concepts and logic as universal and culture free (Derrida 1967; Foucault 1974); postmodernists and sociologists of knowledge who challenge the alleged objectivity of knowledge and would want to draw attention to its social construction and de-centre the knowing subject (Berger and Luckman 1966; Young 1971; Usher and Edwards 1994). A challenge from a different direction comes in the form of the claim that the academic curriculum's emphasis on propositional or theoretical knowledge (knowing that), leads to the neglect of practical knowledge (knowing how). Thus Pring (1976, 1995) argues for the balance between the former and latter to be restored and makes a plea for the gap to be closed between academic and practical knowledge.

Arguments for the parity of practical and theoretical knowledge often appeal to Ryle's (1973) distinction between 'knowing how' and 'knowing that', to 'use' theory, exemplified in Wittgenstein's (1953) conception of language games and Austin's (1962) view of performative utterances. Wittgenstein's claim that language cannot be understood outside the context of the non-linguistic human activities into which language is interwoven, is used as a springboard for the justification that knowledge be acquired in contexts outside traditional academic subjects. And Austin's account of the performative nature of utterances is used to support the case for language use and development taking place in real, active learning environments. Hirst himself now holds that practical knowledge is a prerequisite for developing theoretical knowledge and both must be developed by initiation into what he calls 'social practices' (Hirst 1993). The danger with attempts to establish parity between propositional and practical knowledge is that, in accepting the dichotomy between them, there is the risk that the gap will be widened rather than closed or removed altogether. A more promising challenge to the essentialist foundations of the academic curriculum is to question the categorization of knowledge they presuppose. The challenge by Kant ([1787] 1929) and Quine (1953) to this categorization is a challenge to the empiricism which underpins it. According to traditional post-Enlightenment epistemology, propositions were either analytic or synthetic, either akin to the truths of logic and mathematics, true by virtue of the terms or symbols employed, or they were statements about our experience of the world. In arguing for synthetic judgements known a priori, Kant raised the possibility that our knowledge and understanding of the world were developed through the systematic application of concepts in 12 categories, relating to quality, quantity, permanence in time, possibility – impossibility, for example. Quite apart from questioning the empiricist distinction between theoretical and practical knowledge, Kant's epistemology casts us in an active, organizing, instrumental role in knowing and understanding. Quine's attack on empiricism was based on the view that, on the one hand, the analytic statements of logic and mathematics were contingent upon our experience of the world and, on the other, that none of our experience of the world would be possible without theoretical underpinning. The impact of Kant and Quine's arguments is first the questioning of the empiricist notion of the passivity of the knowing subject, the conception of the mind as a *tabula rasa* on which knowledge is imprinted. And second, it calls into question the distinctiveness of the concepts and logic which academic forms of knowledge rely on for their identity. Indeed, one can see the essentialist flaw to be its reliance on a logical, as opposed to an epistemological grounding for such forms of knowledge.

This challenge to the dualism of theoretical and practical knowledge, as well as the promotion of a conception of knowledge and truth as constructed by an active, knowing subject, is most clearly expressed educationally in the work of Dewey ([1916] 1966) and ([1936] 1963). For Dewey, knowledge and truth were to be constructed by learners from their experience: both their own previous personal experience as well as their interaction in a series of social contexts. It is mistakenly thought that Dewey intended such contexts to be exclusively vocational in the sense of being narrowly work-based. However, his conception of the vocational is extremely broad: 'A vocation is any form of continuous activity which renders service to others and engages personal powers on behalf of the accomplishment of results' (Dewey [1916] 1966: 319). These were to take place in learning contexts which needed to 'exhibit a co-operative community, utilise activity to enhance intellectual growth and give rise to problems that stimulate thinking and development' (Harkin *et al.* 2001: 38).

It was the pre-vocational and vocational initiatives of the 1980s, occasioned as they might have been by ideological, social, economic and labour market factors (see Benn and Fairley 1986; Finn 1987; Ainley 1990; Avis *et al.* 1996) which nevertheless offered the opportunity to realize key elements of Dewey's vocationalism. Such initiatives made central, social and practical learning contexts of the kind Dewey described, within and beyond the classroom, in which a synthesis of theoretical and practical knowledge was developed by active learners through problem-solving processes. These features also show the influence of a number of thinkers, each of whom is closely associated with one of the classical or grand learning theories. Indeed, it is possible to argue that central to all such theories are insights which lend support to the value of the kind of experiential learning Dewey first conceived of.

Kolb (1984) acknowledges his debt to Dewey in the development of his model of experiential learning. Such learning for Kolb involves a cyclical process where the learner's concrete experience becomes the object of their reflective observation. This, in turn, leads to the development of abstract concepts which are then tested experientially in new situations. Kolb also argues that each of us has a dominant learning style related to stages in the learning cycle as: accommodator, assimilator, converger, diverger. However, the most effective learning takes place on full completion of the cycle because 'learning is the process whereby knowledge is created through the transformation of experience' (Kolb 1984: 38). This is a definition, Kolb goes on, which emphasizes certain key features of experiential learning:

> First is the emphasis on the process of adaptation and learning as opposed to content and outcomes. Second is that knowledge is a transformation process, being continuously created and recreated, not as an independent entity to be acquired or transmitted. Third, learning transforms experience in both its objective and subjective forms.
>
> (Kolb 1984: 38)

The role of the learner as active, creative and transformative are, then, central to Kolb's model. In this, he is close to cognitivist or structuralist learning theorists, in particular Piaget (1971) and Bruner (1960). In fact, Kolb himself states that

> For Piaget, action is the key. He has shown . . . that abstract reasoning and the power to manipulate symbols arise from the infant's actions in exploring and coping with the immediate environment.
>
> (Kolb 1984: 13)

Carr (1998) has noted that we can see in cognitivists like Bruner and Piaget the connection not only back to Dewey's constructivism but also further back to Kantian categories of human thought and forward to the generative grammar of Chomskian linguistics. Through such areas of philosophy, psychology, linguistics and education theory runs the same thread of the centrality of the transformative action of the learner in gaining knowledge and understanding.

Kolb also acknowledges his debt to Kurt Lewin (1951), whose work is more often associated with adult learning and who emphasized the central role of subjective personal perceptions in experiential learning. In this, he was influenced by a second classical learning theory, derived from the Gestalt school of psychology. Gestalt theorists stressed the integrative, synthesizing role of the mind in creating wholeness from pieces of information, recognizing the pattern or form ('Gestalt') in our experience. Once again, the active role of the learner is paramount in the creation of order through experience. Lewin's work, in turn, was a stimulus both to the development of the 'reflective practitioner' of Schon (1983) and to the notion of the self-directed learner at the centre of Malcolm Knowles's (1984) 'andragogy': key theorists in describing ways in which adults act upon their experience in learning.

In headlining the importance of self-directedness in learning, Knowles is perhaps more appropriately placed in a tradition of thinkers influenced by a third classical learning theory, associated with humanistic psychology. Knowles's andragogy involves a number of assumptions about learners: that they have accumulated experience which will act as a rich resource for their learning; that their readiness to learn has resulted from the need to perform certain key life tasks; that they are intrinsically motivated; and that they will take a problem-solving approach to learning. A key part of learning for Knowles is the learning contract, negotiated between learner and teacher; the important role that such a contract, with its associated needs analysis, negotiation and monitoring of learning, has played in vocational programmes is testimony to Knowles's influence.

Self-directedness, in the sense that effective learning can result only from the individual construing their experience as personally meaningful to them, is at the centre of the work of Gibbs (1988, 1992) and Rogers (1983). For Gibbs, as for Knowles, intrinsic motivation is vital, with learners engaging with material or experience they care about. Key learning strategies for Gibbs include reflection, learning by doing, personal development tasks, group and project work, and problem-based learning, all familiar features of vocational programmes. Rogers also puts a premium on the significance of learning to students and their ability to create meaning through their learning. For Rogers, this involves the whole person engaging both with their own experience and their feelings. The role of self-evaluation is central for Rogers and, in common with both Gibbs and Knowles, he emphasizes the importance of personal involvement in learning, which is most effective when initiated by learners themselves.

For Lave and Wenger (1991), situated learning involves the whole person and takes place as part of their active, lived participation in a community of practice. For them, the role of context in the development of knowledge and understanding is central, chiefly since they reject the notion that it can be decontextualized and acquired in isolation. Here is experiential learning in its most direct form, or rather learning-*as*-experience since Lave and Wenger would quarrel with a notion of learning as a discrete activity occurring independently of other activities. Knowles,

Gibbs and Rogers emphasize the importance of the social dimension and interaction in learning: for Lave and Wenger learning *is* a social experience.

Central to vocational programmes has been the competence-based approach to education and training, underpinned by a fourth classical learning theory, behaviourism. CBET has been the subject of vocal and extensive criticism during the 1990s (Tuxworth 1989; Prais 1991; Smithers 1993; Barnett 1994; Hyland 1994a,b; Raggatt 1994; Skilbeck *et al.* 1994; Hodkinson and Issitt 1995). This criticism has focused largely on what are seen to be limitations on the scope of such learning and assessment as a result of its behaviourist influence. So it is accused of failing to be able to distinguish levels of performance: competence is an either/or, it cannot be graded. CBET focuses solely, it is argued, on the outcomes of learning, on the attainment of behavioural objectives, rather than on the process of learning itself. The reliability of such assessment is called into question by the variation in assessor interpretation of criteria and the uniqueness of the performance context, with one proponent arguing that 'we should just forget reliability altogether and concentrate on validity, which is ultimately all that matters' (Jessup 1991).

Specifying the domain behaviour to be assessed has been problematic, involving what Wolf (1995: 55) describes as an 'attempt to map out free-standing content and standards [which] leads again and again to a never-ending spiral of specification'. However, CBET was introduced as a way of remedying severe shortcomings in *vocational* learning and assessment and it is worth remembering that many saw its arrival as laudably reformist, for reasons I shall explain below when considering the programmes themselves.

Wolf shows clearly that from both a theoretical and an empirical point of view, competence-based assessment is the most valid approach to the assessment of vocational skills and performance (Wolf 1995: 41–52). I want to argue that such an approach has been adopted in more general vocational and academic programmes such as GNVQ and Advanced Vocational Certificate in Education (AVCE) as well as modified and en-hanced programmes such as AS/A2, because of how it validly assesses learning which, far from being conceived of as narrowly behavioural, is character-ized by its affinity with the experiential learning of Kolb and others as well as the deep and personally meaningful models of Gibbs and Rogers, both described above. Two features establish this affinity. First, in such pro-grammes, a premium is placed on performance through real or simulated but practical and active experiences, not merely as a context for assessment but also as a context for learning. This performativeness is central to the creative, transformative role of the learner with regard to their experience. Second, just as CBET performance criteria assume knowledge require-ments are met through the demonstration of competence, so performance criteria in these programmes specify that knowledge and understanding are both developed and demonstrated dynamically in active contexts, removing the dichotomy between theoretical and practical knowledge.

The work of other theorists has provided further insight into and support for the development of programmes which provide a range of contexts in which learners synthesize theoretical and practical knowledge through active, problem-solving strategies. Howard Gardner (1983, 1993) has challenged traditional notions of intelligence which, he claims, relate to only a narrow range of abilities. He conceives of intelligence as 'the ability to solve problems or fashion products that are of consequence in a particular cultural setting or community' (1993: 15).

For Gardner, there are seven distinct types of intelligence: linguistic, logical–mathematical, spatial, musical, bodily–kinaesthetic, interpersonal and intrapersonal. Traditional schooling places most emphasis on the first two of these both in the mediation and transmission of learning and in assessing it. Each of us, however, has a varying, distinctive blend of these intelligences, according to Gardner, which is largely genetically determined but reliant on social and cultural factors for its arrest or development. Gardner's theory arose out of work with special populations such as the brain damaged, as well as prodigies, idiots savants, autistic children, children with learning disabilities, all of whom, he argues, 'exhibit very jagged profiles – profiles that are extremely difficult to explain in terms of a unitary view of intelligence' (1993: 8).

This blend of different intelligences predisposes us to develop ranges of associated knowledge and understanding via particular approaches or entry points to learning which themselves map onto the multiple intelligences: a story or narrative approach; a logical–quantitative entry point; a foundational approach which examines concepts from a philosophical point of view; and finally, an experiential approach. If intelligences are multiple, then so is their associated knowledge and understanding and related learning approaches and the assessment of this learning must also reflect this breadth, in contrast to standardized testing which samples only a narrow range of abilities. Instead, Gardner advocates assessment which

> must include the individual ability to solve problems or create products using the materials of the intellectual medium [which should] . . . highlight problems that can be solved *in the materials of that intelligence.*
>
> (1993: 31)

Gardner characterizes such assessment in a way that recalls the CBET model of assessment discussed above when he describes

> human cognitive competence as an emerging capacity, one likely to be manifest at the intersection of three different constituents: the 'individual', with his or her skills, knowledge and aims; the structure of a 'domain of knowledge' within which these skills can be aroused; and a set of institutions and roles – a surrounding 'field' – which judges when a particular performance is acceptable and when it fails to meet specifications.
>
> (1993: 172–3)

Daniel Goleman has taken Gardner's interpersonal and intrapersonal intelligences and used them as a starting point to develop a theory of emotional intelligence. Goleman's theory is partly based on empirical studies of brain functioning which show the influence of the emotions on the range of human achievement. What one might call 'emotional capital', emotional intelligence, claims Goleman, is as important as academic attainment and as social and environmental factors in affecting an individual's life chances. Importantly, Goleman believes such intelligence is not genetically determined and that educational programmes have a key role to play in compensating and complementing limited emotional learning in other contexts. Both Gardner and Goleman's work have important implications for those general vocational and academic programmes I am claiming have been profoundly influenced by vocationalism. First, an academic curriculum with its focus on linguistic and logical–mathematical intelligence caters only for a narrow population of those whose strengths reside here. Second, a conception of intelligence in terms of problem solving and fashioning products in a particular cultural setting or community, underlines the importance of a broad range of active, experiential contexts for the development of learning and for assessment. Third, it is clear that emotional intelligence must largely be developed experientially in social contexts where emotions can be engaged and reflected upon. And finally, the importance of emotional intelligence once more undermines the distinction between theoretical and practical knowledge and the elevation of the former over the latter in the academic curriculum.

A wide range of learning theorists and practitioners have therefore influenced the nature initially of those programmes which sought to reform vocational learning, principally NVQ and GNVQ. These key features, I want to argue, have proved to be real strengths not limitations. Both programmes set out clear performance criteria as part of the specification of the domain of achievement. These are framed by range statements indicating the preferred contexts in which such performance should be demonstrated and qualified by the underpinning knowledge or knowledge evidence required. Critics regard such features as weaknesses:

> Instead of a holistic framework, CBET atomises and fragments learning into measurable chunks; rather than valuing process and experience, NVQ's are concerned only with performance outcomes; and, most importantly, instead of encouraging critical reflection on alternative perspectives, the NVQ model offers a monocultural view based on the satisfaction of narrow performance criteria and directed towards fixed and predetermined ends.
>
> (Hyland 1994a: 54)

But it is the unitization of learning that for many students makes it more manageable. They are more able to handle short- rather than long-term learning goals. Unitization, or modularity, facilitates credit accumulation and enables the self-pacing of learning progress. Core and option modules maximize student choice allowing customization of the curriculum offer for individuals. Outcome-oriented assessment against publicly specified criteria make assessment transparent for both students and their teachers and emphasizes ability and achievement rather than penalizing failure. Structured learning experiences in real or simulated practical contexts need not preclude students from critically interrogating such experiences or reflecting on alternative perspectives. They provide contexts in which they are more likely to be able to do so. Nor need such experiences lead to individualism and accent personal as opposed to intellectual development.

All the above features can also be identified in what were introduced through the Curriculum 2000 reforms as vocational A levels or AVCEs. These are unitized and foreground, in particular, creativity, production and problem solving in learning experiences, with knowledge and understanding taken to be incorporated in such productive activity. An important dimension of the desired learning is social, and a key element is students' review and evaluation of their learning. Assessment is on a unit basis against graded criteria. The convergence of the underpinning curriculum model with that of more vocational programmes can be seen in the extent to which Key Skills assessment criteria can be signposted in the stages students go through to complete each unit.

These features are shared by the AS/A level programmes which replaced existing A levels. This would, of course, be expected since the Curriculum 2000 framework was intended to allow flexibility and choice in the way individual students combined different programmes and elements of programmes. AVCE, AS, and A levels therefore share a six-unit structure and an identical grading system, for example. Most telling, however, with regard to the influence of vocational programmes, is the extent to which academic AS/A specifications feature those aspects of experiential, activity-based learning described above. This is evident in the AQA AS/A specifications for English language and literature (AQA 1999). The fusion of theory and practice is emphasized in the introduction:

> By combining practical situations for linguistic exploration and analysis with interdependent skills of reading and literary study, the specification seeks to develop the integral study of both, allowing opportunities for autonomous, seamless linguistic and literary analysis.
>
> (AQA 1999: 9)

The award's underlying principles continue this theme:

> in all cases, analytical interpretation and creative skills are of paramount importance and, wherever possible, *a practical approach should be adopted so candidates gain first hand experience of engaging with and exploring texts.*
>
> (AQA 1999, my italics)

The programme's aims are framed in language which conceives of students as active and their learning as highly contextualized by using linguistic and literary concepts, relating texts to contexts, evaluating analytical approaches and making textual comparisons. In the modules themselves, students are essentially active, whether as writers for specific audiences, constructing arguments, persuading or entertaining. One mod-ule requires candidates to study the language of speech in a variety of situations. In another, equally actively, they are asked to adapt texts for different audiences. There is a strong flavour throughout the specification of the contextualization of language and literature and of the necessity of students to actively engage in these contexts in order to understand this.

It is too early to assess the extent to which Curriculum 2000 reforms have better equipped students to make the transition to higher education since the first cohort has only now begun degree programmes. The evidence regarding the success of their predecessors from GNVQ Advanced programmes in so doing is sketchy and inconclusive. Although former GNVQ students on business studies degrees were more aware of insti-tutional needs and teamwork skills on their work placements, their A level counterparts had a better grasp of leadership requirements and self-sufficiency skills (Hobrough and Bates 1998). Other former GNVQ students showed stronger core skills ability but had not transferred their experience of action planning and lacked sophistication in autonomous learning (Smith 1998). The perceptions of admissions tutors was that although GNVQ students had some strengths as a result of completing their programmes, the tutors had doubts about them in comparison with those students with traditional A level qualifications (Williams 2000). It will be interesting to see how admissions tutors perceive and act upon the equivalence accorded by the UCAS tariff to AS, A, AVCE, GNVQ and Key Skills awards. Widening participation is currently at the top of the higher education (HE) providers' agenda with a government target of 50 per cent of 18–30-year-olds in HE by 2010. But many believe the effort to widen participation has been over-concentrated in certain areas of universities' operations. There has been an effort to aim recruitment at under-represented groups. And institutions have increased their support for student learning and study. However, if this expanded population is to be retained and to progress through degree programmes satisfactorily, the HE curriculum and its delivery need to be congruent with reforms affecting their learning before they arrive. Subject benchmarks do broadly reflect requirements for greater activity and self-directedness on the part of learners and their adoption of key and transferable skills at all levels has played a part in this. However, unless degree programmes in their operation and delivery can translate such requirements into reality and assessment procedures move away from traditional summative exami-nations towards greater differentiation and valid measurement of this broader curriculum, any advantage gained by widening recruitment will be lost.

Chapter 3

THE CHANGED NEXUS BETWEEN WORK AND EDUCATION

Dennis Hayes

The world of work has changed . . . We need to take notice.

(Handy 1990: 43)

The changed world of work is a theme that has dominated popular management literature. It is the basis of books like Charles Handy's *The Age of Unreason* (1990) and Alvin Toffler's *Future Shock* (1971) and *The Third Wave* (1981) that are to be seen alongside the pulp fiction at airports and motorway service stations. It appears resurrected every month or so in the business pages of the dailies, in the lifestyle supplements of the Sunday papers, and in glossy magazines. The variations on the theme of 'change' are, by now, familiar ones; the 'Fordist', 'industrial' or 'work society' has been transformed by new technology into the knowledge society; work in the public sector has expanded whereas work in manufacturing has shrunk; 'flexibility', 'quality', 'teamwork' and 'empowerment' have become management watchwords while job insecurity is everywhere, as workers have to accept the end of a job for life and become, to a greater or lesser extent, 'self-actualizing' or 'portfolio' workers; work has been 'feminized', as women now constitute half the world's workforce and 44 per cent of the British workforce; the nature of work itself has changed, emphasizing more and more what is called 'aesthetic' or 'emotional labour'; the location of work is also shifting from the factory to the deskless office, or into the home (Toffler 1971, 1981, 1990; Handy 1990; Noon and Blyton 1997; Bourdieu 1998; Gallie *et al.* 1998; Cully *et al.* 1999; Beck 2000; Bradley *et al.* 2000; Rifkin 2000).

There have been sophisticated attempts to understand what seems to have changed at work. Ulrich Beck, the sociologist of 'risk society', suggests that 'work society' is at an end, and 'endemic insecurity' marks the majority of people's basic existence and lifeworld (Beck 2000: 3). This is, surprisingly, held to be a positive picture of another 'modernity' in which people can plan their own lives and have the possibility for the first time of engaging in 'civic labour' paid for by 'civic money', as well as paid labour (2000: 126–31). Beck's optimistic and idealist vision of the future is unusual in a market full of survival or 'change or die' guidebooks.

Recently, there has been a backlash of sorts against three decades of writing on the revolution in the workplace. Books such as *Myths at Work* (Bradley *et al.* 2000) and the columns of the *Financial Times* (Overell 2002: 10) are revising our assumptions that the workplace has changed. There is, therefore, a need to make a realistic assessment of the nature and extent of any supposed change, and its impact on workers, if we are to make any comments on the changed nexus between work and education.

The obsession with work

One obvious thing that has changed is that we are all obsessed by work. Evidence for this claim can be found in the growing popularity of work-as-entertainment. Television series such as *Ally McBeal*, *ER*, *Teachers*, *The West Wing*, and a seemingly endless stream of 'fly on the wall' documentaries about ordinary work such as *Airport*, *Airline* and *A Life of Grime* are evidence of how life at work dominates the popular consciousness. We find it entertaining when it might be expected that people at home would want to escape from office politics and the tedium and petty problems of work. But they don't switch off, they switch on. Of course, these programmes are not primarily about work, they are about people, and personal relationships that are developing in the workplace. What they exemplify is the fusion of the professional and the personal (*Ally McBeal*).

Further evidence of our obsession with work is what Cary Cooper calls 'presenteeism', or what others call the 'long hours culture' (Cully *et al.* 1999). We are simply spending more time at work, particularly if we are professionals or managers. This is confirmed by Chartered Institute of Management 'Quality of Working Life' reports that show that 40 per cent of professionals are working 51 hours a week or more, and over 70 per cent of managers work longer than their contracted hours (Kinnes 2001a,b). More importantly, in some of the OECD countries 'the decline in average annual hours of work per person in employment, which can be traced back for over a century, has slowed' (Evans *et al.* 2001: 4). The *State of Working America 2000–2001* report also shows that 'family work hours' increased by 246 hours between 1989 and 1998 (Mishel *et al.* 2001). There is, however, a doubt as to whether professionals as a whole, other than this key 40 per cent, are working longer, and whether this extra time spent at work is productive or unproductive. One view for which I have some sympathy is that extra time spent at work is taken up with activities that we might call 'play' (Woudhuysen 2000). But this is not a question we need address here. The fact is that people do spend more time at work and seem to do so as 'willing slaves' without coercion or fear or indeed payment. In a survey of worker attitudes it was found that the concept of getting paid for over-time was disappearing (Hudson *et al.* 1996; Hayes and Hudson 2003).[1] 'Overtime', like the newly coined 'presenteeism', is becoming an archaic term. Both terms reflect a consciousness of a time when there was much more awareness of the separateness of 'work' and 'life'. The division between our working and personal lives is no longer clear, and it is far from certain that people desire a separation any more. Sit on any beach in the summer and your tranquillity will be disturbed by your neighbours' regular mobile phone calls to, and from, work. This is an indication of a profound shift, at least in people's attitudes: they have become preoccupied by work and spend more time there, both physically and mentally.

There are three possible explanations of why we are obsessed with work. The first is the most appealing to educationalists. It is the idea that we have experienced a 'knowledge revolution' and now live in a new, knowledge-based, 'e-society' or in a new 'creative age'. Most of the literature that discusses the relationship between work and education is usually con-cerned with the 'knowledge economy' or 'knowledge capitalism'. The issue of whether there is any is reality behind the claim about a knowledge revolution or whether this is just self-flattering rhetoric of government departments and human resource managers, is addressed in the next section. Here, I wish to concentrate briefly on the notion that new tech-nology itself, i.e. information technology (IT), is bringing about changes in attitudes to work.

The idea that technological change drives society forward in a deter-ministic way is not new. The problem with this particular determinism is that it is not the technology that is the determinant. It is the vague term 'information', into which we can pour whatever we want and whatever social consequences we like. We do not have to accept the government's and business schools' hype about the excitement of IT to recognize that we enjoy the gadgets the new technology produces. The popularity of e-mail and personal computers shows how much we like these toys and delight in playing with them (Woudhuysen 1999: 18–19).

E-mail is a good example for our purposes, as it is the most used applica-tion of the internet. Glee about this leads to an indiscriminate, unnecessary and inefficient usage, that is time-wasting from an employer's and an employee's point of view. Its benefits are doubtful. Does this sort of tech-nological novelty explain why we are obsessed with work? It is unlikely, because e-mailing, just like many earlier innovations, soon becomes another routine and tedious office chore. We can, therefore, put aside the mechanistic view that the 'technology' part of IT has brought about a shift in worker attitudes in any substantial way.

The second explanation is that we have become more interested in work as a result of management attempting to counteract the impact of 'cor-porate downsizing' on employee commitment and morale. The aim of management in downsizing companies was, from the moment of recruit-ment, to get employees to internalize management values and attitudes. This involved continuous learning so that employees could 'work smarter' and the recognition by managers that they could do this best if they taught others (Poynter 2000: 40–3).

This almost therapeutic process involved several strategies including the use of employee assistance programmes (EAPs). When these began in the 1970s in the US they aimed to tackle alcohol- and drug-related problems. They soon expanded to a wide range of programmes aimed at tackling personal problems unrelated to work. They 'focussed on the individual, emphasising the importance of physical and mental fitness and the improvement of personal lifestyles' (Poynter 2000: 42). There are, therefore, some attitudinal changes brought about by these initiatives, along with other 'soft' forms of 'human resource management' (HRM), that could explain passivity in the workforce, but that hardly explain the current obsession with work.

A third explanation is that work has become more important for reasons that derive from outside the workplace:

> work is being made to perform or fulfil additional social roles which have nothing to do with the previous prime function of work as the place for value creation. Work has become more important because of the way the other parts of social life are not working as well as they used to: everything from the family and personal relationships to politics.
>
> (Mullan 2000: 1)

We must recognize that this is a paradoxical relationship. Work is often blamed because, for example, overwork and increased working hours seem to threaten family life, damage personal relationships and leave little time for active social and political involvement. There is no paradox here, merely an inversion of the truth. Work is not the cause of these problems. It is the relocation of personal and social concerns into the workplace that accentuates the feeling of a loss of a personal, family or community life. The pathological concern with 'stress' at work is another example of how work cannot bear the strain of trying to be the focus of the whole of civic life. In such potentially fractious circumstances, management must takes steps towards adopting therapeutic methods. The 'therapeutic company' is becoming a possibility (Mullan 2000: 8).

The argument that it is a changed social and political context that explains the obsession with work seems to be the most convincing and complete. The collapse of collectivity and community leaves work – the eternal necessity – as the only fixed point of civic life. We cannot assume as a consequence that, from a personal point of view, work has become more fulfilling. People's jobs are also less of a source of identity than they once were, but this fixed and fragile identity is all that is left after the collapse of collective welfare state and community institutions. What is happening is that people look to work for self-development opportunities and self-fulfilment just because the rest of life is nowadays less satisfying. One aspect of the disappearance of collective and community institutions is that the workplace becomes the main focus for people's desires and aspirations. The desire for education at work, or lifelong learning, is the most distinctive aspect of this relocation of aspirations. This desire is not for training but for something vague. When it is defined it is expressed as a desire for traditional liberal forms of education including 'a course' and 'a degree' (Hayes and Hudson 2001).

Educational aspirations on the part of individual workers make them susceptible to therapeutic initiatives from management that are *seen by both* as broadly educational, whether they take the form of 'training' or 'staff development'. Any suggestion of duplicity or deception on the part of managers in this focus on education must be rejected. The commitment to education is clearly there at managerial and professional levels. Managers are concerned to promote workplace learning, even if they are unwilling providers. The transmission agent for the therapeutic culture of the new workplace is 'education' itself; it is not the direct result of human resource or any other management style.

In parallel with the coming of the 'therapeutic company', education, right across the age range, has taken a therapeutic turn. The reason for this is that educationalists, as we shall see, have lost confidence in the pursuit of knowledge. Education is now said to have other values and aims, and these turn out to be therapeutic. Most disturbingly, it is in higher education institutions that we find the strongest and most articulate rejection of knowledge and the promotion of therapy. To understand the changed nexus between work and education, this loss of confidence in knowledge must be explored further.

The know-nothing society

A common assumption amongst academics and educationalists is that the contemporary lack of confidence about human knowledge comes from an awareness of deep and unresolved philosophical issues in the area of philosophy known as epistemology. This deals with difficult questions such as, what are the grounds on which we make any knowledge claims? One traditional answer, given by the empiricists, was that our knowledge claims are valid because they have a secure foundation based on evidence from experience, that is, from our senses. These 'foundationalist' views of knowledge are no longer held to be acceptable. A traditional and unresolved difficulty for foundationalism is the familiar 'problem of induction'. Simply put, the problem of induction arises if we ask questions like, just because the sun has always risen in the morning is this sufficient grounds for believing it will do so tomorrow? In the view of the British empiricist philosopher David Hume, 'there can be no *demonstrative* arguments to prove, *that those instances, of which we have had no experience, resemble those, of which we have had experience*' (Hume [1739] 1973: 89). Hume provided an explanation of causality that tried to show that causality was not rationally but psychologically determined. In Hume's view, a causal inference had a cause but was not grounded in the rational inspection of the relations of objects (see Jessop 1970). It was a natural habit of thought. Hume's philosophical psychology is notoriously difficult and we need not discuss it, or the problem of induction, here. What is interesting to note, however, is that nonfoundationalists also leave the problem unresolved. For example, Phillips and Burbules declare that, 'it is safe to say that there is no unanimity about how to resolve "Hume's problem" – even post-positivists disagree amongst themselves over this issue' (2000: 24). Post-positivists believe in 'warranted' knowledge. Earlier 'positivists' and, in particular, the 'logical positivists', held that there were analytical truths (mathematics) or scientific truths (facts about the world) and that all other statements were literally 'nonsense' (ethical or religious beliefs). They were clearly foundationalists. Postpositivists accept that knowledge is fallible and conjectural (Phillips and Burbules 2000: 29).

Postpositivism is mentioned as an example of a general approach adopted by many educationalists who would eschew the term 'postivism' with or without a prefix. Phillips and Burbules rightly claim that 'Much of contemporary epistemology is *nonfoundationalist*' (Phillips and Burbules 2000: 7). One question that might usefully be asked here, is that, if 'knowledge' is obtained by the best procedures available and supported by the 'strongest (if possibly imperfect) warrants', is it not entirely secure? What is being described as 'warranted' or 'conjectural' knowledge – or we might even talk of it as 'nonfoundationalist' knowledge, – *is just knowledge*. There is no need for terminological nervousness just because we have rejected psychologistic foundationalism. In any case, rejecting foundation-alism does not imply the rejection of knowledge or truth. There are other possibilities open to us (Haack 1995).

A concern with these epistemological issues, particularly with issues about the foundations or grounds or justification of knowledge claims is rife in universities and colleges. We might expect and want such a concern from philosophers of education, who have the task of providing a robust educational epistemology, or at least an understanding and defence of human knowledge in the face of attacks by relativists and metaphysicians. However, everyone nowadays seems to be an epistemologist-manqué. In the common room, classroom, conference or corridor, any confident assertion of a true proposition, or any attempt to defend the pursuit of knowledge and truth, is likely to be met with questions about 'whose truth?', or 'whose knowledge?' This does not refer just to sophisticated 'postmodern' playfulness but also to a ubiquitous and woolly-minded rela-tivism and scepticism that seems particularly prevalent in discussions in university education departments and at education conferences.

What it is important to understand is that a profound concern with epistemological issues is not the cause of this universal lumpen-scepticism and relativism. The concern with epistemology arises because of a lack of confidence elsewhere in society. In his discussion of the significance of theory, Terry Eagleton (1989: 30) reminds us that ' "Theory" was born as a result of political intervention, whatever academic respectability it may since have achieved'. Attitudes to 'knowledge' are also a result of political interventions.

In the contemporary political sphere there is a lack of confidence in the potential of human achievements, such as IT, and a negative view of progress. This diminished view of human potential leaves politicians seeking to set limits to people's ambitions and to emphasize caution and self-regulation. The 'precautionary principle' in science is a well-known example of the contemporary hesitancy about progress. In this political climate, academics respond spontaneously to the mood of the times and seek an abstract explanation for the lack of confidence in society. If they are radical, they turn to the work of 'postmodernists' and 'critical theorists' and find a set of writings that seem to reflect this mood, as these works embody the outcomes of an earlier political retreat from Stalinism, into epistemology. What they find in the writings of Foucault, Habermas and others, is a two-fold retreat from politics into a relativistic rejection of objectivity (the retreat from Marxist historical materialism) and to multiple or contingent self theories (the retreat from the working class as the subjective agent of politics). If they are less radical, they find the more philosophical works of the American pragmatists such as Dewey, Quine, and Rorty which challenge the basic tenets of what we called 'foundationalist' views. But this concern with epistemology is discovered *post hoc* and explains nothing.

A simple comparison will make this clear. Consider the period that runs roughly from the launch of Sputnik in 1957, to man's landing on the moon in 1969. In the educational world this is a creative time and it is then that philosophy of education begins to develop as a field of study. The major works of the educational philosophers Dearden, Hirst, O'Conner, Peters, Reid and Scheffler were all written in the 1950s and 1960s. Their works rehearsed the philosophical debates about epistemological issues, for the problem of induction was unresolved and criticisms of foundationalism were being made. What is different, however, is that there was no lack of confidence in society about progress or what human beings could achieve. This contrast does away with any suggestion that the contemporary concern with epistemology is really about epistemological matters.

Furthermore, the interest in epistemology stifles enquiry and reinforces the lack of confidence in progress. Over 40 years ago, C. Wright Mills wrote of the withdrawal of some sociologists from the tasks of the social sciences. He argued that 'abstracted empiricists' and others were so concerned with the philosophy and epistemology underlying their work that it produced a 'methodological inhibition'. This was stifling the sociological imagination:

> What has happened in the methodological inhibition is that men have become stuck, not so much in the empirical intake, as in what are essentially epistemological problems of method. Since many of these men, especially the younger, do not know very much about epistemology, they tend to be quite dogmatic about the one set of canons that dominate them.
>
> (Wright Mills 2000: 74)

The same is happening today but in a more generalized way. Most people, including most academics, do not know much about epistemology and the concern with epistemological issues stifles their imagination. When we hear the word 'epistemology' used by those who are not epistemologists we should reach for our guns.

The loss of confidence in the academy

If it is not an epistemological issue, what explains the loss of confidence in knowledge that is widespread amongst academics? As very few people recognize what the cause is, it is worth stating at the outset: *academics have lost confidence in the academy and the academy has lost the confidence to argue for its own project*. It is also worth stating that this project is *the disinterested pursuit of knowledge*.

No single statement encapsulates this lack of confidence about the role of the university better than this: 'Knowledge and control are not, thankfully, available. (That belief partly led to Auschwitz.) What is both necessary and possible – just – is an enlightened societal self-monitoring' (Barnett 2000a: 68). This sentence is taken from Barnett's bestselling book *Realizing the University in an age of supercomplexity*. Barnett understands and describes very clearly the academic project of disinterested enquiry. He identifies internal threats to the intellectual heritage of disinterestedness, seeing this as a conflict between the managerialist value of performativity and the academic value of collegiality (Barnett 2000a: 25–30). If this conflict was central we could look at issues such as 'job insecurity' and think of how to tackle the conflict of values from the point of view of academic workers. Even this discussion could begin only if we assumed that a defence of disinterested enquiry should be undertaken. Barnett does not want to do this. He wants to reposition the university within wider society, devoid of the 'ideological baggage . . . of spreading the light of reason' (2000a: 69). Instead of spreading the light of reason, the university is to reorganize itself around the 'uncertainty principle'. This will transform it into an institution that

> (i) contributes to our uncertainty in the world (through its research and consultancy); (ii) helps us monitor and evaluate that uncertainty (through its work as a centre of critique); and (iii) enables us to live with that uncertainty, through both the operational capacities and the existential capacities it promotes (in its pedagogical activities).
>
> (Barnett 2000a: 69)

The blurb on the book adds 'to revel in our uncertainty' to point (iii). Barnett is not a lone or eccentric voice. A recent book on the university in the knowledge society, pointedly entitled *Challenging Knowledge*, argues that he is correct, and that the university must 'allow society to live at greater ease with uncertainty' (Delanty 2001: 155). This is because it is one of the 'few locations in society' where the discourse of the 'challenge of technology' and the discourse of 'culture' interconnect (p. 158). This claim exaggerates the role and importance of the university in helping to overcome the cultural damage done by capitalism and managerialism. The new role on offer, however, is the only one possible when you give up on the pursuit of knowledge, namely, that the university has a 'communicative role' (p. 11) in the 'knowledge economy'. This can only mean that it has a 'therapeutic' role. Barnett and his epigones are providing us with an account of what would be better called the 'therapeutic university', an institution that has an ethical purpose (to make people feel safe and secure), and in which knowledge doesn't figure. This vision of the university is an articulate celebration of the loss of confidence in the academy.

Before leaving this discussion, it might be useful to consider if there is not some basis in reality for the lack of confidence in knowledge and the academy. The traditional role of the university as the market leader in the production of knowledge might be challenged in fact rather than in theory.

A knowledge revolution?

Do we live in a knowledge economy or is it best to say that we have always lived in 'knowledge' economies? The introduction of steam power and electrical power, and the industrialization of car production, all involved knowledge. Or does the 'knowledge' or 'information economy' refer just to the IT sector of the economy? We begin to play with words here. Do not contemporary car production and oil exploration involve knowledge? An answer should be sought not in the fantasies of academics or management gurus but in an analysis of what is happening in the real world of business.

A recent survey of the impact of advances in IT on business and productivity shows that many of the claims made about changes that are happening are false or exaggerated. Improvements in the productivity of individual businesses are shown to be a function of 'one-off' downsizing activities and a longer and more intensive working day. They are not a result of the impact of new technology. New technology appears to be a lifestyle choice for businesses and businesspeople, as colossal increases in expenditure on computing and IT do not correlate with increased productivity (Woudhuysen 1999).

It is always salutary to remind ourselves that, for all the celebration of the role of knowledge workers, profits are still obtained through old-fashioned production lines where workers put CDs in boxes or install microchips. The potential of the new technology to drive change is not proven. Most expenditure on the internet is used to provide data warehousing. The projected expenditure on the world market for storing data is $24 billion whereas a mere $3 billion will be spent on online analytical processing. Even less than this, $0.8 billion will be spent on data mining. The conclusion is that 'storing data will be a bigger market than learning from it' (Woudhuysen 1999: 8–9). Information is not being transformed into knowledge.

Arguments based on the speed and complexity of change are equally disputable. Despite its benefits when accompanied by harder work, IT is not producing the kind of 'creative destruction' of old technologies that steam, electricity and motorization brought to economies' (Woudhuysen 1999: 18). Progress in the spread of IT is relatively slow. Change is not as huge and global as we might presume. The World Trade Organization suggested that there would be a total of 300 million internet users by 2001. But with the world's population reaching 6 billion, 'this represents a global penetration of only 5%' (Woudhuysen 1999).

The conclusion of the survey is that it is human creativity that has the potential to transform our lives through new technologies, but in the present climate of insecurity and caution in business, this may be being squandered. Meanwhile, we are left with IT as a displacement activity at work and 'edutainment' in colleges and universities.

Knowledge and 'knowledges'

Most workers have not been transformed into knowledge workers and the work of new knowledge production by business is static or declining.

Research and development in the economy as a whole has been under 2 per cent of gross domestic product during most of the 1990s. Likewise, the funding of research and development (R&D) by business has been relatively static at 1.2 per cent of GDP. However, figures for R&D funding in the manufacturing sector declined by 3 per cent between 1994 and 1996. In 1997 manufacturers' spending on R&D fell dramatically from 11.8 per cent of turnover to 5.4 per cent according to the CBI's 1998 *Innovation Trends Survey* (CBI 1998). Spending on innovation also fell from 5.9 to 4.9 per cent of turnover. Employment in R&D in business declined from 157,000 to 145,000 between 1993 and 2000, reaching a low of 137,000 in 1997 (National Statistics 2001). Recent increases, therefore, calculate from a low point. Much of what academics wrote at the time about the new knowledge economy did not reflect the fact that R&D in business and industry in the UK was at a relatively low level. They were, therefore, mere flights of fancy.

If the university is now one amongst many sources of knowledge production, R&D funding should be increasing. A 'knowledge revolution' would mean a huge growth in this sector of the economy. Where there is real growth is in the university sector.

In the UK there are 132 publicly funded HE institutions. HE income and expenditure is about £12 billion. This is 1.4 per cent of GDP; its contribution to the economy is held to be 3.5 per cent of GDP. 'Productivity' in the sector averaged 6 per cent between 1991 and 1995, compared with 2 per cent for the UK service sector as a whole. Recent figures show that increases in expenditure in both cash and real terms were, as a percentage, significantly higher than increases in business R&D expenditure between 1988 and 2000 (National Statistics 2002).

Figures from the 1996 and 2001 Research Assessment Exercises (RAEs) recorded 48,000 active researchers. This is an increase of 11 per cent over the 1992 numbers and accounts for half the staff in universities. (HEFCE 1997). The quality of the research has also improved, as the 2001 exercise also showed that 55 per cent of staff work in the top-graded institutions compared with 36 per cent in 1996.

Staff employed in the university sector number 300,000. Academic staff numbers have grown by 60 per cent between 1986 and 1997. In 1998 they stood at 105,287 and this rose to 112,374 the following year. In 1998 there were 28,690 researchers and 20,701 academic-related staff (Bett 1999: 13–21).

This growth, although we might question some aspects of it, should put academic staff in a confident mood. Barnett, of course, does not expect the university to cease being a big knowledge producer. But for the traditional knowledge producer to be growing while other knowledge production declines leaves his vision with no foundation.

He does say that: 'It is not that the clerks have lost their monopoly over the definitions as to what is to count as knowledge . . . it is that they have lost their monopoly over the definition as to what is to count as knowledge' (Barnett 2000a: 35). What follows this is an exercise in *nominalism*. Barnett lists things we could, and some people do, call knowledge. But if any trivial activity such as writing a mission statement counts as knowledge production, then the concept of knowledge is debased. Can we really equate the recent advances in our knowledge of genetics with this sort of thing? One task for academics should be to provide a critique of this trivialization of the concept of knowledge.

The triumph of therapeutic education

In the companion book to this (Armitage *et al.* 1999: 22–6) there is a section on the 'triumph of vocationalism' in post-compulsory education (PCE). The debate, in that book, about vocationalism was set in the context of the irreconcilability of 'education' and 'practical' or 'vocational' to 'vocational training' of whatever sort. It is still true that vocationalism is triumphal. Even philosophers of education have turned sociologists to defend concepts of 'aims' in education that are descriptive, or arise out of a utopian social vision (Winch 2002). The intention of the earlier argument was to give the changing historical context to those who saw a young person as ' "the heir of all the ages" and the treatment of him as job fodder' (Anderson 1980: 156). A different social context has since emerged in which there seems to be a greater focus on 'education' than on 'training'. It is worth summarizing the previous discussion. Four periods in PCE were identified through different analyses of the changing nexus between work and education. The first related to the 1950s and 1960s, when the approach to vocationalism in education was straightforward, and involved *training for jobs*. The second period related to the 1970s and was a response to mass youth unemployment and involved the same sort of training but was *training without jobs*. The third period covers the 1980s and early 1990s, although it was initiated by Callaghan's 'Great Debate' in 1976, and involved a general pre-vocational form of training that was called the *'new' vocationalism*. The fourth period is the contemporary one that is characterized as a period of *education without jobs*.

At the risk of terminological confusion, and a loss of specificity of the sort that is common in writing on PCE, we could see the contemporary period as a 'new' new vocationalism. The education that is now on offer is a form of preparation for work and arises out of the changed nexus between work and education. The new vocational skills that are required in the workforce are sometimes called 'emotional' or 'aesthetic' labour. If PCE students are being trained in personal and social skills as well as in relationships, this is training in emotional labour. The so-called 'key skill' of 'working with others' is an example of emotional labour. At its most trivial, emotional labour consists of nothing more than the fast-food or call-centre training in speech codes of the 'Have a nice day' variety. But training in emotional labour goes deeper than this and requires and receives a personal and wholehearted commitment to workplace values. This training will be consolidated when a student starts work, whether in private or public sector institutions. PCE institutions are, in fact, paradigm examples of the modern 'learning organization', offering training in emotional labour to students, and professional training and staff development that is quite often nothing more than training in emotional labour (Hayes 2002a,b). At this level, 'training' can only be described as 'education' and, as we have seen, 'education' today has nothing to do with the pursuit of knowledge: it is about enabling people to live with uncertainty. Crucially, this involves building up people's self-esteem, and it is here that the relativistic attitudes that now draw support from epistemological critiques of foundationalism and other aspects of Enlightenment modernity such as rationality, objectivity, science and progress come into their own. They support anyone's values and viewpoint without any damage or offence to their 'self-esteem'. This is *therapeutic education*. The contrast with the pursuit of knowledge is sharp, as it necessarily causes offence, and should do so.

Just as knowledge is under attack, so is the Enlightenment concept of the human subject, mankind, that can have that knowledge and use it in rational ways to advance society. This two-fold attack of the new epistemologists undermines both the subject and object of knowledge. Although, we have concentrated on the lack of confidence in knowledge, it is important to recognize that similar arguments apply to the *knowing subject*. For example, where we have discussed not knowledge but 'knowledges', in this parallel discussion, the self becomes our 'multiple selves', or identity becomes 'multiple identity'. Learning to live with such notions demands a therapeutic approach to education. But the deconstruction of the human or knowing subject is not part of the lessons from postmodernism or any other philosophy. It is a political response to the demise of the notion of human agency that occurred as a result of the collapse of the collective forms of working-class organization, in the form of the labour and trade union movement, as well as of more radical projects. The working class that was once the 'subject' or subjective factor pushing society forward, disappeared as a political force after the collapse of communism in 1989. The demise of that subject inevitably meant the demise of the human or knowing subject.

The crux of the changed nexus between work and education is that the 'knowledge' society is actually its opposite. It is a society in which institutions set aside to pursue or promulgate knowledge have given up on their project. This is evidence of social stagnation because a society that does not have confidence in the pursuit of knowledge is a society that is going nowhere. All that society can offer is therapy and therapeutic organizations and initiatives to help adjust to the low expectations they are now expected to have. This explains how the government can focus so much on improving 'basic skills', an ill-defined idea that often includes personal qualities and attitudes. Talk about 'basic skills' means: 'Get used to having limited expectations and no aspirations'.

The pursuit of knowledge, just like real training for skilled jobs, always goes on. There are never enough philosophers and scientists or good nurses, cooks or plumbers – but, at the present time, it is taking place in an environment that is hostile and ever-encroaching. The therapeutic ethos is difficult to resist and we are moving towards the creation of what can be called the 'therapeutic college' that will close the gap between the 'therapeutic school' (Nolan 1998) and the 'therapeutic university' (Hayes 2002a, 2003 forthcoming). As therapeutic education becomes the norm, the basis is set for resolving the stresses caused by the obsession with work. The individualized and fractious workforce, will be replaced by a workforce of the future in which every worker will be concerned with enhancing their own self-esteem and that of others. This future is not going to be a new creative age. To be creative you must take risks, and taking risks means the possibility and the actuality of failure. The therapeutic future will be static and dull.

Note

1. This chapter draws on published and unpublished research undertaken with my colleague Alan Hudson into working-class attitudes. The data are drawn from two research projects: the first is a survey of the attitudes to work of 1000 workers in 12 geographical areas of Britain and the second is a longitudinal study of the social and political attitudes of skilled workers in Basildon, Essex.

THE ORGANIZATION OF POST-COMPULSORY EDUCATION

Chapter 4

OVERVIEW: THE ORGANIZATION OF POST-COMPULSORY EDUCATION

John Lea

Introduction

In Part 2 we look at PCET more from an organizational point of view by considering what exactly is the nature of the organizations in which PCET practitioners are employed? This will involve a discussion of organizational structures, systems of accountability, and organizational purposes. As we saw in Part 1, the sector has seen many changes in the past 25 years, perhaps none more so than in the way the typical PCET organization has reframed its *modus operandi*. It is common to refer to the changes that have been brought about as 'the new managerialism', and this will be the main focus for this part.

There are two broad strands to the new managerialism. First, there was the expressed desire of the Conservative government elected in 1979 to seek to call to account the many public sector professionals working, particularly, in health, education and the social services. After all, ran the argument, their salaries were paid by the taxpayer and the taxpayer should have the right to know what they were getting for their money (and how to measure increases in their productivity). Second, the same government sought the means to improve the efficiency of these public servants by bringing a 'market-oriented' philosophy and practice to public service provision. This produced a new business language enabling managers to track funds using funding formulae which quantified all aspects of their provision (McGinty and Fish 1993). Indeed, because of these changes we might argue that the notion of management now had a much clearer identity in the public services.

We should not underestimate the significance of these changes within PCET. First, the changes were broad-ranging, necessitating that PCET practitioners assimilate them mentally. Second, they were introduced into a PCET context where many practitioners felt that they already had a strong professional value base. Finally, they were introduced at the same time as other educational agendas – most significantly, the 'new vocationalism' and 'widening participation' (see Part 1), and we need to ask what effects this might have had on these agendas. These issues are discussed throughout this chapter. Although the further education incorporation legislation of 1992 is often seen as the watershed for these changes, we should not forget that they could be seen across the whole of PCET and, to a large extent, they had begun before this date. Indeed, authors such as Elliot and Hyland have argued that the 'competency movement' had already set important wheels in motion (Elliot 1993; Hyland 1996).

There is probably no corner of PCET practice that has not been influenced in some way by the 'competency movement'. What we are concerned with here is how the 'competency movement' has changed the nature of the social relations between professionals within PCET organizations. More specifically, we need to address the degree to which CBET has helped to either reprofessionalize or deprofessionalize the PCET practitioner.

Hyland (1996) charges the 'competency movement' with being responsible for attacking the professional autonomy of the PCET teacher and as being an important means by which the government of the day sought to control not just the content of parts of the PCET curriculum, but also the nature of the performance of the PCET teacher. This was achieved by ensuring that the core of student experience should be the achievement of predetermined competences as laid down by employer-based Lead Bodies.

> professional studies and education and training generally have been forced to change in order to accommodate what Elliot (1993) calls the 'social market' model according to which the 'outcomes' of professional learning are construed as quantifiable products which can be pre-specified in tangible and concrete forms. A major vehicle for such change has been the competence-based education strategy popularised through the work of the National Council for Vocational Qualifications.
>
> (Hyland 1996: 168–80)

Discussion point

To what extent would you accept that a teacher/assessor's work is governed by Lead Bodies? Is this a good or bad thing? Would you say that CBET assessment has changed much over the years?

Some authors have taken the argument a step further and argued that the 'competency movement' is part not just of a deprofessionalization process, but also of a deskilling process (Carter 1997). This thesis has been prompted by the discussions surrounding the publication of the seminal work *Labor and Monopoly* (Braverman 1974). In this book he analyses the way that the twentieth century saw a 'degradation of work', where all the skills and knowledge previously held by workers were slowly wrested from them and placed in the hands of managers who used this newly founded 'science of work' to control the workplace and the output of the now deskilled workforce. Braverman predicted that this trend would continue into routine non-manual work and we might now say that it has begun to encroach on (lower or public sector) professional work as well, where the government and its agencies become the 'controllers' of the workforce.

For example, in the early 1990s there was a concerted effort to make teacher training courses competence-based, where the core skills of teaching were packaged as a series of behavioural outcomes (Moore 1996). Stripped of its fuzzy ethical base, teacher training could become a technical exercise where trainee teachers methodically acquired the tools of the trade, signed off by assessors, using pre-specified observable performance criteria. Indeed, this might just have been the way (favoured in some right-wing quarters) to exorcise teacher training from some of the radical teacher education departments located in the university sector in the UK. More recent history has seen the creation of the Further Education National Training Organization (FENTO), and the attempt to revisit professionalism, not with competences but national standards. This is not the place to discuss the difference between a competence and a standard but, in passing, it may be noted that, in terms of the call to public accountability, it perhaps matters very little.

It is important to contextualize these developments. Textbook definitions of 'professional' usually include a combination of the following characteristics: long training programmes in specialist knowledge; an ethic of altruism; autonomous work practices; the presence of a professional association (see K. MacDonald (1997) for a detailed discussion). These characteristics might be argued to be at the heart of any professional value system and if they were in place amongst PCET practitioners prior to the reforms we have been discussing, it is perhaps not surprising that they would come into conflict with the 'new managerialist' paradigm. Putting it crudely, the last thing that a committed professional would want is somebody else telling them how to do their job. What was perhaps equally frustrating to many professionals was the introduction of forms of accountability which 'sat on top' of what was already in place. For example, if lecturers hold themselves up to the critical scrutiny of their students, are accountable to a departmental hierarchy, are internally and externally scrutinized for the purposes of course validation and implement the recommendations of external examiners or verifiers, what merit was there in introducing another layer of accountability? All of this, of course, would come on top of their own sense of professional pride.

Discussion point

To what extent do you share the view that 'trust' in professionalism is too flimsy a base for the purposes of accountability?

Clearly, the basis for conflict was established here. No doubt this was fuelled by the popular perception that the Thatcher governments had little respect for public sector professionals, to which we might now add the popular perception that the Blair governments have also found it difficult to trust these professionals to strictly adhere to nationally agreed targets for the public services. The 1990s saw the establishment of many government educational quangos: the Further Education Funding Council, now replaced by the Learning and Skills Council (LSC), along with its inspection tools the Adult Learning Inspectorate (ALI) and Ofsted, and the Higher Education Funding Council (HEFCE), along with its inspection tool the Quality Assurance Agency (QAA). All of these are charged with producing the quality criteria by which PCET organizations will be judged as being worthy of merit and further funding. On top of this we now have the Institute for Learning and Teaching in Higher Education (ILT) as well as FENTO, who are charged with overseeing the professional training required by new entrants to the PCET professions. It might be argued that these were long overdue institutions aimed precisely at making publicly funded organizations more accountable for the public funding they receive. However, again, it might also be argued that they are, in part at least, the means by which a profession could be deprofessionalized.

Behind all of these changes was the determined effort to bring a 'social market' philosophy to education – a sense that what lies at the root of accountability is a desire to see education responding efficiently to consumer demand. One of the effects of this has been an increasing sense that education is a commodity, just like any other, and the sense that the public should get what the public wants. Students thus become customers with needs, and it is the job of the educational organization to satisfy those needs with appropriate 'products', i.e. courses, programmes and qualifications.

One of the ways in which the demands of this more 'business-like' approach has encroached on the practices of educational organizations is the use of business plans, mission statements and a sense of corporate image – in essence a statement of aims and objectives for a whole organization for the foreseeable future. This could be argued to produce a new set of social relations because it asks teachers to reflect (possibly through a formal appraisal system) on where they see themselves in terms of these aims and objectives. There is a sense here in which the individual is being asked to see themselves not as an individual but as a member of a corporate team. The aim of this 'collegiality' would be to improve the working practices of an organization, helping employees to realize an organization's aims, but it might equally be argued that the collegiality could easily become contrived, where teachers with their traditional emphasis on public service are increasingly co-opted into accepting a new set of values which are, in effect, very different but are disguised in a language of 'community and co-operation' (Hargreaves 1994).

> **Discussion point**
>
> To what extent would you agree with the policy of importing a 'business' approach to public service providers such as educational establishments?

Taking on board what has been raised above, we might argue that the past 25 years have not just been about educational reform, but also about wholesale political and economic reform, concerned with how best to provide and fund public services. Indeed, in some political circles the question has been raised of whether there should be any traditional public services at all. Readers familiar with economic theory will recognize this as an introduction to the debate between monetarists and Keynesians on how best to run a modern capitalist economy. There was a time when the political right and the political left were reasonably clear about such ideological matters. Elected governments, of course, are another matter.

With the benefit of hindsight we can see reasonably clearly that throughout the post-war period from 1945 until about 1975, right-wing and left-wing governments all governed within much the same social democratic consensus. Here was a period in history where there was a broad acceptance that public goods such as healthcare and education should be publicly funded by progressive taxation, and free at the point of delivery to every citizen according to need. Herein lies the fundamental reason why Thatcherism was so revolutionary, for it broke with this tradition and, paraphrasing Friedman and Friedman (1979), it offered the nation the simple maxim that 'individuals know best how to spend their own money'.

It might be argued that this simple maxim has helped to reframe the whole nature of PCET organizations. No longer would colleges be forwarded money because they said they needed it. From now on every college must see itself as a 'learning provider', offering programmes of learning to its customers who will either pay individually or be sponsored. Should the provider not provide the service adequately there is no reason why it should be paid, leaving the customer to shop around to find a more appropriate provider. In this marketplace, only the most efficient will survive and the service they provide will be the best that money can buy. After all, why should taxpayers' (or indirectly an individual's) money be wasted on shoddy goods?

I have recounted this economic tale not simply to rehash the right/left political debates of the post-war past, but also to remind us, as PCET practitioners, what exactly has been at stake. Bringing the marketplace to education required that PCET organizations were willing and able to compete for students and resources and understood that there would be penalties for 'poor' performance. However, the Blair government has argued that it is not a government made up of old right or left ideologues but practises the Third Way. The new Learning and Skills Council was formed against the backdrop of this new political language. The final section of this chapter considers how much this new language represents a real political shift.

The rest of this chapter looks in more detail at the background to, and some of the implications of, these market-oriented, and, more recently, Third Way reforms. More explicitly it looks at the interrelated nature of PCET institutional *cultures*, and PCET institutional *accountability*. This will involve discussions of: the nature of the organizational structures of PCET institutions; (post)modern working conditions; the changing nature of student accountability; and finally the nature of public accountability. In the process the chapter draws on wider sociological concepts and, more specifically, on the work of Hargreaves (1994) and Ritzer (2000).

PCET cultures

Background

In his book *Changing Teachers, Changing Times*, Hargreaves (1994) reflects on the types of social relations which now typify educational organizations and how social change is being responded to in these organizations. He raises the issue that the employment of increasing numbers of managers in education has actually produced two distinct groups of professionals who do not necessarily share the same values. This has resulted in the quality assurance mechanisms currently in operation being implemented and monitored by a new tier of middle management usually drawn from the ranks of former teachers.

These developments would appear to raise two distinct concerns. First, as identified previously, the new forms of supervision and surveillance can be viewed either as a more efficient form of accountability or as a more sinister form of state control of educational output. Secondly, we might now add to this the fact that the values inherent in the new forms of supervision might be argued to be distinct from the values more traditionally associated with education and educationalists. Hargreaves summarizes this distinction by using the work of the anthropologist Hall, who distinguishes between monochronic and polychronic time frames (Hargreaves 1994: 102). Table 4.1 lists some of the features of each time frame.

Discussion point

How far would you say that the following dichotomy resonates with your own recent experience of PCET practice?

Table 4.1 Monochronic and polychronic time frame

Monochronic time frame	Polychronic time frame
One thing at a time	Several things at once
Completion of schedules	Completion of transactions
Low sensitivity to context	High sensitivity to context
Control over completion of schedules	Control over description and evaluation of tasks
Orientation to schedules and procedures	Orientation to people and relationships

Hyland alludes to this dichotomy:

> To manage a budget and to achieve the public service equivalent of profit has become the central concern of a whole stratum who previously thought of themselves as committed mainly to providing a public service. Seducing and cajoling the public sector middle class into the embrace of the market has been a key objective of public service reforms.
>
> (Hyland 1996: 76–7)

Whereas Hyland indicates that this is a shift in the nature of the sector's work, Hargreaves seems to be pointing out that it is actually about the creation of a new tier of public sector professionals, who have found themselves pitted against the more traditional public servant. In this respect the new managerialism has been about co-opting ex-public servants into becoming a new breed of corporate managers, who will then supervise the 'output' of those they have left behind. Indeed, they may have to invest a lot of their time in thinking about ways in which they can persuade their recalcitrant (ex)colleagues that education has 'outputs'.

It might be argued that this new managerialist paradigm has not so much been fostered within PCET as foisted on it. There may be several reasons for this. If, as seems to have been the perception amongst senior Conservative ministers in the Thatcher government, professional autonomy was actually a veil to disguise inefficiency, there would have to be a battle to wrest control away from these professional groups. Also, if publicly funded (and feather-bedded) educational organizations were to be brought into the monetarist fray there would have to be an enormous amount of work to be done to put into place practices which were not only absent but actually alien to the sector. In this context it is perhaps not surprising that the past ten years have seen not just a radical restructuring of the PCET organizational landscape, but also high social costs in terms of personal stress, staff turnover, disciplinary procedures and trade union/professional association activity.

Reflecting on the recent work of the organizational management guru Charles Handy, it might be said to be somewhat ironic that PCET organizations have been adopting the very management structures and styles that large private sector organizations have been steadily ditching in favour of what are often referred to as flatter and more democratic systems. However, it could equally be argued that if PCET organizations need to be brought kicking and screaming into the twentieth century then the twenty-first century will have to wait a while.

The first person to appear on the corporate PCET stage was the line manager, and this person has become many PCET practitioners' most obvious love/hate object. At one extreme the line manager is clearly a mentor, an appraiser and a critical friend, in the middle they are the human resource manager, but at the other end of the continuum they are an incompetent ogre who either cannot teach or will not teach, and has clearly been promoted above their capabilities.

Charles Handy (1993) uses the work of Mant to reflect on a fundamental difference at the heart of the management styles, which were flippantly alluded to in my continuum:

> There are two sorts of people in this world, says Alistair Mant, and one of them ought never to be promoted to high rank. One sort thinks of life, and success, in terms of his or her relationships with other people – the object being to control, dominate or seduce the other in the interest of personal survival. These are the bipods, or raiders.
>
> The other sort are tripods or builders (ternary thinkers as opposed to binary thinkers). For them the question is not so much 'Shall I win?' but 'What's it for?' For these people there is a third corner to all relationships – the task or purpose. They can, says Mant, run personal risks in pursuit of some high purpose and can observe themselves in their relationships. They can, as it were, see the joke.
>
> (Handy 1993: 74)

As I hinted earlier, the bipod thinker may have been foisted upon the PCET world owing to the urgent need to reform organizational structures and practices. In the process this has produced a 'rapid results' mentality, a sense that there are uncharted career paths in the making, and possibly an acute sense of insecurity. We might argue that having to establish a management CV at breakneck pace is perhaps no way to foster the kind of tripod thinker that Mant refers to above.

The process of change

It is at this point that we should remind ourselves that change of any sort is a process. Change is rarely readily accepted, and although perhaps manifesting itself outwardly, it is only in the subjective mental assimilation of change that it is really accepted by individuals.

> No one can resolve the crisis of reintegration on behalf of another. Every attempt to pre-empt conflict, argument, protest by rational planning, can only be abortive; however reasonable the proposed changes, the process of implementing them must still allow the impulse of rejection to play itself out. When those who have power to manipulate changes act as if they have only to explain, and when their explanations are not at once accepted, shrug off opposition as ignorance or prejudice, they express a profound contempt for the meaning of lives other than their own. For the reformers have already assimilated these changes to their purposes, and worked out a reformulation which makes sense to them, perhaps through months or years of analysis and debate. If they deny others the chance to do the same, they treat them as puppets dangling by the threads of their own conceptions.
>
> (Marris 1975, in Fullan 1991: 31)

I am sure we can all remember situations where good ideas got lost because they were poorly managed and bad ideas have survived through careful management.

Discussion point

To what extent would you accept that the problems associated with the radical restructuring of PCET organizations in the past ten years have largely been ones related to the assimilation and management of change?

Although organizational structures are clearly socially constructed, with their own hierarchies, systems of communication and working practices, there is also a sense in which they can take on a reified form, i.e. a sense that not only is this 'the way that things get done round here' but it is actually the only way that things can get done. This may in part reflect the vested interests and prejudices of certain individuals, but it can also be the product of the way in which individuals use organizations and groups to exhibit their own conscious and unconscious desires, anxieties and defence mechanisms.

> In aggressive, individualistic organizations the corporate culture is often characterized by what Wilhelm Reich would describe as a phallic-narcissistic ethos, where satisfaction is derived from being visible, adored, and a 'winner'. Such organizations regard and encourage this kind of narcissistic behaviour exactly as rigid bureaucracies institutionalize anality.
>
> (Morgan 1996: 226)

Morgan refers to such organizational structures as 'psychic prisons'. In the same way that Plato's cave dwellers cannot contemplate that the shadows on the walls of the cave are actually shadows, we find individuals in organizations unable to break free from their own mental traps. (Is this another footnote to Plato?) (Plato *The Republic*) There is a difficult chicken and egg scenario here. Are individuals attracted to organizational structures which reflect their own crystallized psyche or are they produced from within these structures? No matter, the important point is to understand that organizational structures are more than simply the rational means to achieve avowed ends.

What I hope is instructive about this discussion is the extent to which it promotes the view that organizational structures should be seen as cultures and cultures which are multifaceted and multilayered. To use an analogy, just as teachers are constantly being reminded that students have individual learning styles, we should perhaps also remind ourselves that colleagues have management and communication styles which also require careful understandings.

Hargreaves (1994: 13) has skilfully depicted the various types of, what he calls, 'teacher cultures'. In this depiction we see:

- 'fragmented individualism' – where teachers act as if they are simply ploughing their own furrow with little concern for others;
- 'balkanization' – where departments and sections define themselves in part by their separation and distinctiveness from others;
- 'collaborative culture' – where there is a sense that everyone is in the same boat sailing on a mutually agreed route;
- 'contrived collegiality' – where there is a sense of teamwork but also an overarching sense of control;
- 'moving mosaic' – where there is a sense of a fast-moving set of flexible relationships responding quickly and imaginatively to changing circumstances.

Discussion point

Do any of Hargreaves's teacher cultures resonate with your own experience of PCET organizations?

Hargreaves's own view is that too often we see forms of 'contrived collegiality'. This is perhaps not surprising when we reflect on the fact that there have been enormous changes in PCET, particularly in the past ten years, and that the desire to carry teachers through these changes via their own initiatives has been more than matched by the desire to control, cajole and manipulate the same teachers into accepting an already established management agenda.

> In the more dominant *cultural* perspective, collaborative cultures express and emerge from a process of consensus building that is facilitated by a largely benevolent and skilled educational management. In the *micro political* perspective, collaboration and collegiality result from the exercise of organisational power by control-conscious administrators. In these cases, collegiality is either unwanted managerial imposition from the point of view of teachers subject to it or, more usually, a way of co-opting teachers to fulfilling administrative purposes and the implementation of external mandates. From the micro political perspective, collaboration and collegiality are often bound up with either direct administrative constraint or the indirect management of consent.
>
> (Hargreaves 1994: 190)

Hargreaves's preferred culture is the 'moving mosaic', as it is most in tune with the demands of an increasingly postmodern social existence, where organizations will survive to the extent to which they are able to respond quickly and imaginatively to an ever-changing and often short-lived set of demands and social circumstances. Thus, we might speculate that forms of new managerialism, although in part a reflection of the expressed need to radically transform the structures of PCET organizations, might easily become trapped in forms of 'modern' balkanization and contrived collegiality and be unable to tap into the kinds of moving mosaic needed to respond to the postmodern challenges.

The postmodern organization

The essence of the postmodern argument can be stated briefly. Throughout the first half of the twentieth century most organizations produced bureaucratic hierarchical structures, laying down rules and procedures as the efficient means by which set aims were to be achieved. In this process, all questions become technical ones: how will we achieve the aims we have set ourselves? Educational organizations typified this 'modern' approach on two distinct counts. First, through a confidence concerning what the aims of an educational establishment were, and second, through a confidence in the nature of the knowledge transmitted by these organizations – that the knowledge was true and needed.

However, since that time, many of these 'certainties' have come to be questioned. Increasing reflection in educational circles not just on means, but also on the aims themselves have forced many teachers into questioning whether educational establishments could ever specify with any degree of certainty that any particular means and/or ends could be seen as superior to any other and therefore that most means and ends can only ever be seen as temporary and transient. Furthermore, developments within groups variously representing 'distant voices' (feminist, black, gay, environmental, etc.) have come to question the nature of the knowledge transmitted in educational establishments, seeing it as being nothing more than the views and values of particular powerful social groups. This, ultimately, raises questions concerning how the teaching profession helps to reproduce these powerful social groups' interests in terms of both what is taught and the way it is taught. Some of these issues were raised in Part 1.

What is of more immediate concern to us in Part 2 is the extent to which elements of this postmodern existence have impinged on the way that PCET practitioners experience their workplaces and whether this is to be celebrated or bemoaned. On the one hand, we might want to rise to the challenge of increasingly having to form and work in fast-moving teams, thinking creatively about responding to changing client (student) needs, and producing the kinds of allegiances not permitted in 'balkanized' settings. On the other hand, we might come, increasingly, to experience this fast-moving existence as unsettling, making it difficult to establish a routine to be fitted around domestic commitments, and ultimately producing acute anxiety about a job's security. This 'ontological insecurity' (Giddens 1991) is like skating on thin ice with a stark choice: practise the skill or look for something else with a more firm footing.

Looked at in this way, PCET institutions might be said to display all the characteristics of 'disorganized capitalism' with *flexible specialization* (Lash and Urry 1987), i.e. production is increasingly smaller scale with short production runs and subcontracting, and aimed at specific markets. Furthermore, we might suggest that the real educational marketplace is much more fast moving than the 'social market', indicating the extent to which the latter is more about controlling PCET professionals through forms of 'contrived collegiality', rather than freeing them to produce 'moving mosaics'. And, of course, in a new mangerialist setting, keeping an organization very 'lean and fit' with a 'flexible' workforce might easily translate into a low-cost institution with a casualization of labour. In this respect, downsizing certainly makes capitalist firms more adaptable to change, but how many times has this resulted in more redundancies, lower pay and part-time work? The PCET equivalent would appear to be 'restructuring'.

Discussion point

What connotations does the word 'restructuring' have from your PCET experience?

There seems to be something very appealing about the (post)modern notion of teamwork. It conjures up images of democratic collaboration and quick responses to need:

> Modern forms of teamwork are in many ways the opposites of the work ethic as Max Weber conceived it. An ethic of the group as opposed to the individual, teamwork emphasizes mutual responsiveness rather than personal validation. The time of teams is flexible and oriented to specific, short-term tasks, rather than the reckoning of decades marked by withholding and waiting.
>
> (Sennett 1998: 206)

However, Sennett describes most real forms of modern teamwork as composed of nothing more than 'demeaning superficiality', a facade that is at the heart of modern communications in work settings. The emphasis on teamwork, on getting things done, on sharing knowledge, hides the extent to which the concept has no depth – no long-term development of relationships, no overriding principles, no meaningful commitments – everything is short term and on the surface.

> Teamwork exits the realm of tragedy to enact human relations as a farce.
>
> (Sennett 1998: 106)

In this depiction, the time-serving bureaucrat is replaced by an endless stream of ice-breaking, trust-forming, brainstorming team meetings where, increasingly, the teamworker comes to the realization that the important decisions are actually being taken elsewhere. Of course, this would be most clearly seen where forms of contrived collegiality were firmly embedded in institutional practice. If professionals find themselves outside of this orbit we might suggest that the challenge that (post)modern ontological insecurity brings might be more easily risen to. Sennett himself is sceptical:

> How can a human being develop a narrative of identity and life history in a society composed of episodes and fragments? The conditions of the new economy feed instead on experience which drifts in time, from place to place, from job to job . . . short term capitalism threatens to corrode [his] character, particularly those qualities of character that bind human beings to one another and furnishes each with a sense of sustainable self.
>
> (Sennett 1998: 27)

This is surely in stark contrast to the kind of teambuilding where there is a serious attempt to develop the kinds of 'emotional intelligence' (Goleman 1995) that should be the bedrock of a profession centred around communication skills.

However, freed from contrived collegiality, we might suggest that professional groups such as PCET practitioners might increasingly come to learn to 'skate on the thin ice' of a more postmodern existence. The first precondition, however, might well have to be a serious relaxation in the new managerialist paradigm. This brings us to a discussion of the different ways in which we might conceive of forms of PCET professional accountability.

PCET accountability

Background

It might be argued that throughout the past 25 years we have seen public sector professionals not just called to account but also, through various changes in their working practices, increasingly calling themselves to account. I am thinking here of the Thatcherite call to public sector professionals to be accountable for taxpayers' money being matched by the professionals' own sense of accountability to their clients. In the context of post-compulsory education we might say that a natural consequence of moving away from pedagogical practice towards andragogical practice has been a desire not just to invite feedback from students on professional performance but also increasingly to seek the means by which curricular provision might reflect more clearly the needs and objectives of students (see Armitage et al 2003).

This student-centredness has taken many forms: experiential learning, participatory delivery, 'horseshoe seating' in classrooms, individual learning contracts, student presentations, systematic tutorial support. On top of this we have seen allied movements towards more flexible timetables and course structures, more varied assessment techniques, and accreditation of prior (experiential) learning. All of these are attempts not just to cater for a wider range of learning styles but also to reflect a wider range of lifestyles and to encourage learning to be seen as part of everybody's everyday life and not just something that someone does, full time, for certain periods in their life (and which, in many respects, is detached from their life).

Discussion point

How far would you say that your own organization is a model for these contemporary developments? What advantages and disadvantages can you see in these changes?

The student-centred organization

Forms of student-centredeness raise important questions concerning the nature of the work undertaken in the sector. An important philosophical issue is the extent to which there has been a fundamental ideological shift not just away from forms of classical humanism towards forms of instrumental vocationalism but also away from the former towards forms of progressivism and individual self-development. This is itself problematical, for, on the one hand, the extent to which vocationalism can be reconciled with personal self-development is debatable and, on the other, it raises perhaps a deeper question as to whether andragogy should be seen as a series of participatory teaching methods or as a fundamental reorientation of educational aims:

> If I distrust the human being, then I must cram her with information of my own choosing lest she go her own mistaken way. But if I trust the capacity of the human individual for developing her own potentiality, then I can provide her with many opportunities and permit her to choose her own way and her own direction in her learning.
>
> (Rogers 1957, in Kirschenbaum 1990: 313)

There are extremely serious implications here. First, to what extent does this challenge our own sense of what we are as teachers? Second, to what extent could any nationally prescribed educational programme provide the space for meaningful dialogue with students concerning their aims? And, third, to what extent is this a question not so much about teachers being accountable to students, as about students taking responsibility for their own learning?

Discussion point

How far would you say that the current AVCE framework recognizes and addresses these questions?

This raises the question of the desirability of putting students in charge of their own learning. Apart from the obvious quip that if you told a typical group of students that they could do as they wished they would probably all vote to go home, we might suggest that this is a highly problematical area. Even inviting feedback on a course raises questions:

> Although student ratings are desirable in a number of ways, they also have some unfortunate consequences. For example, they tend to favour professors who are performers, who have a sense of humour, or who do not demand too much from students. The serious professor who places great demands on students is not likely to do well in such ratings systems, even though he or she may offer higher-quality teaching.
>
> (Ritzer 2000: 68)

We should not forget that even the great champion of student autonomy, Carl Rogers, believed that this is an ultimate aim, not a starting point. Students, like therapy patients, are likely to enter classrooms in various states of teacher dependence. The art of teaching (if there could be such a thing) is to turn this dependence into autonomy. This is a process that may take some time; it also raises the question of the extent to which, once a student has produced their own learning goals (and the means by which they might be achieved), the teacher might still be required to monitor and assess (and grade) these voyages of self-discovery. In this context we might ask, 'Just whose intended learning outcomes are they?'

Clearly, within a more traditional Socratic pedagogy, the teacher plays an important role in guiding the student to their own self-understanding. The Socratic method, the *Elenchus*, is at the root of most question-and-answer routines in almost all classrooms – it is the probing process that seeks to subvert the foundation for the assumptions upon which an argument rests:

> She [the psyche] cannot profit from the knowledge offered to her until the Elenchus is applied and the man is refuted and brought to shame, thus purifying him from opinions that hinder learning and causing him to think he knows only what he does know and no more.
>
> (Plato, quoted in Abbs 1994: 18)

What I am attempting to establish here is that even in situations where one is driving students towards their own self-understandings and self-discovery, teachers can and do play important roles in establishing the ground rules for a 'true' educational encounter. Put crudely, students could not be in charge of this process. In this context, being accountable to students is clearly a complicated matter.

McDonaldization and PCET

Ritzer's earlier reservations concerning student evaluations are part of his broader McDonaldization thesis. He is keen to encourage us to see education as an eager exponent of the process:

> The University is a means of educational consumption.
>
> (Ritzer 2000)

The main principles of McDonaldization can be easily stated:

- *Efficiency* – 'each step in producing the limited menu was stripped down to its essence and accomplished with a minimum of effort' (p. 42).
- *Calculability* – 'the pre-cooked hamburger measures precisely 3.875 inches in diameter, the bun exactly 3.5 inches' (p. 79).
- *Predictability* – 'Much of what is said in fast-food restaurants by both employees and customers is ritualized, routinized, even scripted' (p. 88).
- *Control* – 'the soft drinks dispenser that shuts off when the glass is full, the French fry machine that rings and lifts the basket out of the oil when the fries are crisp' (p. 14).

(adapted from Ritzer 2000)

Discussion point

To what extent do you recognize the potential for these operating principles to take hold in your own organization?

If we define the *raison d'être* for McDonald's as 'finding the most efficient means to turn hunger into full up', we could argue that we have established at the same time an operating principle for education:

- *Efficiency* – maximize output of students with minimum input of resources.
- *Calculability* – precisely form and measure 'learning' products.
- *Predictability* – standardize and uniformly deliver products.
- *Control* – manage and inspect the delivery of products for quality assurance.

Readers who are familiar with Marxist and Weberian sociology will recognize elements of both theoretical structures within this formulation. For Weberians we can see the 'iron cage of bureaucracy' with its obsession for rationalizing, measuring and calculating. For Marxists we can see the 'commodification' of education where useful items are turned into saleable products. In both formulations we see the tendency for 'modern' organizations to want to *control* the production process for the purposes of rationalization and commodification. We could argue that both processes have important implications for accountability within post-compulsory education.

From one perspective we see students identifying learning opportunities from a range of providers, all clearly identifying the nature of the their products, and the means by which they might be attained, but, from another, we see students consuming education in the same way that they might purchase any product in a large shopping mall: '[Students] want high-quality products but are eager for low costs. They are willing to comparison shop – placing a premium on time and money' (Levine, in Ritzer 2000: 152).

Discussion point

How far would you say that colleges are beginning to look and act like retail outlets?

Along with marketable products comes the need to market them. If colleges come heavily under this sway we might expect them to seek to eliminate any 'downside' to their students' purchases – 'customer satisfaction guaranteed or your money back'. Will we see a time when students cannot fail a course? Furthermore, if we remember that companies like Nike don't so much make running shoes as create *images* of running shoes, we might further challenge colleges to follow suit. In this respect, colleges are not just commercial enterprises in that they sell products but they also 'make' commercials about those products. '[The] focus on positivity will produce an educational world that, in Baudrillard's words, resembles "the smile of a corpse in a funeral home" ' (Ritzer 2000: 156).

Discussion point

To what extent would you say that educational establishments now guarantee customer satisfaction?

The final implication in the McDonaldization thesis is the extent to which information and communications technology (ICT) is being used in the rationalizing cause: 'they [students] will educate themselves more and more on their own in interaction with images emanating from their own computer and television screens' (Ritzer 2000: 161).

With the increased use of 'imploding technology', i.e. the compression of time and space (Harvey 1989), it becomes possible to extend the boundary walls of the school or colleges – why limit your college's potential market by containing it within the physical confines of its 'real' environment? If students do not want to come to college, why not take the college to the students? Why teach 20 students in a seminar room when you can teach 200 in a lecture theatre, 2000 through video links, 200 million through interactive web packages? We should note here an important element in the McDonaldizing process: the extent to which the consumer is asked to do a lot of the work in the consumption process, using their own computer, their own home, etc.

Discussion point

How far away are we from discarding real teachers in favour of virtual ones? Would this be a good thing?

The increased use of computer-based and computer-enhanced learning might be extremely useful in giving a wider audience of students access to educational opportunities, not just geographically, but also in terms of inclusivity. It also promotes a more flexible approach to seminar discussion and feedback. That is, it is no longer necessary for everyone to meet, physically, in the same room in order to engage in a discussion, when web bulletin boards, virtual discussions and chat rooms can be easily generated. Students should no longer feel that they must be physically present to hand in and receive feedback from tutors – this can be done in a much more interactive way through e-mail communication. Many courses now have these processes firmly established as forms of communication.

All of these developments might be argued to have produced a much greater sense of accountability to a wider range of students. However, they have also coincided with a much more aggressive marketization of educational products, which has turned students into consumers of those products. This might be seen as an inevitable by-product of importing a more business-like approach to education, i.e. the idea that one is selling education and is in competition with others when doing it. Furthermore, it could be argued that being accountable to students in a climate where one is being called to public account is much more likely to make teachers responsible for student learning rather than students themselves. At this point let us turn our attention more fully to a consideration of the nature of PCET professionals being called to public account.

Discussion point

How seriously do you take the view that we have turned students into consumers of learning products? Does it matter?

Inspection regimes in PCET

Many of the processes we have been discussing might be said to have been initiated within the profession. However, we should remember that the same professionals have come under increasing scrutiny from government agencies who are the means by which the 'social market' has been used to call the professionals to account. Perhaps the two most important agencies within the sector in the recent past have been the FEFC inspectorate and the QAA for higher education. Most PCET practitioners have quickly become used to the processes of inspection, which have been instigated by these agencies and others. What I want to discuss is how such agencies have affected the social relations within PCET organizations and thus affected the way in which we all now approach our work.

There is a compelling logic to the argument that if colleges are placed in competition with each other and funding is, at least in part, determined by the achievement of targets, that the whole sector would become more robust and able to respond quickly to change. There is also a convincing moral imperative implicit in the notion that public sector professionals should be accountable for the ways in which they spend taxpayers' money. If this is long overdue then at least we can now say that it has finally arrived. However, as with all change, it is important that we look at it in terms of how it has affected everyday work practice.

There comes a time when lesson plans and schemes of work lose whatever initial interest they may have had and become a burdensome chore. However, knowing that inspectors will call forces all practitioners to make explicit whatever may have been implicit before, i.e. if it cannot be seen it cannot be inspected. And, to some extent, *saying what you do* now becomes a natural corollary of doing what you do. However, what I am interested in exploring here is the extent to which saying what you do actually changes what you do and, furthermore, whether saying what you do is a different practice from doing what you do.

Discussion point

How far would say that the language of inspection is the same as your own language of practice?

We should not lose sight of the fact that the language of, for example, 'learning outcomes', although popularized by bodies such as the Institute for Learning and Teaching in H.E., is not necessarily a language imposed on practitioners. For most of my own lesson planning I am happy to operate with this term, and it fits naturally into my *modus operandi*, but I can also see the way that it is also able to shape my thinking for the purposes of more public accountability. For example, a learning outcome is much easier to frame when it is seen as a pre-specified behavioural objective, much more difficult when it is used as a call to students to join in a process of existential intellectual angst. Of course, the former is also easier to measure and perhaps this is the real point.

In this respect, being accountable is closely allied with measuring the measurable. But should not all aspects of educational practice be measurable? Surely, if it cannot be measured, we cannot then conceive of any notion of productivity or movement in the direction of final achievement? Lecturers are split on this one. What might be conceived as nebulous to one could be construed as a sublime educational moment to another.

This discussion reaches to the heart of what education is actually perceived to be: on the one hand (from the Latin) *educare*, emphasizing placing in, and on the other, *educere*, emphasizing drawing out (see Barrow and Woods (1988) for a fuller discussion of this distinction). In the former conception it is directed by teachers, whereas, in the latter, it is facilitated by teachers. In the past 25 years we have seen an enormous emphasis on the latter as being the more appropriate model for PCET in terms of educational methods, and in some circles, in terms of educational aims. However, the call to accountability has often necessitated a formulation of education where we are asked to measure the amount of learning that a *teacher* has enabled a learner to acquire, and the PCET organization is held accountable for the (easily measurable) educational value added to the learner.

Discussion point

To what extent would you share the view that accountability in PCET has forced teachers to be responsible for students' learning rather than students themselves?

Professionalism in modern PCET

A recurring theme in the sociological literature on the role of professionals is the extent to which there is a discrepancy between what professionals say they do and what they actually do. A famous study of this was undertaken by Garfinkel in his analysis of official records in an American hospital (Garfinkel 1967). Summarizing his main point, we might say that the last place we would go if we wanted to learn anything about patients or the workings of the hospital would be the official records. Or, perhaps better, these might be the first place we would go to in order to begin an examination of how official records are constructed and used by professionals. It would seem that these ideas could easily be transferred to an educational context.

Discussion point

How far would you accept that your own official records record a particular version of reality?

This is not a question of inefficiency, or outright deceit, but the result of the way that organizations inevitably produce conflicts, ultimately, of time, and the way that they have to justify their funding to outside bodies, all of which must be managed by the professionals who work in those organizations. There is a clear sense in Garfinkel's work that professionals often keep the 'front desk' misinformed, but for good organizational reasons. On the one hand, official records are kept for official reasons; there is no need for them to record 'reality' as such, and, on the other, not paying too much attention to official records gives professionals the time and space to do what they believe they ought to be doing, which is engaging in client care.

The QAA for higher education has been minded to refer to its inspection regime as 'Subject Review'. What is clearly encouraging about this approach is the way that it fosters a sense that colleagues are mutually engaged in the process of critical reflection on curriculum development. However, the desire to create league tables of achievement on a grading scale perhaps indicates the not-so-hidden agenda to produce a conformity to a pre-specified model of what an HE curriculum must look like. In this respect, what an institution does must be seen to be in accord with what is laid down. For many this is a clear undermining of professional autonomy; for others it is simply what you would expect in order to produce uniformity amongst quality learning providers.

Utilizing Garfinkel's original conception we might suggest that there are now clearly 'good organizational reasons for bad educational records'. This reminds me of the joke that the Queen always thinks that Britain smells of fresh paint because wherever she goes somebody is busy ten yards ahead preparing the way. In this respect, preparing for inspection is not about displaying what one does, but manufacturing it. Furthermore, it might be seen as a process whereby the institutional records' referent is not the institution's reality but a subsisting inspection reality. At worse, this creates a two-tier reality requiring professionals to operate at both levels. At best, it sets a challenge to the institution to shape its own reality to approximate an ideal inspection reality.

One should not forget the opportunities available for professional development in this new world of accountability. There is a growing market for consultants and advisers who can run workshops on how professionals should present themselves for the purposes of public accountability. In this respect they are a necessary adjunct to professional accountability offering advice on models of good practice. On the other, they are an expensive means by which professionals might further learn how to 'keep the front desk misinformed'.

> **Discussion point**
>
> How far would you go in suggesting that consultants exist to help professionals look good rather than be good?

Third Way accountability

With the election of a Labour government in 1997 and its subsequent re-election in 2001, we have seen a steady flow of documents arguing that the ideological underpinning of this government is neither a market philosophy nor a traditional welfare model but a form of communitarianism, or, to use the popular phrase, it is the Third Way (Giddens 1998, 2000; Etzioni 2000). Many commentators see little difference, in practice, not between New (Third Way) Labour and old (welfare) Labour, but between New Labour and the 'social market' Conservatives. With this in mind we might suggest that it could be some time before PCET sees any significant change in its accountability agenda. However, we should consider the ways in which the 'social market' philosophy has perhaps been *relaxed* by the Third Way philosophy:

> Social democrats need a different approach to government, in which 'the state should not row, but steer: not so much control, as challenge'. The quality of public services must be improved and the performance of government monitored. A positive climate for entrepreneurial independence and initiative has to be nurtured.
>
> (Giddens 2000: 6–7)

We might suggest that we are currently moving in the direction 'not so much [of] control, as challenge'. Indeed, it is in finding examples where the word 'challenge' has significance that we are likely to locate any changes. The establishment of the Learning and Skills Council in April

2001 is perhaps the best example to date of where this philosophical shift might have been given some significance. In this context, the competition between PCET institutions, the hallmark of quality in the heyday of Thatcherism, seems to be giving way to new forms of partnership:

> Local Learning Partnerships have a key role in driving forward improvements in the quality of provision and bringing greater coherence at the local level. Working together, partners can identify and address gaps in provision, eliminate duplication and co-ordinate local action to raise achievement – making sure that it meets local needs.
>
> (DfEE 1999: 30)

It is also the avowed intent of the present government to target learners through funding rather than reward institutions: '[The LSC] will develop . . . truly responsive and flexible provision, facilitated (not hampered) by appropriate funding mechanisms' (DfEE 1999: 65).

Both of these developments could be seen as serious attempts to relax the use of the 'market' to call PCET to account – a little less stick and little more carrot, perhaps. However, there seems little relaxation of the call for public accountability through the use of inspection regimes. Indeed, the *Learning to Succeed* document is littered with references to the importance of these mechanisms.

The future PCET organization

In the past 25 years we have seen many changes in the nature of PCET organizations and these have been welcomed as voraciously as they have been resisted. However, one thing which seems reasonably clear is that the sector now has a much firmer footing in the popular consciousness and the institutions are clearly central to the notion of the 'learning society'. However, we might still anticipate that there could be many more changes in the PCET landscape in the near future.

The university sector may well produce a much clearer dichotomy between those organizations that see themselves primarily as research establishments and those that see themselves primarily as teaching establishments. Achieving a balance may prove to be increasingly difficult in the chase for the large research contracts. Those who have scored highly on the Research Assessment Exercises might anticipate not just more funding, but also the need to concentrate their efforts in continuing to score highly in the future, leaving other institutions to fly the flag of widening participation and secure their funding from increased student numbers. Practitioners may also find themselves increasingly torn between the demands of producing high-status research and the demands of producing innovative teaching practice.

In further education we might anticipate that the recent government '14–19 agenda' could have important implications (DfES 2002). On the one hand, it might secure the mid-term future of the institutions as they strive to play their part in cementing the 'learning society'. On the other hand, they may find themselves increasingly squeezed from one side, with schools anticipating that '14–19' will increasingly move us towards (in effect) a rise in the school leaving age and thus see themselves as the main providers of general 'liberal' education. And, they might be squeezed from the other side as well, as private training providers queue up to offer work-related training programmes, thereby edging out the suite of training opportunities currently provided by FE institutions. We might also see, under the Third Way philosophy, an increased emphasis on third sector or not-for-profit organizations supporting public service provision, much of which might be local educational services:

> Developed in an effective manner . . . third-sector groups can offer choice and responsiveness in the delivery of public services. They can also help promote local civic culture and forms of community development . . . Social entrepreneurs can be highly effective innovators in the realm of civil society, at the same time contributing to economic development.
>
> (Giddens 2000: 81–2)

In this scenario FE institutions might find themselves increasingly offering more specialist educational services such as 'inclusion units' for excluded school pupils, and, more generally, alternative educational environments for the 'socially excluded'.

Lastly, adult and community education might increasingly be able to position itself to provide the kinds of education that a more postmodern society demands, where

> the aesthetic and cultural displace the functional as central to economic activity, with style and design playing an increasingly significant role in ensuring consumption of products and services, and with image and lifestyle playing an increasing role in the choice of consumers. On this reading, the economy, and this includes providers of learning opportunities for adults, is increasingly recentred away from 'meeting need' towards supporting 'lifestyle practices'.
>
> (Edwards 1997: 15)

On the other hand, it might equally find itself outmanoeuvred by the other institutions in the sector and come increasingly to see itself as primarily attempting to meet the 'basic skills' national targets by providing flexible provision in local settings.

Conclusion

Perhaps the most significant change we have seen in PCET organizations in the past 25 years has been a heightened sense of public accountability. For some this has been part of the process of the professionalization of the sector, or, perhaps better, the reprofessionalization of the sector. For others it has been seen as a period in which professional autonomy has slowly been eroded by a series of curricular and organizational reforms aimed at producing a dull bureaucratic uniformity and the aforementioned McDonaldization. Ritzer's claim is that this is relentless and is encroaching on more and more areas of life:

> Kinder-care tends to hire short-term employees with little or no training in child care. What these employees do in the 'classroom' is largely determined by an instruction book with a ready-made curriculum. Staff members open the manual to find activities spelled out in detail for each day. Clearly, a skilled, experienced, creative teacher is not the kind of person that such 'McChild' care centers seek to hire. Rather, relatively untrained employees are more easily controlled by the non-human technology of the omnipresent 'instruction book'.
>
> (Ritzer 2000: 108)

Readers familiar with the Research Assessment Exercise in HE might at this point be forgiven for thinking that the most appropriate context in which to consider McDonaldization is surely here. When funding and status are closely aligned with quantifiable measures, how often might an academic have to consider just where that article should be published – perhaps not where it will be read, but where it will score more points. Ritzer makes the general point from an American context:

> The 'publish or perish' pressure on academicians in may colleges and universities tends to lead to great attention to the quantity of their publications rather than their quality . . . The sciences have come up with another quantifiable measure in an effort to evaluate the quality of work: the number of times a person's work is cited in the work of other people.
>
> (Ritzer 2000: 68–9)

It is perhaps necessary to pause at this point and consider the extent to which this rationalization and commodification are much more readily accepted in the US than in the UK. I would suggest that education, as a commodity form, to be consumed like any other, is not in itself the problem in the US. What is, is the ensuing disenchantment that it can cause, i.e. the unintended but inevitable consequences of rationalization. What is interesting about the UK is the extent to which the McDonaldizing tendencies have encroached onto the educational landscape, more from the state's perceived need to be monitoring and measuring the educational output of the teaching professions. The consequences are the same – disenchantment and dull bureaucracy – but the driving force has a much more overtly political agenda in the UK.

We should perhaps also at this concluding point make explicit some important definitional dichotomies. First, the process of *standardizing* educational products for the purposes of measurement and comparison between organizations is not the same as *standards*, i.e. maintaining high standards in PCET organizations might be achieved through means other than standardization. Second, *professionalization* is not the same as *professionalism*. It is one thing to seek to enhance the professional status of PCET practitioners (perhaps through professional organizations such as FENTO and the fledgling IFL), but it might be another to engage in forms of continuous professional development, which seek to encourage the critical exploration of the professional value base within the sector. The recent introduction of FENTO standards might well be a serious attempt to balance these dichotomies in a meaningful way, but they might also contribute to the very deprofessionalization, which deeply worries authors such as Hyland.

It seems that we are in a position to argue that one person's calling to account is another person's means of social control. Not only are many professionals within the sector worried about the business ethos which now permeates many PCET institutions, arguing that we are in the business of education and not the education of business, but there is also a split between those who see professional accountability as a hallmark of effectiveness, and those who see it as little more than the invidious arm of a centralized state *continuing* the Thatcherite agenda of controlling public sector professionals at the same time as freeing up private sector entrepreneurs.

From the curriculum perspective, we have seen many changes attempting to move in the direction of learner-centredness. This moves our gaze away from professional accountability in terms of the public purse and directs it towards student learning needs. We might argue that many of these changes have brought us closer to an understanding not just of learning styles but also of the need to have wide variation in the means of access, modes of representation and forms of assessment available to students (see Part 1). However, we might also argue that this has coincided with a 'commodification' of education, where students increasingly see education as a shopping mall inviting them to purchase educational products from a range of outlets. *Edutainment* then becomes the byword for the PCET practitioner in terms of delivery and *ease of completion* becomes the marketable slogan, all resulting, for the student, in a sense that one collects educational credentials in the same way that one collects consumer durables.

Finally, we should not forget that change is always a process. Individuals need the time and the space to assimilate change, particularly when it is perceived as a threat. The extent to which the new managerialism has enabled this assimilation to take place is debatable, it clearly having been experienced by many PCET practitioners as a controlling mechanism rather than an exercise in making PCET institutions more responsive to change. In this context it is perhaps ironic that the new managerialism may come to be seen as the last throw of a 'modern' die rather than as a preparation for a more postmodern future.

Further reading

Altrichter, H. and Elliot, J. (eds) (2000) *Images of Educational Change*. Buckingham: Open University Press.

Barnett, R. (2000) *The University of an Age of Supercomplexity*. Buckingham: Open University Press.

Bush, T. (1995) *Theories of Educational Management* (2nd edition). London: Paul Chapman.

Edwards, R. (1997) *Changing Places: Flexibility, Lifelong Learning and a Learning Society*. London: Routledge.

Fullan, M.G. (1991) *The New Meaning of Educational Change*. London: Cassell.

Giddens, A. (2000) *The Third Way and its Critics*. Cambridge: Polity Press.

Handy, C. (1993) *Understanding Organizations* (4th edition). London: Penguin.

Hargreaves, A. (1994) *Changing Teachers, Changing Times*. London: Cassell.

Hodgson, A. and Spours, K. (eds) (1999) *New Labour's Educational Agenda*. London: Kogan Page.

Morgan, G. (1997) *Images of Organization* (2nd edition). London: Sage.

Ritzer, G. (2000) *The McDonaldization of Society*. Boston: Pine Forge.

Sennett, R. (1998) *The Corrosion of Character*. New York: Norton.

Usher, R. and Edwards, R. (1994) *Postmodernism and Education*. London: Routledge.

Part 2 exercises

1 The literature review

Locate up to ten journals that have PCET as their focus. Choose a topic that is of interest to you in your PCET professional practice. Write a critical review of the articles that relate to your chosen topic written in the past ten years. Use the following as a guide:

(a) Produce a Harvard style reference to each article used.
(b) Identify the similarities and differences between the authors' perspectives.
(c) Discuss your perception of the strengths and weaknesses in the authors' perspectives with reference to your own professional context.
(d) Use short quotations which summarize an author's ideas.

The following have been popular journals in the past ten years, most with a PCET focus. Begin your search with some of these:

Adults Learning
Assessment in Education – Principles, Policy and Practice
British Journal of Education and Work
Curriculum Studies
Journal of Education for Teaching
Journal of Further and Higher Education
Journal of Vocational Education and Work
Research in Post Compulsory Education
Studies in Higher Education
Teaching in Higher Education

2 Critical reflection

Choose a PCET reform of which you have had direct experience in your professional context. Write a critically reflective commentary focusing on how this reform was implemented and managed.

In the first of the following two polemical pieces Dennis Hayes places recent developments in 'managerialist' practice under critical scrutiny. He questions whether there is any real substance behind the Third Way philosophy of New Labour, and goes on to challenge us to consider whether we have transformed PCET organizations into 'therapeutic' centres rather than education centres. By stark contrast, Laurie Lomas applauds the recent reforms in PCET organizational practice, which have produced long overdue forms of public accountability. He argues that students and lecturers are no longer left to plough their own furrows leaving educational organizations without any clear direction or *modus operandi*. He concludes that it is now possible to make PCET organizations more effective largely because, at last, we have *measures* of effectiveness.

QUESTION TO THINK ABOUT

After having read the two polemical pieces contained in this section to what extent would you accept that PCET practitioners have been either reprofessionalized or deprofessionalized in the past 25 years?

Chapter 5

MANAGERIALISM AND PROFESSIONALISM IN POST-COMPULSORY EDUCATION

Dennis Hayes

Today, when we talk of 'managerialism' or the 'new managerialism' in further or higher education, or in any other context, this should not be confused with, or seen as a continuation of, the market-oriented managerialism of the Thatcherite 1980s. The imposition of managerialism at that time was contested and opposed by defenders of the welfare state. In the late 1990s and the early part of the twenty-first century, managerialism has to be seen in the context of the politics of TINA (There Is No Alternative!). The crucial point about TINA, and the difference between the two political periods, is that there is no longer any serious belief in an alternative to liberal democracy and its economic form (capitalism). In this new political context, running the state, a business, a college or a university is seen as a purely technical matter. Even managing itself is no longer a matter of achieving a temporary settlement or compromise as a result of a social or political contestation over 'big' ideas.

The practical result of this depoliticization is an obsession with the 'image' of management and the adoption of an ethic that can best be described as 'therapeutic'. As a result of this changed situation, academic workers in further and higher education are less likely to feel alienated, and more likely to accept the rationalization of their work, because managers will naturally focus more and more on the 'image' and the 'therapeutic' ethic of the institution. Examples of this new focus are bureaucratic concerns with 'student-centredness', 'inclusivity' and 'life-long learning' in the context of staff development, all ideas that have progressive antecedents.

The seemingly progressive aspect of these notions makes them difficult to resist. They have become part of an academic worker's personal professional

perspectives. Sennett has described the outcome of such a fortunate correspondence of concerns as resulting in a 'compulsive bonding' with institutions ([1977] 1993: 332). 'Compulsive bonding' and other psychological
traits, such as the concern staff and management have with their own and
their students' self-esteem, result in passivity. This passivity benefits no one.
In further or higher education the passivity of lecturers and academics
undermines the possibility of revitalizing what is left of the academic community. Having nothing other than a pathological desire to avoid conflict,
passive lecturers and academics undermine their societal role, which is the
pursuit of knowledge through the rigorous contestation of ideas.

The legacy of Thatcher and the politics of the Third Way

Any form of managerialism implies a form of professionalism. In the
Thatcherite 1980s the ruthless corporate ambition of the yuppie was the
caricature, and sometimes the reality, of professionalism. Contemporary
managerialism requires a softer and more ethical professionalism. In what
follows we shall explore both managerialism and professionalism as they
cannot really be examined separately.

To understand the trajectory of PCE managerialism, and the new professionalism that it sets out for lecturers, we have to see it in the context
of some theoretical discussion, a lot of policy making and a few practical
ideas that are best understood through the concept of the politics of
the Third Way. To talk meaningfully of the politics of the Third Way, however, requires some understanding of the 'second' and 'first' ways (for
a fuller discussion see Blair 1998; Giddens 1998; Hayes and Hudson 2001;
Armitage *et al.* 2003: ch.9).

The 'first way' as a historical period ran from the time of post-war
reconstruction until the middle of the 1970s. In this period we can identify
a managerial approach that accepted an idea of professionalism that was
based on a lecturer's or teacher's independence and autonomy in all areas
of their work that was based on their (subject) knowledge. Their teaching
methodology, their relation to students and their judgements, as far as
assessment and examination were concerned, were all their responsibility.
It is important to understand that the consensus about professional
autonomy was an accidental feature of a historical period. It was not
worked out from an epistemological or philosophical position. The
elevation of knowledge was part of the progressive feel of the times. This
explains in part why those thinkers we associate with this period – perhaps
Paul Hirst and his 'forms of knowledge' thesis is the exemplar of this – have
moved with the times and changed or abandoned their views. What made
this period unique was the post-war boom, which allowed the expansion of
education and the luxury of Socratic and disinterested enquiry for a short
period, even if it never amounted to a 'golden age' (Hayes 2002a). For

those of us of a certain age, this decade dominates and often distorts our thinking because we give little thought to its uniqueness and assume that the characteristics of the time are generalizable to other periods.

The end of the post-war boom – we can date it technically from 1972 and the end of the Bretton Woods agreement – or, for our purposes, in 1976 with James Callaghan's 'great debate', put an end to this consensus. In a real sense, the 1980s and the 'second way' of Thatcherism began then. Thatcherism was an entirely destructive project. The Thatcherite 'second way' set out to destroy what she called 'socialism', that is, trade unions and the communities of the period of welfare consensus, or the 'first way'. However, Thatcherism left nothing in their place, only the illusory 'market mechanisms' imposed on all public sector institutions, including schools, colleges and universities. The legacy of the second way is not just a morass of managerialist and bureaucratic practices. Mrs Thatcher's claim in the popular magazine *Women's Own* that 'There is no such thing as Society. There are individual men and women, and there are families' (*Women's Own*, 31 October 1987) is a statement that characterizes both the consequences of the second way and the contemporary context of social individuation and atomization. The response to this defeat from lecturers was not a defence of the old professionalism but the assertion of an ethical imperative. The focus of professionalism became the need for an ethical dimension to managerialism or the more left-wing assertion of the overriding importance of equal opportunities, what became in practice a form of 'political correctness' that was willingly embraced by managers seeking points of consensus in the workplace.

And so to the Third Way, in which no return to the welfare consensus seems possible, and the market is equally unacceptable. This political impasse is what we described above as the politics of TINA. In these circumstances what characterizes the Third Way is the artificiality and fragility of *all* policies and practices. Most discussions of managerialism and professionalism in PCE do not set themselves in the context of Third Way politics, although this politics defines the particular historical moment in which we live. Since the collapse of 'communism' as the seeming alternative to capitalism in 1989, a period of history that had run for 200 years – we could date it from the French Revolution of 1789 – had come to an end. Politics as it we knew it came to an end and, more importantly, the historical subject that drove society forward during this time, what we used to call the working class, was simply absent in any institutional or organizational form. This context, which we can remind readers of but cannot really begin to explain here, means that the content of any political policy or practice is no longer, even in a distanced way, focused on enemies within or without. Such a freedom is not a happy state but leads to uncertainty and constant change. Policy making and a whole raft of government initiatives become arbitrary because they are not aimed at any community. They cannot be, because traditional communities no longer exist.

This political climate of the Third Way is fundamentally about the uncertainties of a political elite that is anxious about ordinary people. Lacking organizations that represent, and also discipline, people, they can only, in an entirely spontaneous way, encourage low horizons and low expectations. This only partly removes a feeling of threat, but cannot entirely reassure an over-anxious elite, that constantly falls back on authoritarian measures more appropriate to the past. Only half consciously and experimentally do they allow and encourage the more effective approaches that promote self-limitation and self-regulation.

The attitude of the political elite to the management of professionals over the period of the three ways moves from a consensus about independence, to seeking to control through the market, to making tentative moves towards self-regulation. Academic responses to managerialism and the new professionalism seem mostly to be responses to the destructive period of the second way. They reflect a sadness about the decline of autonomy in their talk of deskilling and deprofessionalization, or they show a distaste for the Thatcherite attacks, but all without any recognition of the real extent of contemporary political change. This is not merely a failing of the historical memory, which famously concerned Eric Hobsbawm in the early 1990s, it is an intellectual and theoretical failing that can only damage a new generation of lecturers by persuading them to address the wrong issues.

There are some exceptions. For example, Hodgson and Spours (1999) writing during New Labour's first term of office, championed a 'strong' Third Way. They do not want to leave it to management to make ethical and other changes but suggest some form of legislative compulsion. This approach, which is, as we shall see, exactly the approach of New Labour in its second incarnation, is bound to fail. No matter how forceful you are about artificial and arbitrary impositions of new styles of management and professionalism, this is merely an expression of exasperation that illustrates the fragility of the whole New Labour project. They want to trust managers, professionals and people in general, but only to do what the New Labour government wants. The problem is, however, that it just does not know what it wants.

One thing that we can say with certainty that government needs is to get people on side. In Anthony Seldon's monumental tome *The Blair Effect*, he concludes that 'the net Blair effect' is a matter of style. New Labour has 'become more national and classless and less of a sectional and class based party, and it reached out as never before to embrace the establishment, including the City, business, the professions, the media and the Church of England, and even independent schools' (Seldon 2001: 594). Kavanagh, in an earlier piece in the same volume, adds south-east England to this list (Kavanagh 2001: 16). Trying to get professionals on side is one of the major motivations behind New Labour policy. Perhaps the best example of this is the concern with 'inclusive' policies that target the excluded, while their numbers seem in every area of exclusion to continue to rise because other policies may seem paradoxical or contradictory. But this is to mistake the object of these policies, whether they are concerned with those excluded from school, the long-term unemployed or the illiterate. These policies exist to 'include' mangers and professionals and to get them on side.

This, in part, explains the constant changes of policy. Alan Smithers has commented that New Labour, in its educational thinking, 'desperately wanted to be seen to be doing good things' to the extent that 'everyday without a new education headline was regarded as a day wasted'. And he asks: 'What are we to make of all this activity? Has the Blair government really had 'a big picture', with the many initiatives necessitated by numerous faults in the system? Or has it tended to dissipate its political capital by failing to focus sufficiently on the main issues, rushing off in all directions?' (Smithers 2001: 425). Smithers inclines to the second proposition and blames the privately educated 'ideas-people' that surround Blair for producing a situation where 'idea after idea seems to have come tumbling out, often encapsulated in a catchy two- or three-word phrase, without a full appreciation of the education system's capacity to absorb them or their relevance to ordinary pupils' (p.425). Smithers' conclusion is widely accepted and it is becoming a commonplace that 'New Labour does not appear to know what kind of direction it wants the education and training system to follow' (Hodgson and Spours 1999: 145).

But these responses simply miss the point. It is true that in one sense New Labour does not know what it is doing and that the result can only be personality conflict amongst politicians. However, these changes were not about solving problems or promoting any sort of 'big' educational idea. These constant shifts were experiments in trying to win over a new audience. This narrowly functional approach to policy is of the greatest importance as New Labour had lost its traditional electoral constituency. Ever since Callaghan's 'great debate' about education in 1976 there had been a political drift away from policy aimed at the traditional Labour supporter. Now is seems impossible for New Labour to identify any clear constituency at all. For a successful political party this presents an appalling situation within which continuation of temporary electoral success, however dramatic, is clearly threatened. Turning to management and professionals is one of New Labour's responses to the contemporary political problem of disconnection. Any policy and any audience will do if it gives you support or even votes for you.

The uncertainty and constant change that are a consequence of this in turn exacerbate this deep-seated lack of trust in people outside of the elite. For, even if some people such as managers and professionals come on board, the ways in which they do so are arbitrary. Having them on board for one fragile and arbitrary project may be a temporary solution, but the uncertainty will lead to the invention of another project. This may or may not get people on board. The problem of the lack of any real politics with a 'big idea' leads to this uncertain shifting. This explains why so much New Labour talk is about one major reform after another or rhetoric piled on rhetoric.

This turn towards a new constituency is one aspect of the concern with management and professionalism. However, it is only partial as there is a more profound disconnection behind the superficial and psephological one. This is the disconnection between people and politics (Bentley *et al.* 2000; Hayes 2001; Hayes and Hudson 2001). The atomized populace that

Mrs Thatcher celebrated are, rightly, uninspired by the dull managerial approaches that are a consequence of TINA. This is what creates anxiety amongst the political elite. Although the political elite may seek votes, it also seeks legitimacy. People not only do not bother to vote, as shown by the historically low turnout in the 2001 general election, but they also have no time for politicians or any interest in political policies. Setting yourself up as a 'managerial' team in charge of the country is to invite indifference to your approach. Apathy is not a personal or psychological problem, it is merely the way that the political elite views the response of ordinary people to their own lack of political vision.

The solution for New Labour is slowly emerging in its policies. These provide clear evidence of what can be identified as a *therapeutic turn*. To understand how this is a solution, it must be set in the *social context* of Third Way politics, what is variously described as 'risk society', 'culture of fear' or 'victim culture'.

The fearful organization in an anxious age

Working in higher education is now seen to be a risky business. In 2001, the Higher Education Funding Council for England (HEFCE) launched a major project to review and improve 'risk management' across the HE sector. This task was enthusiastically accepted by college managers, who set about initiating risk assessments in all institutions and at all levels. It is now accepted that HE is a 'risky business' and that 'risk management is good management'. HE institutions, however, must be some of the safest places on the earth and the irrationality of this exercise is an example of the exaggeration of risk that is holding back developments in contemporary society and contemporary business (Ben-Ami 2001; Furedi 2002).

The idea that we are all at risk is the key to understanding the social context of the Third Way. An atomized and isolated population – individuals and their families – is a population that is naturally vulnerable to feelings of being at risk. The sociologist Ulrich Beck has characterized the social and historical context in the following way: 'The driving force in the class society can be summarised in the phrase: *I am hungry!* The movement set in motion by risk society, on the other hand, is expressed in the statement: *I am afraid!*' (Beck 1992: 49). However, the theory of 'risk society' has been shown to be idealist because it suggests that *consciousness* (of risk) can propel society forward (Rustin 1994). This critique questions Beck's hypothesis that consciousness or 'fear', rather than a more materialist need, 'hunger', is the driving force of history at the present time. More recently, Furedi (2002), has argued that risk consciousness is a pathological response to the collapse of collectivity, and the absence of the subject from history, by which he means the absence of working-class political struggle. In this understanding of the Third Way, the consciousness of risk and a demand for safety become an automatic way of responding to events. This response seems logical but is essentially irrational. Table 5.1 contrasts the key notions of Beck's 'risk society' with Furedi's notion of a 'culture of fear' (Lawes 2003).

Table 5.1 Beck's 'risk society' and Furedi's 'culture of fear'

Risk society	*Culture of fear*
People have become more knowledgeable: a society of 'clever people'	Knowledge is seen as dangerous
Rationality is possible	Irrationality becomes presented as rationality
Manufactured risks are beyond control	There is now a dangerous belief that humankind cannot control nature
A new form of modernity may come into being	All we can hope for is safety
People can be more fully themselves now that the traditional institutions of industrial society have gone	The very concept of humanity is diminished as we seek security and avoid experiment and challenge
Risk society is developing	We live in fear

It is Beck's ideas that dominate Third Way theories and policies. This dominance is usually implicit but occasionally it surfaces (see Jacobs 2001). It is also Beck's ideas that form the ideological background for the managerialism and professionalism of the Third Way. In a risk society it is held to be a *good thing* that people are afraid, so that they can avoid the errors of the rush to 'industrialize and progress' that was characteristic of class society. Being afraid is what makes you a clever person. But this is an idealistic view of risk that projects the consequences of being afraid into the future. The reality of the present is simply, and Furedi is right here, that we live in fear.

The acceleration of the progress towards a situation where we have a fearful, risk-conscious group of managers and professionals in HE and in PCE may well be the outcome of the HEFCE initiative. But the tendency to interpret all life situations as risky is already the norm. Staff and students in PCE increasingly see themselves as victims or potential victims as a result. Staff are concerned with stress and harassment, and inflate minor managerial harms. Students feel they are victims of an endless series of harms from staff prejudice, sexual harassment, examinations and poor examination results, to poor lighting and gas fires. Student Union annual reports often are no more that a catalogue of risks felt or avoided. Management consciously or unconsciously benefits from this victim mentality, as it gives them a role as the group that provides the therapeutic solutions in terms of its own mediation, referral to therapeutic workers such as counsellors, or by arranging therapeutic courses in 'coping with stress' or 'managing your time'. However, the benefits to management from supporting the victim culture are, as we shall see, short term and in reality no one benefits from a therapeutic environment.

In the context of *risk society* the things that are the perennial butt of academic criticism such as inspections by Ofsted, the QAA, ALI and the internal institutional units that mirror these such as 'quality committees' and 'academic standards' are clearly changing. The thrust of their new practice is 'light touch' inspections that require 'self-regulation'. The move to the Third Way of self-regulation is under way but it is actually more demanding and intrusive as it requires the internalization of the standards of these government bodies and quangos. What is being internalized is not just meaningless, rigid, bureaucratic rules about the nature of courses and teaching but the uncertainty of the political elite that lies behind these intrusive measures and organizations. They reflect a lack of confidence about what educational institutions are supposed to be doing. This lack of confidence is apparent in a speech made in 2001 by the then Secretary of State for Employment and Skills, Estelle Morris, to the Social Market Foundation in which she defined the contemporary problem of professionalism from the viewpoint of New Labour's nervous political elite:

> Gone are the days when doctors and teachers could say, with a straight face, 'trust me, I'm a professional'. So we need to be clear about what does constitute professionalism for the modern world. And what will provide the basis for a new era of trust between Government and the teaching profession. This is an arena ripe for debate and we welcome views from all round the education system and from others, including parents and business people.
>
> (E. Morris 2001: 19)

All the key aspects of New Labour's attitude to professionalism are expressed in this quotation from the aptly entitled *Professionalism and Trust*. First, there is the scathing rejection of the teacher as an autonomous expert. Second, there is an abstract semantic search for the meaning of trust – something that must follow once the autonomy that is of the essence of trust has been rejected. Finally, we get an elevation of 'others' – 'stakeholders' or more properly 'know-nothings' to the role of experts in a search for meaning. New Labour is only categorical about what is not on in the development of this new professionalism:

> It is important to trust our professionals to get on with the job. That does not mean leaving professionals to go their own way, without scrutiny – we will always need the constant focus on effective teaching and learning and the accountability measures described above. But what it does mean is that we shall increasingly want to see professionals at the core, to join us in shaping the patterns for the schools of the future.
>
> (E. Morris 2001: 26)

Here we have the 'Millennium Dome' or 'big tent' view of professionalism. As long as you are on the inside of the dome/tent that is OK, but you cannot have any independent thought or autonomy. Indeed, the six criteria that define New Labour's 'professionalism' are entirely arbitrary.

They are: high standards at key levels such as entry; a body of knowledge about what works best and why; management of complementary staff; effective use of 'cutting edge' IT; incentives and rewards for excellence; and a relentless focus on the best interests of those who use the service – pupils and parents – backed by performance and accountability measures. This is not a list that shows a confidence in professional people but an expression of an anxious authoritarianism.

Why raise the issue of creating a 'modern' professionalism at all when you have no confidence in professionals? The obvious reason, as we have repeatedly said, is New Labour's simple desire to get people on side. In Estelle Morris's speech this is expressed through the concern to give professionalism 'meaning'. This is the Third Way problem of political disconnection projected through what appears to be a semantic or philosophical matter onto any group that is prepared to offer advice and, therefore, to come on side. But once you reject the fist way of autonomy, and dislike the 'market', there is nothing to fill the vacuum and all you encourage, through endless discussion and consultation, is confusion. Out of such confusion can only come the therapeutic strategies to enable us to cope with the loss of meaning.

The anxious college manager

Institutions are anxious places that now have to have mission statements and strategic plans as thick as telephone directories to reassure themselves as to what they are about. Middle managers are always the most anxious, most stressed and overworked. Marx once described the middle class as 'human dust' that would move in the wind depending on the balance of forces in the struggle between capital and labour. The middle manager is also 'human dust'. The label 'manager' is now affixed to anyone from porters, now labelled 'security services managers', to the deans of large education departments. In this sense the use of the term 'manager' and the label 'professional' start to merge. One difference, although this is no longer as clear as it was, is to see managers as having the role of the traditional foreman. A foreman is someone who has been promoted and no longer takes part in the work they once did; instead, they oversee such work. Their job was fragile in that they no longer produced anything, but it was seen as necessary by employers and tolerated by employees. In depoliticized times, middle management, although it proliferates, has no obvious role. When 'compulsive bonding' and 'presenteeism' are the features of working and professional life, what role has the manager? Bureaucracy, however, has a life of it own and a new role is developing for managers in providing advice and therapy. 'Appraisal' is the institutionalized form of the manager-as-therapist, but mentoring new staff and organizing training and staff development of an increasingly therapeutic nature are roles that are evloving. We have already discussed the new role of the middle manager in managing risk assessments, and we can be sure that making staff and students feel safe will be the focus of a manager's role in the future.

It would be wrong just to see such roles as pointless or 'unproductive'. That they are economically unproductive workers does not serve to distinguish them from other workers who undertake more classroom work or more menial or practical jobs. Most of PCE prepares people for work in the public sector. PCE is paid for out of taxation and not by people buying it on the market. There is no 'market' for education. That is why the Thatcherite introduction of 'market' mechanisms into education was irrational. If education is a commodity, and is sold on the market, where would it be bought? It is not on sale in the shops. If lecturers work harder, or longer hours, they cut costs, and this saves institutions money, but they do not produce any value that can be realized as 'profits'. There is a small exception to this when the education and training that produces productive workers takes place, but for the most part we can ignore this, as most education produces unproductive workers (Howell 1975; Yaffe [1976] 1998). To talk of the 'productive' academic workers is merely to separate out those academic workers that do the core tasks of teaching and research from support workers or managers.

Whether or not management is now becoming a pointless activity depends on the degree to which employees and students continue to see themselves as vulnerable and at risk. As victims they will be seen as in need of management support. In any case, there is very little evidence of hostility to management. Even in 1996 one survey found that although workers blamed management to some extent for their problems at work, it was intervention by management, rather than anything else, that they thought could provide solutions (Hudson *et al.* 1996: 40). The most likely scenario is that the number of managers will continue to increase, but that their roles will be 'supportive' ones. The current increase in numbers of managers and others involved in 'student services' is one example that indicates the course of developments.

From managerialism to therapy

It is not managers, but the new professionals that will be the harbingers of the 'therapeutic' college. Those that are creating the conditions for this change are the teacher educators, and particularly those who describe themselves as radicals. At a time when the introduction of mandatory teacher training in FE is seen as the first step towards professionalism in PCE, the influence of teacher educators will be a growing one.

The therapeutic approach first came into PCE teacher training as a response to the imposition of competence-based education and training. Usher and Edwards (1994) have pointed out that the introduction of CBET is paradoxical. The commodification and control of knowledge that is seen as the political purpose behind the introduction of CBET exists alongside a 'humanistic' approach to teacher education. The notion of competence is 'cast in behavioural terms but the discourse is itself not behaviourist. It is precisely because it is not, but rather interwoven with liberal humanist discourse that it is powerful' (Usher and Edwards 1994: 110). They add that: 'In its liberal humanist form, competence is more a form of "seduction" than of oppression' (p.111). CBET is, in fact, largely delivered using 'humanistic' methods and this is a device to make the approach acceptable. What Usher and Edwards saw as 'humanistic', is better called therapeutic. The humanistic or subject-based liberal educational curriculum would be impossible to deliver through CBET. What we get as a complement to CBET is the therapeutic curriculum, the concern with personal development and the growth of self-awareness and understanding (reflective practice). The influence of John Dewey is of some importance (Nolan 1998: 140–5), but the appearance of Carl Rogers' work on the reading lists for the PGCE/Cert. Ed. and his influence on teacher educators constitute substantial evidence of an explicitly therapeutic turn. Further support for therapeutic approaches to FE is found in the works of 'radical' writers on education, who are an influence on teacher educators, or who are teacher educators themselves.

Two examples of therapeutic theory will be given, but there are many more. The first shows the influence of a watered-down and indulgent form of Deweyan pragmatism in PCE, that is, in the end, a sort of therapy. A recent book for people working with young adults in PCE seems to echo Dewey's *Democracy and Education* ([1916] 1966) with the comment that 'much of what passes for education is dull and of little relevance to learners' (Harkin *et al.* 2001: 140). The authors add:

> It is time to build a high-trust, democratic education system that respects learners and their experiences, listens closely to their expressions of interest and need, builds partnerships between teachers, learners, parents, the community, and employers so that young adults learn what they wish to learn, and how they wish to learn.
>
> (Harkin *et al.* 2001: 140)

The language here, 'trust', 'partnership' and 'respect' for 'learners and their experiences', is that of the therapist rather than the educationalist. The belief is that the new cohorts of students condemned to education or training rather than being properly employed may be, if we see them as an asset,

> the catalyst for fundamental change in education. Not content to receive more of what they have already endured with indifference or hostility, they may challenge educationalists to provide an experience which promotes rational autonomy, personal engagement and a healthy social democracy.
>
> (Harkin *et al.* 2001: 141)

This somewhat quixotic vision of the potential of PCE throws in every social hope that disillusioned educators might have in these disconnected times. How real are these hopes? The specific condition of their achievement is that 'we', the educators and educational institutions, should value and accept these new students and their experiences. This is a therapeutic rather than a radical approach.

A more realistic picture of the student of today is given in Allan Bloom's book *The Closing of the American Mind* (1987) which is subtitled: *How Higher Education has Failed Democracy and Impoverished the Souls of Today's Students*. He says in a section headed 'Self-centeredness': 'Students these days are, in general, nice. I choose the word carefully. They are not particularly moral or noble. Such niceness is a face of democratic character when times are good. Neither war nor tyranny nor want has hardened them or made demands on them. The wounds and rivalries caused by class distinction have disappeared along with any strong sense of class' (Bloom 1987: 82). Those who know the text will know that Bloom qualifies this with the comment that class discrimination still exists 'poisonously' in British universities. Bloom made this comment two years before the events of 1989, and we can, as a result of the subsequent changes, assume that they no longer hold true.

The assumption of the transformative potential of working-class students is false. Even if it were a possibility, it would be diluted and displaced by navel-gazing forms of therapy disguised as education.

The second example of therapeutic theory for a therapeutic professionalism comes in a limited way from postmodern thinkers but more forcefully from a new generation of seemingly radical or critical thinkers influenced by the writings of Jürgen Habermas.

Habermas was a philosopher linked with the Marxist Frankfurt School (see Habermas (1986) and Therborn (1978) for an introduction and criticism). Habermas argued that socially coordinated activities were established through communication and in certain central spheres this was 'through communication aimed at reaching agreement', and he adds:

> the reproduction of the species *also* requires satisfying the conditions of a rationality that is inherent in communicative action. These conditions have become perceptible in the modern period with the decentration of our understanding of the world and the differentiation of various universal validity claims.
>
> (Habermas 1986: 397)

This is what Habermas calls the 'communication-theoretic turn'. From his work, an idea of a search for 'communication free of domination' has been applied to PCE. Using this notion, some writers are critical of the fact, that in PCE institutions,

> it is clear that we are far from establishing an ideal speech community but importantly we should be endeavouring to make classrooms more open in language practices . . . [which means that] differences of gender, culture and outlook should be celebrated as part of a democratic endeavour.
>
> (Harkin *et al.* 2001: 135)

The consequence of this seeming radicalism will be identical to what Habermas put forward: a critical self-reflection that is a sort of therapy (see Therborn 1978: 125–8). The appeal of this sort of philosophy to professionals is, in fact, a false ideological sense of themselves as radicals. It relocates political problems to the classroom and pretends that they can be overcome by 'the enlightened efforts of critical students and scholars' (Therborn 1978: 139). As Therborn puts it: 'Hence Habermas's popularity . . . He combines an apparently left-wing pedigree, conventional humanism and a notion that the basic political problems are problems of communication. The blandness of these ideas is evident' (Therborn 1978: 139). These ideas may be bland but they do flatter and exaggerate the role of the PCE teacher or trainer and the potential for social change that lies in the hands of students.

The focus on communication and critical reflection is no more than therapy because at the very core they change nothing in society but merely get people to feel better about things, because they are engaging in the 'politics' of communication. At a time when real material or social antagonism (class politics) seem non-existent, the search for a fuller understanding through communication seems all that we can hope for.

Towards the therapeutic college

The turn towards therapy is based on the premise of low expectations. The horizons managers and professionals set for us and our students are lowered because the social antagonisms that drove society forward and produced big ideas such as 'socialism' are absent. The consequence is a turn towards the personal and subjective, and if we are not aware of the political context of this change, the belief that all we can do is improve intersubjective communication quite naturally follows. A period in which horizons are lowered is a time in which we have a diminished view of the potential of people. The current expression of this is what we have discussed as the 'victim culture', in which we see people as constantly at risk and unable to cope.

The political response to the 'victim culture', according to James L. Nolan in his seminal book *The Therapeutic State* (1998), is that all state institutions, and education in particular, are open to the 'therapeutic ethos'. The therapeutic ethos centres on building up individual self-esteem. In the face of the forces of technical rationalization it helps people cope with the effects on their private lives. It also helps people subject to racial, sexual or any other discrimination, to cope with their 'victimhood'. Moreover, it accommodates to religious and cultural pluralism by offering 'a religion-like system of collective meaning' devoid of divisive sectarianism (Nolan 1998: 19). The therapeutic ethos is wrongly seen as oppositional:

> Though sometimes portrayed as a reaction against utilitarian capitalism, the therapeutic cultural impulse does not directly challenge or

threaten the utilitarian orientation of the capitalistic order. To the contrary, the therapeutic ethic appears to complement the utilitarian ethic. It offers to soften the harshness of life in the machine without removing the machine. In fact, it is often defended as a viable source of action because of its purported efficacy. Though these two dispositions seem intuitively disparate, they may actually be complementary.

(Nolan 1998: 20).

More succinctly he argues: 'The therapeutic orientation provides a personalized remedy to a highly impersonal, rationalized, bureaucratic system, but without fundamentally altering the system' (1998: 20).

The trends towards a new ideology of managerialism and professionalism, based upon the therapeutic ethos, may ultimately lead to the establishment of the *therapeutic college*. The prime movers in this direction will not be college authorities or the state and its quangos, but PCE teachers and teacher educators who have been influenced by ideas from a variety of radical sources, but mostly by the retreat into the politics of communication that derives from Habermas's rejection of Marxism. The tragedy is that no one benefits from this development. The students attending the therapeutic college will be impoverished human beings taught to seek not dangerous things like knowledge and truth but more communication experiences that build up their self-esteem and that of others. Lecturers will have to engage in classes that more and more resemble 'circle time' in the primary school. The therapeutic ethos arises out of the more negative and atomized nature of society. To go along with it is to undermine the potential to overcome individual adversity and to take control of our lives. 'Circle time' is a poor substitute for human achievement and social progress.

Chapter 6

ACCOUNTABILITY AND EFFECTIVENESS IN POST-COMPULSORY EDUCATION

Laurie Lomas

Introduction

When an undergraduate at university in the late 1960s and early 1970s, I was amongst a relatively small proportion of my age group enjoying the benefits of higher education. Looking back on those three years, one of my recollections is of tutors who were generally preoccupied with their research and publications and did not appear to be either enthusiastic or effusive in tutorials – when one could be arranged. Generally, I was left to 'get on with it' and work out for myself what was expected of me as an undergraduate in terms of written work. Essays were marked and returned, at the tutor's convenience, with minimal comments that were usually very general and vague. What had been expected from me had to be inferred from these scant remarks and the approach to the subject adapted appropriately in order to improve my score for the next assignment. Perhaps I need not have worried too much about my essay scores as the final class of degree was determined by my performance in several examinations at the end of my third year. Essay scores were taken into account only if students were at the borderline of a degree class. When I had finished my degree course and received my degree certificate, it was with some relief that I left university and entered my chosen profession.

Higher education colleges and universities should be accountable for their actions and their performance, as are other service organizations in the public and private sectors. Senior managers in commercial organizations are responsible to the company's shareholders: managers in HE colleges and universities may be held to account by their principal funders: central government and the students. Performance management, which is now being adopted in public sector organizations such as HE colleges and universities after extensive and continuing use in commerce and industry, utilizes performance indicators to relate outcomes to particular inputs. Quality assurance systems are required to ensure that the government and students are receiving value for money and that the education being provided is fit for purpose, and feedback from customers (the students) should indicate any need for the future development of the existing service on offer.

There is nothing special about higher education that differentiates it from any other service organization. Managerial principles applied in commercial service organizations and other public sector service organizations such as health trusts, hospitals and local councils, are just as relevant in a higher education context. Managerialism is universalist and, as Ritzer (1996) argues, higher education institutions are no different from other service industries with consumers requiring the same standardization, reliability and predictability as they do when purchasing a burger or dealing with their bank. This leads Ritzer to postulate the notion of the 'McUniversity'. Further support of this universalistic perspective is provided by Harvey (1999) who clearly identifies consumerism in HE colleges and universities, and Scott (1998) who claims that the recent massification of higher education in the UK has confirmed that higher education as just another 'mass production industry'.

Massification

Scott (1998) uses the term 'massification' to describe the development of mass higher education during the latter part of the twentieth century. Between 1981/82 and 2000/01, there was a 135 per cent increase in the number of higher education students. Figures during the last five of those years illustrate this steep rise. In 1996/97, there were 1.53 million students, and by 2000/01 there had been a 5.3 per cent increase to 1.66 million (THES 2002). Participation in higher education now involves nearly one in three of those in the 18–21 age group (Gibbs 2001). This increase in numbers has diminished the elitist nature of higher education institutions and this trend has been assisted by an increase in the proportion of non-standard entry students who do not have the usual minimum requirement of two A levels for undergraduate courses. At Liverpool John Moores University, the proportion of non-standard entrants was nearly 75 per cent (Rust 1997). With such a significant growth in student numbers, it is essential that management systems are in place to monitor the quality of higher education provision and the work of the students. These systems can help to ensure that 'more means different' rather than 'more means worse' (Lomas and Tomlinson 2000).

Performance management

Recent developments in public sector management have involved reviewing and revising management and remodelling it to reflect 'best' commercial practice. There has been an emphasis on decentralization, leadership, explicit standards and measures of performance. There has been greater emphasis on output measures with resources and rewards being linked to performance (Docking 2000). Performance management has tended to replace long-standing management approaches that have been concerned more with inputs and processes.

The greater use of performance management in the context of public service is not a recent phenomenon. In the higher education sector, the Jarratt report (1985) exhorted higher education institutions to adopt managerialist approaches (action planning, mission statements, appraisal schemes and performance indicators, for example), which were being used in business, commercial and industrial organizations. Two years later, the Croham report (Croham 1987) recommended performance indicators for university teaching and research, finance and management. At the beginning of the twenty-first century there is the emergence of perfor-mativity with academic staff in universities being asked to demonstrate their value to their institution in the marketplace (Barnett 2000b).

Performance management, which includes performance appraisal, is the process of monitoring employee performance in an objective manner (Marcousé *et al.* 1999). There are a number of stakeholders who have an interest in this process, including staff, employers, boards of governors, and local and central government funding agencies (Burgoyne 1995). A key aim of performance management is to align the performance of individuals with the organization's strategy and attempt to ensure their congruence (Simmons and Iles 2001).

Performance management has been the subject of criticism on the grounds that, for example, it embodies all the insensitive elements of 'hard' human resource management (Guest 1987). It has been regarded by some writers as a panoptic control mechanism used by management in flat-structured organizations (Townley 1992). Nevertheless, the emphasis on performance (outcomes) allows for the close monitoring of the impact of individual human and other resources on overall organizational performance.

Performance management in the education sector has been achieved via much tighter regulation by central government through the develop-ment of national standards such as the national qualifications framework and subject benchmarking. This has resulted in a clear specification of what is regarded as effective teaching and learning and a standardization of the relationship between managers and managed. As Hoggett (1996: 20) notes:

> In virtually all sectors, operational decentralisation has been accom-panied by the extended development of performance manage-ment systems [which include] . . . performance review, staff appraisal

systems, performance-related pay, customer feedback mechanisms, comparative tables of performance indicators, including league tables, quality standards and total quality management.

The *Times Higher Educational Supplement* and broadsheet daily and Sunday newspapers regularly publish league tables that show the performance of HE colleges and universities in, for example, the Research Assessment Exercise, widening participation, degree classifications and 'value added' and graduate employability.

Service quality and evaluation

There are numerous interpretations of quality in the higher education sector and these can include a blend of excellence, fitness for purpose, value for money, and transformation. This transformation often involves cognitive transcendence, with the provider 'doing something to the customer rather than just doing something for the customer' (Harvey and Green 1993: 24).

In at least one particular sample (Lomas 2002), quality as value for money does not seem to be a popular concept with university and college senior academics but it is very much part of the interpretation of a former head of the Quality Assurance Agency for higher education (QAA). He considered that the publishing of quality measures of higher education was essential if parents and students are to judge which higher education institutions represent good value for the annual fee. Problems of measuring quality as transformation in terms of intellectual capital may well mean that this interpretation has relatively little impact, even though it is popular with academics in higher education institutions (Lomas 2002).

Higher education colleges and universities have made use of standard quality management models that have been used extensively in other sectors for many years. In 1994 the University of Wolverhampton was the first university to be awarded the Charter Mark (Doherty 1995). This university, together with Aston, South Bank and Ulster Universities, have developed total quality management (TQM) approaches (Kanji and Tambi 1999). Aston University has made use of the notion of continuous improvement (*kaizen*) and, as early as 1987, introduced quality circles as a means of achieving this end. TQM was adopted throughout the university and involved academic and non-academic staff. As well as the adoption of *kaizen*, there was academic restructuring, a great emphasis on customer care and the development of a clear corporate identity (Clayton 1995).

South Bank University considered that TQM was a means of developing and eventually achieving an organizational culture that was more amenable to change. Teamwork and cross-functional cooperation were used to develop this openness. TQM was seen by their dean of educational development, not only as a mechanism to control the level of quality, but also as a way of motivating staff and increasing their commitment to the students (Chadwick 1995). Again, there is an emphasis on care of customers and changing lecturers' attitudes towards them. More recently, Sheffield Hallam University has been applying the European Foundation for Quality Management model in order to achieve organizational excellence (Pupius 2001).

The priority of the customer's needs has been codified through, for example, the greater use of service level agreements in HE colleges and universities. These agreements detail the rights and responsibilities of the two parties – the students and the organization. An exemplar of these specified and unambiguous rights and responsibilities are that deadlines are published for the submission of assignments by students, as are dates for the return of marked assignments by lecturers. When examining the notion of quality as it relates to all services including those in the higher education sector, it is the customer's judgement about the particular service's overall excellence or superiority that is crucial. Organizations need to address two key questions. What is the gap between the customer's expectations and her perceived level of service? Also, what needs to be done to improve the customer's perception of service quality and thereby close this gap (Zeithaml 1987; Parasuraman *et al.* 1991)?

Evaluation

There is a certain universalism about the provision of services (Lovelock 2001) and practitioners in the higher education sector can learn from good practice in other sectors. In the private sector, hotels, fast food restaurants, and providers of car components, Kwikfit for example (Farmer 1999), have for some while made use of simple satisfaction survey questionnaires in order to assist in their pursuit of continuous improvement (Heller 1997). More recently, in the public sector, hospitals and local councils have followed their example of using regular satisfaction surveys (Wilkinson *et al.* 1998). Indeed, in local government Best Value requires councils to consult their charge payers on the services they provide (DETR 1999).

A thorough evaluation of service provision involves an examination of efficiency and effectiveness. Whereas efficiency relates to the degree to which a service generates the largest possible outputs from a given amount of inputs, effectiveness is concerned with the achievement of particular desired outcomes (Lovelock 2001). As Adam *et al.* (1995) summarize it, efficiency is about doing things right and effectiveness is about doing the right things. From a student's perceptive, there will be a concern about the institution doing the right things and doing them right so the identification of their views on a range of issues in HE colleges and universities is concerned with both the efficiency and the effectiveness of provision. An example could be students might want a wide range of book and non-book resources (effectiveness) to assist with their studies but at the same time they will require easy and reliable access to these resources (efficiency).

Most HE colleges and universities throughout the world collect some form of feedback from their students about the higher education experience. This feedback can be a most powerful quality enhancement tool, with the institution identifying, devising and then implementing strategies to achieve improvements (Centre for Research into Quality 2001).

The Higher Education Funding Council for England (HEFCE) project 'Collecting and Using Student Feedback on Quality and Standards in Learning and Teaching in Higher Education' will provide some of the information required by institutional audit teams to form judgements about quality and standards when conducting QAA external reviews from the start of the 2002/03 academic year. In addition to the views of students, reviewers will take account of the institution's self-evaluation documents, information submitted by the professional and statutory bodies of other stakeholder groups, details about specific academic disciplines, and written and oral information acquired during the visit to the institution (QAA 2002).

In order to locate good practice in higher education institutions, it is necessary to design and implement a national survey on students' views on the quality and standards of learning and teaching. There are certain key areas of the student experience that need to be examined by means of this survey. These are (HEFCE 2002):

- Arrangements for academic and tutorial guidance, support and supervision.
- Library services and IT support.
- Suitability of accommodation, equipment and facilities for teaching and learning.
- Perceptions of the quality of teaching and the range of teaching and learning methods.
- Assessment arrangements.
- Quality of pastoral support.

Managerialism and professionalism

In HE colleges and universities, there has been a growth in managerialism at the expense of professionalism that has led to their being regarded as just like any other public or private sector organization in the way in which they function in order to achieve their strategic goals. This rise in managerialism has strengthened the notion of the universalism of management. The increase in the level of managerialism in education has been fuelled by the necessity to do more with less (Williams 1997). Managerialism is based on the primacy of student throughput with the consequent generation of income. Quality is assessed on the basis of outcomes with value for taxpayers' money being a key factor (Randle and Brady 1997). The notion of accountability is central to this definition of quality, with accountability being predicated upon the need for restraint in public expenditure in order that the UK can remain competitive in world markets

(Harvey and Knight 1996). It involves the development of a more formal organizational structure with a centralizing of control (Holmes 1993).

A number of writers argue that managerialism leads to a reduction in the level of consultation, fewer committees and the concentration of power at the centre of a college or university. This shift in the locus of power has been encapsulated in the phrase 'the decline of the professor and the rise of the registrar' (Dopson and McNay 1996: 30). Morley (1997) neatly summarizes managerialism in terms of the 3E's of economy, efficiency and effectiveness, and government restrictions on public expenditure have exerted pressure on educational institutions to be far more cost effective. Strengthening management has been seen as an aid to achieving this objective. Recent government reforms have been designed to develop HE colleges and universities into business-like organizations (Shore and Roberts 1995) and to tighten up the relationship between the various academic, administrative, support and ancillary units that make up a college or university. Weick (1988) argues that, before the rise of managerialism, these units were 'loosely coupled'. Generally, the relationship between the academic and administrative functions, for example, was relatively weak with infrequent contact between academic and administrative staff and only minimal interdependence. Loose coupling allows the staff of a college or university a significant degree of autonomy (Weick 1988), and one consequence of a tightening of the coupling is to increase the visibility and accountability of each unit. This is because the behaviour and contribution of its staff towards the achievement of organizational goals is open to greater scrutiny by the staff of other units.

Lessons in management have been sought from the private sector and then applied to the public sector as the budget-capping of the 1970s gave way to an insistence on commercial models of management in the 1980s (Barnett 1994). Such commercial models placed emphasis on the value of small business units, a balance between central control and devolution of decision making and the importance of the quality of a service or product as well as its price (Fielden 1990). Scott (1998) also views the adoption of the notions of line management as a substitute for those of professional responsibility. The development of line management, together with strategic planning, mission statements, objectives, action plans and performance indicators are examples of the development of managerialism in the educational sector. Trowler (1998) cites modularization, semesterization, and the use of Accreditation of Prior Learning (APL) and Accreditation of Prior (Experiential) Learning (APEL) for credit accumulation and transfer schemes (CATs) as relatively recent specific manifestations of managerialism in HE colleges and universities. Rowley (1997) claims that a redefinition of higher education is taking place. This redefinition still includes the intellectual development of students. However, accountability is no longer restricted to the academic community as there is accountability to the students amongst other stakeholder groups. With the emergence of a contract culture, there has been the establishment of learning contracts and the Students' Charter. Students, as customers, expect lecturers to arrive for lectures on time and to mark and return work within a reasonable period. Until the creation of the Higher Education Quality Council (HEQC) and HEFCE, universities were exempt from external scrutiny (Sharp 1995). The development of these two bodies, and the later emergence of the Quality Assurance Agency, reflect the greater emphasis that is placed on meeting the needs of society, the economy and the state. Consequently, there has been an extension of the people and institutions to which higher education institutions are now accountable (NATFHE 1992).

The move to greater accountability – as exemplified by course review systems, staff appraisal and research ratings – has tended to narrow the perceived gap between the functioning and strategic purpose of HE colleges and universities and other organizations (Barnett 1994). As a consequence, the opposition to quality management awareness-raising and training has waned. Overall, the drive for efficiency with the consequent emphasis on greater government control has meant that managerialism has flourished at the expense of professionalism (Thorne and Cuthbert 1996).

The various issues involved in the debate over professionalism and managerialism are summarized in Table 6.1.

Table 6.1 Conflicting professional and managerialist paradigms

Professional paradigm	*Managerialist paradigm*
Goals and values	**Goals and values**
• Primacy of student learning and the teaching process	• Primacy of student throughout and income generation
• Loyalty to students and colleagues	• Loyalty to the organization
• Concern for academic standards	• Concern to achieve an acceptable balance between efficiency and effectiveness
Key assumptions	**Key assumptions**
• Lecturers as experts	• Lecturers as flexible facilitators and assessors
• Resources deployed on the basis of educational need	• Resources deployed on the basis of market demand and value for taxpayers' money
• Quality of provision assessed on the basis of input	• Quality assessed on the basis of output/outcomes
Management ethos	**Management ethos**
• Collegiality	• Control by managers and the market
• Professional autonomy	• Management by performance indicators
• Pluralism	• Unitarism

Source: Randle and Brady 1997.

Barnett (1997) acknowledges that modern HE colleges and universities are large, complex organizations that require firm, clear management in order to provide strategic thinking and to ensure that their mission, aims and objectives are fulfilled efficiently and effectively. However, he gives a practical example of how managerialism can be in conflict with certain cherished tenets associated with professionalism. One such tenet is the primacy of critical thought in higher education. Managerialism involves the creation of a clear goal that is articulated in the mission statement and goal congruity is achieved through the use of staff appraisal. As agreement to common goals is sought, so criticism is seen as dissent and, perhaps, disloyalty. There is an expectation that all staff will assist in the achievement of corporate goals and promote the corporate image.

In higher education, it is necessary to take into account the notion of professionalism that can lead to some resistance to change. Professionals are usually defined as those people in non-manual, scholarly occupations who have undertaken an educational programme in order to acquire specialized, theoretical professional knowledge. The success in acquiring this knowledge is often demonstrated in examinations. They possess a body of knowledge that others do not and the consumer expects the professional to use this body of knowledge to fulfil their needs (Squires 1990). Becoming a professional involves more than just accumulating and updating a particular body of knowledge. It also requires a special perspective with a characteristic type of thinking (Hammer 1997). An example of this would be an ethical sensitivity with regard to professional/client relationships. Burrage and Torstendahl (1990) consider that there are four professional faculties – theological, medical, juridical and philosophical – and these have the associated occupations of priest, doctor, lawyer and lecturer/teacher. Lecturers can be seen as commanding cultural knowledge that they then transmit to their students. They can, it is argued, 'be considered to be among the élite of modern secularised culture' (Siegrist 1994: 3).

Indeed, higher education lecturing has been termed the key profession because it provides the initial education for other professions (Becher 1999). Thus, lecturers often perceive themselves as professionals in the same way as doctors, barristers and solicitors do, and there is an underpinning dominant person culture, which can lead to resistance to extra-professional training initiatives. It can also lead to an unwillingness or inability to deal with incompetent or unconscientious members of the profession (Handy 1993).

Lecturers can be seen as operating within a professional bureaucracy that is one of the five types of bureaucracy discerned by Mintzberg (1983). Mintzberg developed a typology of bureaucracies as a result of his research in North American colleges and universities. The professional bureaucratic form of organization tends to be common in education and healthcare services and relies on specialists. It affords them a high degree of autonomy. These specialists are free to develop their skills with only limited interference from outside the profession. Becher (1989) notes that within the lecturing profession there are a number of subject-based 'academic tribes' that have their own epistemological territories, artefacts and heroes. This tribal system further reinforces professionalism. However, there is a danger that the discretion and autonomy possessed by professionals lead them to ignore the needs of their clients, customers and organization (Mintzberg 1983). Recent developments in the higher education sector have elevated the application of managerialism whilst undermining professionalism.

Any change, such as the growth of managerialism, tends to be met initially by denial (Carnall 1999) and occurrences of cultural change in HE colleges and universities can be gauged by looking at indicators such as management and teaching styles, the type of student feedback and the willingness of lecturers to give tutorials. The embedding of managerialism can be gauged by the extent to which academic and non-academic staff understand the mission statement and are committed to its achievement (Hart and Shoolbred 1993). Also, the existence of a culture of continuous improvement with the emphasis not just on external scrutiny but also on effective internal action is another indicator of the impact of managerialism on an organization (Harvey and Knight 1996).

More recently, professionalism in higher education has tended to be codified, bounded and specified. This is typified by the work of the Institute for Learning and Teaching (ILT), a professional association for higher education staff that was established in response to one of the recommendations of the Dearing report (Dearing 1997). ILT accredits experienced staff on the basis of a reflective portfolio and postgraduate certificate programmes of study in learning and teaching designed for new entrants to the profession. The main aims of the ILT are to enhance the status of teaching and supporting learning, contribute to the improvement of teaching and learning quality and set standards of good professional practice. The ILT's six elements of core knowledge and five professional values underpin their accreditation of individuals and institutional programmes, exemplifying the specificity and tight coupling that is now endemic in HE colleges and universities. Thus, an applicant to the ILT, or any programme of study for which ILT accreditation is sought, must demonstrate the mastery of the six core knowledge elements. These are the particular subject material, teaching and learning methods, models of how students learn, the use of learning technologies, evaluation methods, and the implications of quality assurance. Similarly, the following five professional values need to be manifested: commitment to scholarship, continued reflection and evaluation, the development of learning communities, the encouragement of participation in higher education, and respect for individual learners. The professionalism that is required of experienced practitioners and new entrants to the higher education is clearly stated, unambiguous, demonstrable and measurable.

In addition, there has been the growth of more utilitarian attitudes towards the notion of professionalism in higher education. Academic work has experienced a period of demystification that has been accompanied by a questioning of the notion of 'academic guilds' (Henkel 1997). This move to a more utilitarian approach has been manifested by changes in the discourse in HE colleges and universities from the 'old discourse' which included issues of collegiality, community, scholarship and A levels to the 'new discourse'. This new discourse includes mission statements, business plans, non-traditional entry, semesterization, modularity, credit accumulation and transfer points (CATs), franchizing, Accreditation of Prior Learning and Accreditation of Prior Experiential Learning (Duke 1992). Again, the emergence of the 'new discourse' illustrates and illuminates how many elements of higher education have become more atomized and measurable.

Conclusions

The thrust of the argument of this chapter has been that HE colleges and universities are just like other organizations in that they require effective management systems and structures if they are to function effectively and achieve their goals. The massification of higher education in the late twentieth century together with the desire to achieve a 50 per cent participation rate amongst 18–30-year-olds by 2010 (*The Lecturer* 2002) means that higher education is just another mass production industry. In order to coordinate numerous human and other resources and a wide range of academic and support tasks in large institutions, tighter coupling between the academic and support functions is required in order to integrate their activities and thereby maximize the organization's efficiency and effectiveness.

Managerialism – with its emphasis on responding to the market, accountability to the customer, the measurement of quality in terms of outcomes and value for money, performance indicators and performance management – helps to ensure the tight coupling of all these various components. Clear structures and systems help to ensure the effective functioning of the organization and the achievement of its goals and mission. In modern HE colleges and universities, professionalism is no longer the 'woolly' notion it used to be. Instead, it is clearly and unambiguously defined and then 'measured'. It is widely known what it means to be a higher education professional.

There is the universalism of management. As in all organizations, it is the views of the customers in HE institutions that are paramount. Essentially, managing an HE college or university is no different from managing any other large service organization and, as in other organizations, it is the HE colleges and universities that are seen to meet their customers' needs that will flourish and prosper.

Undergraduates in the first part of the twenty-first century are fortunate that there are unambiguous statements relating to learning outcomes and assessment criteria so that they are well aware of what is expected of them. Their lecturers are required to return their assignments by a specified date and provide appropriate formative and summative comments. Students' views are sought on a range of issues including library provision, computer access, the quality of teaching, and the food in the refectory. The greater concern for accountability and the notion of students as customers have been part of the substantial and significant changes that have occurred in HE colleges and universities over the past 25 years – and they are surely changes for the better.

CONDUCTING RESEARCH IN EDUCATIONAL SETTINGS

OVERVIEW: CONDUCTING RESEARCH IN EDUCATIONAL SETTINGS

John Lea

Introduction

To a large extent, conducting research in an educational setting is no different from conducting research in any other setting. However, it is likely to be *social* in its nature. Unless you are interested in the molecular structure of classroom desks you will, probably, either be looking at the underlying causes of a particular form of social behaviour or you will be looking at people's perceptions and experiences. The difference between these two types of research will feature heavily in this chapter along with a discussion of the uses and limitations of the methods that you might choose to conduct these types of research.

It is common in discussions of research methodology to introduce, at an early stage, questions of epistemology. Not wanting to buck this trend I will be looking at some of the issues raised by these discussions. Essentially, an epistemological question concerns the validity of knowledge: how do we know what we know and how trustworthy is it? Although these discussions usually revolve around a consideration of the appropriateness of the use of a particular research method, there are occasions, increasingly in educational research, where they involve a consideration of the purposes of research in general. In this latter context we need to ask whether we are conducting research in order to uncover educational 'truths' or whether we have a more instrumental aim – does the research make us more effective as PCET practitioners? You may be wondering why this should be an issue. Research could surely achieve, simultaneously, both aims? We will be looking at this issue in some detail.

The final section of this chapter concerns the thorny question of theory. Essentially, we need to look at what exactly a theory is, where theories come from, and what is the role of theory in research? This is perhaps the most esoteric part of this book but I hope to convince you that there are important issues at stake here. None more so than in the question of how theory makes its way into practice. If you have undertaken a course in initial teacher training I feel sure that you will have asked yourself the question: 'What's all this theory got to do with me and my practice?' If you are worried by this section of the chapter, you might like to keep this question in mind.

I will close the chapter with a more detailed look at the more instrumental approach to research often associated with the rise of action research in education. Action research could be considered to be something of a popular movement in education. It now has a large number of devotees and there are departments in some HEIs which specialize in preparing students to conduct such research. Essentially, action research, in education at least, is research conducted by practitioners, for practitioners. In this respect it is aimed at making practitioners more effective. We will consider the issues raised by this movement in some detail.

To some extent, we might argue that action research is also of its time, i.e. its rise has coincided with a more general scepticism towards traditional research, particularly concerning its truth claims. On the one hand, there has been a steady rise throughout the last century in what is often referred to as ethnographic research, i.e. research centred on documenting individuals' meanings, and a burgeoning of a postmodern sensibility which has encouraged a general scepticism towards our ability to 'know' anything which could detached from some form of vested interest. In this context a more instrumental approach to research knowledge might be argued to be a 'healthy' contribution to this more general movement.

Methodological and epistemological concerns

Background

Choosing a research method is like choosing a tool from a tool box. If you are unfamiliar with the tools you will probably start by asking some obvious questions: what does this one do; where would I use this one; why use this one when this other one looks simpler? However, the tools might be more aptly described as measuring devices where you hope to able to use them to detect the nature and quantity of a 'substance'. In educational research the 'substances' are likely to be either forms of human behaviour or the concepts we have constructed to help us explain or categorize human behaviour. To choose a classic example, if I am interested in how intelligent somebody is, the traditional measuring device would be the IQ test. In this context the test is simply a ruler – it will measure the existence and the amount of the 'substance' intelligence. This is a good example because it clearly raises the question of the appropriateness of the ruler and, for some people, the nature of the concept 'intelligence'.

This question of the appropriateness of the ruler is a fundamental research question, and it can also act as our lead into more epistemological matters. For example, if I am interested in whether there is a connection between students having been abused as youngsters and their post-compulsory college achievement, I might, quite rightly, be hauled over the research coals for seeking to measure the existence of 'abuse' through asking questions of students as they enter or leave the college gates. The issue, in strict research terms, is the same as in the IQ example above, that is, is this form of questioning likely to uncover the 'substance', but also, is the definition of 'abuse' that I am using a good one? In case the point is not clear, ask yourself, first, who is likely to reveal such personal information about themselves to a researcher at the college gates, but second, should that person be happy to do so, what exactly is being taken to be the definition of 'abuse' – physical, sexual, mental, etc.? Hopefully what is clear in this example is that the amount of abuse uncovered is in large part a reflection of both the research tool and the definition of 'abuse' being measured. Or, to make the point more epistemologically, how much are we learning about the researcher and the research context and how much are we learning about the reality of abuse?

I chose this particular example for a further reason: there is surely an ethical dimension to be considered in all social research and this might manifest itself in many ways. For example, should those being interviewed be fully aware of the nature of the research and the purposes to which it might be put? And, furthermore, to what extent should they not just be consulted, but also be considered to be collaborators in the research? I have posed the questions in this way as both will feature later in the chapter.

The epistemological context

However, returning to our epistemological theme, an epistemological question is a question concerning the nature and validity of human knowledge. A fundamental epistemological question is the extent to which we believe when we undertake some form of research that the knowledge we produce reflects the reality of the object under investigation, or whether the object comes to resemble the way in which we have come to conceptualize it. To put it crudely, does the world speak to us, or do we speak to the world? If this is unclear, imagine a scientist conducting research into an aspect of molecular biology or atomic physics. I am asking you to consider the extent to which you believe that the scientist is 'listening' carefully to the voice of Nature, or, as most sociologists would argue, is framing the way in which Nature will be spoken about.

Discussion point

Pick a famous scientific theory (for example, Darwin's theory of evolution, the 'Big Bang', or even, Einstein's theory of relativity) and ask yourself whether you believe it describes the natural world or offers an interpretation of how we might conceive it?

Another epistemological dispute might be explored through considering the following fictitious scenario. Imagine a scene a hundred years into the future where two people are rummaging around the attic of an early twenty-first century educational researcher and the following conversation takes place:

First person: Hey! Look at this. I've found some things here called graphs and tables looking at who achieved the most GCSE maths passes, whatever they were, between the years 1988 and 1998. It says underneath that 'females', whatever they were, didn't achieve as many passes as something called 'males', and that people from 'working-class backgrounds' didn't achieve as many as those from 'middle-class backgrounds regardless of sex', whatever all that means!

Second person: But hey! Look over here, I've found some old diaries written by people attending something called an FE college in the same period. This one's about one of those females you mentioned and the experience of being on a BTEC engineering course, whatever that was. And, look! Here's one by a 'gay male' talking about 'his' experiences of being on the same course. These look much more interesting than those, what did you call them, 'tables'?

It seems that there are two main issues here. First, if our two friends in the attic were to compare the two types of research they had stumbled over, they might ask which type is better, or, which type is more reliable, gives more insight, is more useful, is more objective. Although a perfectly valid set of questions, the answer may well be that both are as good as each other, because it depends what sorts of questions you are interested in asking, and what it is about social life that interests you. In social research language you are being asked whether you prefer multivariate statistical analysis or people telling stories. You can probably see from this crude dichotomy why the former approach is often referred to as *quantitative* and the latter *qualitative*.

Discussion point

Do you have a view about whether quantitative or qualitative research would be more appropriate in educational settings?

The methodological context

At this point we should distinguish between research methods and research types. Although in many cases the distinction will not be necessary, we should be mindful that, for example, to decide to undertake a social survey is not itself a research methods question, for survey work might be undertaken using several research methods. In this respect the research method is, technically, the tool(s) that will be utilized in research, and several tools might be used concurrently. We can use Table 7.1 to clarify the distinctions.

The first column of Table 7.1 lists some of the main research types. Broadly speaking, this column distinguishes researchers who undertake *survey* work from those who undertake *ethnographic* work. If we remember the fictitious conversation between the two people in the attic, this dichotomy was being alluded to, i.e. there is social research broadly aimed at uncovering 'social facts' and there is social research which is interested in documenting the ways that people make sense of their lives. Action research (to be discussed in more detail below) is included in the centre of this column to reflect the fact that some research falls between these two broad categories and might lean one way or the other depending on the researcher's main interest at the time or research orientation in general.

However, the main point I wish to make clear is that the actual research methods are in fact wide-ranging and might serve different types of researcher. For example, survey work might include large-scale *questionnaires* sent to many homes (indeed, the National Census is a survey sent to every home), or a series of *structured interviews* – where respondents are all asked the same questions – or it could comprise an *attitude scale* where large numbers of people are asked to rank their responses on a number of questions. Similarly, ethnographic work might include *unstructured interviews* – where the interviewer acts as a prompt and a guide to elicit information – or forms of *participant observation* where the researcher 'joins' the group that they are interested in studying, and moves amongst them to elicit information in its 'natural' setting, or finally, asks respondents to keep *written, oral* or *video diaries*, again in an attempt to naturalize the research and document social life through the language and eyes of those being researched (as opposed to those of the researcher).

At this point it is time to consider carefully what is at stake when using these research methods. We could take the very practical view that we will use the method that is the most convenient given our time, money and personal inclination. For example, to conduct a participant observation successfully may require a minimum of six months' work in the field, which could be a major drawback, particularly if we are conducting research within the confines of an undergraduate dissertation. Or, alternatively, to administer a large postal questionnaire might carry enormous financial considerations, not just in postage stamps but also in the processing of the information – this often requires the use of several people to input data into computer programs.

However, we might also have spent some time considering whether *what* we want to study is amenable to the method. For example, if we are interested in the relationship between social class and educational achievement we might want to rank certain methods above others. By contrast, if we are interested in college 'canteen culture' we might rank the methods very

Table 7.1 Research styles and methods: their uses and validity

Styles (approaches)	Methods (techniques)	Uses	Validity (1) – Limitations	Validity (2) – Epistemology
Surveys	Questionnaires	Correlating variables or uncovering facts = QUANTITATIVE DATA	Problems: • Representativeness • Appropriateness of measuring devices • Correlations and causes	POSITIVISITIC TRADITION (statements of fact) The social world exists independently of us and can be studied using the logic and methods of natural science to uncover causes and effects
	Structured interviews			
	Attitude scales			
Action research				
	Unstructured interviews	Documenting meanings or telling stories = QUALITATIVE DATA	Problems: • Generalizability • Attached observers • Interpreting meanings	INTERPRETIVE TRADITION (statements of the way the world appears) The social world can only be understood by looking at the way people make sense of it, through interpretation and negotiation
Ethnographies	(Participant) Observation			
	Diaries and oral histories			

differently. At this point we might want to ask ourselves the important question: is the method appropriate to the object of study? In many cases this question might easily be translated into, perhaps, the real question: what exactly do we want to know? For example, when we are studying the relationship between social class and educational attainment, do we want to correlate the variables (to see how strongly they are related), or do want to get an insight into, say, what it is like to experience Oxbridge under-graduate life coming from a working-class background? Similarly, although studying college canteen culture might immediately lend itself to the use of the more ethnographic methods, this would not be the case if our main concern were uncovering statistical correlations between, say, class, sex or ethnicity and time spent 'gossiping'.

Discussion point

Do you have a view on whether particular types of research are more trustworthy than others?

In this context, choosing a method revolves around a consideration of its usefulness, but we should not forget that with use comes *limitation*. The fourth column in Table 7.1 is a brief attempt to remind us of key elements in respect of method limitations. The question of *representativeness* is directed at the need to consider the extent to which the population of a survey could be seen as representative of a wider population. For example, if I correlate the variable 'class' with 'gossip' and I do this from a sample of FE colleges in south-east England, I would be opening myself to the potential criticism that 'it's different in the north'. This is a question, on the one hand, of the application of sampling techniques (see Cohen *et al.* 2000), but also, on the other, of the need to recognize the limitations of any concluding comments a researcher might make about a research population.

Similarly, as soon as we become aware of the effect that the measuring device might have on the research, not only might we want to reconsider the ruler we are using, but we might want to go even further and consider the extent to which any measurement will naturally affect what is being measured. This is often referred to as the Hawthorne effect in social research, i.e. the simple recognition that people act differently when they know that they are part of an experiment. This was first highlighted at the Hawthorne Electric Works in Chicago in 1932 when a group of researchers were conducting research into productivity (Mayo 1933). One of the researchers came to question the validity of the experiments by asking: how do we distinguish between the effect caused by a change in worker environment from the effect caused by the workers being in an experiment in the first place? However, we might also want to include in this consider-ation the need to recognize that 'variables' in social research are not things in the ordinary sense of that word, but concepts. For example, 'social class' might be defined in many different ways, and, indeed, rejected by some as an outdated concept. Similarly, the concept 'gossip' is clearly open to debate.

Finally, the act of correlating variables is not the simple task it might ordinarily appear to be either. The point can be made simply by using the example of 'firefighters causing fires', i.e. if you feed a computer with all the information which relates to 'uncontrollable fires' and ask it to correlate the most significant variables, it would always rank 'fire-fighters' as the strongest correlate. The point here is that statistical correlation has little meaning until it is interpreted by social researchers. What we really want to know is what *causes* fires, and this would normally require some reasoned argument to accompany the raw data,

In this respect, statistical correlates might be simply coincidental, but, furthermore, if they are causal we still need to consider which variable is the dependent one and which is the independent one? For example, if we find a statistical correlation between the variable (A) social class and the variable (B) intelligence, we might want to dismiss this as mere coincidence; alternatively, we might want to argue that A causes B, thus making B the dependent variable. However, we could also make a case for saying that it is actually B that causes A, thus making A the dependent variable. Of course, we could take this one step further and argue that, in reality, A and B are co-determined by the variable C which we had, until this point, conveniently forgotten or ignored.

Discussion point

Can you think of examples where reversing the 'arrow of causation' might be possible when correlating educational variables?

With more ethnographic research methods we need to be mindful of the extent to which an in-depth study of the 'mind's eye' of a small group of people might be *generalizable*. For example, the classic study by Willis of 12 non-academic 'lads' in a secondary modern school in the mid-1970s is often taken as indicative of a much wider class-cultural phenomenon and we should be asking ourselves whether this is justifiable (Willis 1977). Similarly, if we use Willis's work again as our example, to what extent should we read the ethnography as a transcript of the views of the lads or as a interpretation of the meaning of their views from the point of view of a young Marxist sociologist writing in the mid-1970s? Furthermore, given that the research was conducted using a combination of (participant) observation and unstructured group interviews, we might want to ask the extent to which the views expressed might, in part at least, reflect the desire of the lads to show-off in front of each other.

Lastly, we might also want to be mindful of the extent to which we are much more likely to witness Hawthorne effects using more ethnographic methods, largely because the researcher will often have face-to-face contact with those taking part in the study. Thus, although the main aim of much ethnographic work is to study people and processes in their 'natural' surroundings, the researcher is clearly an intrusion – an *attached* observer. Those skilled in the art of participation observation are clearly aware of this and take steps to limit the effect and/or acknowledge it (Whyte 1955; Patrick 1973; Williams *et al.* 1984) but this should not stop the reader of the research report judging the limitation that this intrusion may have produced.

> **Discussion point**
>
> Do you think the way that ethnographic researchers tend to conduct their research places a serious limitation on the validity of their work?

The quantitative vs qualitative debate

This discussion is aimed at alerting us all to the need to handle research tools carefully, but I have other aims in mind here also. There is a long tradition in social research which suggests that quantitative data is more robust, trustworthy and scientific when compared with the 'softer', interpretive data associated with ethnographic work. Put simply, there is an objectivity about quantitative data when compared with the more subjective qualitative data which thus makes the former more reliable and truthful. There are several reasons why we should, perhaps, question these statements.

> **Discussion point**
>
> What do you consider is necessary to make research findings objective?

It might be argued that because people's perceptions of the world are likely to be highly subjective, if not on occasion idiosyncratic, then statistical analysis, because its aim is to uncover the facts, must be more reliable and objective. However, it may be that you are simply not interested in 'facts' but are genuinely interested in someone's particular experience of the world, no matter how bizarre, indeed possibly because it is bizarre, and thus there are no facts in the equation. Alternatively, you may be concerned to highlight that all research is a social process, that quantitative data possesses an *air* of objectivity but nothing more. All research involves the researcher making choices about what is to be studied, how it is to be studied, what questions will be asked, and how results will be interpreted. If we widen our definition of the Hawthorne effect to include all the ways in which a researcher might influence their research, we would now have to say that it will occur with the use of all methods. In this case what we should ensure is that we know what research methods can and cannot do, become adept in their use, and write research reports which include discussions of how the research might be limited by the methods which were chosen. For example, it is well known in market research that there are ways of phrasing questions which are likely to elicit certain responses (people like to be positive, for instance) and we all know that data can be presented in certain ways to highlight certain points ('lies, damn lies and statistics', and so on).

It is quite common to see educational researchers championing the use of qualitative data (for example, Hitchcock and Hughes 1995). A key figure in this development was Delamont (see particularly 1984). She contrasts a tradition of *systematic observation*, where the researcher conducts research with a pre-set agenda of what they are looking for in a classroom, with her own interest in *ethnography*, where the researcher works on understanding the agenda of the participants in the classroom. Delamont argues that systematic observation, where the researcher operates with a pre-specified coding schedule, will frame the research in such a way that it can only end up reflecting the questions, concerns and interests of the researcher rather than those of the subjects. It is only through forms of unstructured interviewing, participant observation, oral history and diaries (where individuals document their own feelings on the things which concern them), that one can hope to understand the meanings, motives and intentions of the social actors under study.

> To the extent that classroom research claims to illuminate the processes that associate with classroom life, it cannot afford to divorce what people do from their intentions.
>
> (Delamont 1984: 20)

The notion of intention is crucial here. If systematic observation can effectively distort the attempt to understand what is happening in a classroom situation (because it sets its own agenda), it might be argued that a more 'natural' observation will not. However, our epistemological problem now becomes a question of the extent to which it is possible to observe intentions, i.e. what a piece of behaviour means to the actors involved. For example, imagine observing a classroom, possibly on video, where a student is being disruptive. Our first problem is, of course, to ask what disruptive behaviour actually is. Just like 'social class', 'intelligence' and 'gossiping', it is a concept open to contrasting understanding. However, once we have agreed what disruptive behaviour looks like, we still have to consider what is actually going on, for example, is the form we witness an aberration, a form of resistance, anger aimed at a particular person? That is, we need to consider the intention behind the behaviour before we can argue that we understand what is happening – this is an act of interpretation.

Attribution theory suggests that it is fruitful for teachers to attempt to find out to what students attribute their successes and failures (Feldman 1992). In this context we might argue that it is important to uncover to what the student attributes their disruption. Of course the student may not see their behaviour as disruptive, but also, it may be that the student is not the best person to interpret the motives behind their own behaviour anyway. This perspective lies at the heart of psychoanalytical approaches, where the central focus is that people carry repressed anxieties from their childhood into adult life. The repression pushes the anxieties into the unconscious, and thus by definition it becomes lost to conscious control. The anxieties, however, are not lost altogether, and will resurface whenever someone is placed in circumstances which resemble the original sources of the anxieties. This clearly requires an act of interpretation on the part of the researcher.

There is a fundamental point at stake here. It could be argued that quantitative data is collected using methods that allow the data to surface, without contamination from the researcher, whereas qualitative data is collected using methods where the researcher is attached to what is being researched. However, if no data speaks for itself, we are left to conclude that 'observing' educational reality is not as simple as it might first appear. Or, we might say that, quite literally, there is more to seeing than meets the eye.

Positivistic and interpretive traditions

This debate is at the heart of dichotomy drawn in the final column of Table 7.1. The positivistic tradition in the social sciences is founded on the belief that just as there are natural facts (for example, the law of gravity) there are 'social facts' which confront us with the same force as gravity. And just as natural science has produced methods by which these laws might be uncovered, the social sciences should seek to mirror these methods (i.e. reproduce a social scientific equivalent of laboratory conditions) in order to uncover the social laws. Comte and Durkheim, two key founding fathers of sociology, were keen to see this emerging science develop in this way (Comte 1842; Durkheim 1895). Indeed, Comte, credited with the first use of the term 'sociology', originally called his emerging science 'social physics'.

It was Comte and Durkheim's view that metaphysical statements would slowly give way to statements based on observation, experiment and comparison. This tradition was taken up by their philosophical counterparts in the 1920s in the Vienna Circle of logical positivism, who argued that metaphysical statements were meaningless – they were either statements that could not be *empirically* verified or statements that made no *logical* sense. For our purposes, two key features clearly underpin the positivistic tradition in educational research. First, that certain methods will enable us to uncover the social facts, and second, that the relationship between the methods and the reality they explain is one of 'correspondence', i.e. there is a confidence about the systematic use of certain methods and their ability to 'see' reality – in an unbiased, undistorted and impartial way.

Discussion point

Are you persuaded by the view that bias in research is caused primarily by the mishandling of positivistic methods?

However, it could be argued that an interpretive tradition in the social sciences has just as long a history (see Bottomore and Nisbett (1978) for detailed discussions of this). After all, although it may be possible to view human beings as cogs in a causal chain of social events, it is surely equally as valid to consider the need to document the meanings that these social events might have for people. An interpretive tradition is often differentiated from positivism with reference to the former's aim of seeking understanding rather than explanation:

> The natural sciences develop causal explanations of 'outer' events; the human sciences, on the other hand, are concerned with the 'inner' understanding of 'meaningful conduct'.
> (Giddens, in Bottomore and Nisbett 1978: 277)

There seem to be at least two different ways in which the term 'interpretive' might be understood. First, there is the *phenomenological* strand, which concentrates on documenting the ways that people make sense of everyday life – the way the world appears to them. This is most clearly seen in the work of the sociologist Schutz (1932). Second, there is the *hermeneutic* strand where the focus is on the need to recognize that understanding 'meaning' is an act of interpretation. This is what Freud meant by the use of the word 'interpretation' in his famous book *The Interpretation of Dreams*, i.e. the raw material of any dream is only a set of clues to help us understand the real meaning (Freud [1900] 1976).

If you are having trouble seeing how this might relate to educational research within your own professional context, let us reconsider some of the (conceptual) substances we have already discussed. For example, if we take the example of intelligence again, it is one thing to seek to unravel a causal chain by looking at the variables which might be dependent and independent in the chain, but it is quite another to look at what being labelled intelligent might mean to a 16-year-old student in an FE college (a phenomenological account). However, we might go one step further and mount a more thoroughgoing attack on the positivistic variable analysis by arguing that the concept 'intelligence' does not exist independently of the way that it is understood and that its meaning is negotiable; if there is truly a 'human science' then its *raison d'être* is surely contained here.

Discussion point

What do you think might be the *facts* in a study of student 'exclusion' from school or college for disruptive behaviour?

I suggest that there are two ways to look at this debate between the positivists and the interpretivists. We could take the view that each offers an epistemological critique of the other's forms of knowledge, i.e. that it is invalid. Positivists might argue that because interpretivists break important canons of scientific procedure, most importantly that researchers should be detached from their observations, then the latter's work must be epistemologically suspect. Interpretivists might equally retort that scientific procedures are no guarantee of quality – indeed, the procedures are simply a veil to disguise the social processes which are clearly at work not just by the researcher in framing the research, but also more generally on how concepts such as 'intelligence' or 'disruption' are understood (rather than simply found). However, we could take the view that there is a place in educational research for attempting to uncover social facts, and equally, there is a place for documenting meanings. All we need to do is be clear about what it is we are doing, be aware of the limitations of the methods we have chosen, and simply guard ourselves against the epistemologically committed who will be keen to point out our naivety in these matters.

What is perhaps comforting is that many researchers will say that in the framing of their research project they tend to be guided by the much more mundane matters of time, money and inclination. And, if you are not epistemologically committed, several doors also remain open to you. You may feel comfortable about being guided by the 'object' of study, i.e. if you feel that a particular research project is leading you towards quantitative or qualitative data collection techniques this could form the basis for your methodological rationale.

Furthermore, you may feel that you could benefit from a form of methodological triangulation. Put simply, triangulation refers to the process whereby you might approach your 'object' from several angles. This might be achieved through the use of a combination of both quantitative and qualitative methods in order to arrive at a more rounded, fuller, or more complete picture of the object. Alternatively, you might undertake some small-scale ethnographic work in order to orient yourself and then proceed with a much larger-scale piece of social survey work, or vice versa. In this way one method can act as a check on another, act as a pilot for a larger study, or simply act to move the researcher in the direction of a more complete understanding of the 'object' under study.

Discussion point

How far would you go in accepting that forms of triangulation might enable you to arrive at a more rounded research project?

The philosophies of science

In the light of this discussion of triangulation it could be argued that the previous discussion concerning epistemological commitment is rather esoteric and unhelpful. One of the stumbling blocks seems to lie with the long-running concern to make social research 'scientific' and in order to do this, to be seen to mirror the methods used in natural science, i.e. to find the equivalent of laboratory methods in the social sciences. If you have been following my argument carefully you should be able to see that this desire is largely rooted in the idea that there are social facts and that these could be uncovered with the careful use of particular research methods. However, one of the trends in the social sciences over the past 25 years has been to look more carefully at exactly what is natural scientific methodology.

This debate seems to comprise three distinct elements. First, the expressed desire to produce 'objectivity' in the social sciences through using laboratory-equivalent methods in the social sciences – in order to find the facts. Second, the defence of the interpretivist tradition with the two-pronged attack on positivism: that it is not able to understand meanings, but also that its so-called facts are a matter of interpretation. This second element has spawned the humanistic tradition in the social sciences, indicating that we do not really need the word 'science' to be attached to our work (Winch 1990). But, there is a third element which has grown enormously throughout the past 25 years which argues that all is not as it appears in the natural scientific world. This latter investigation seems to have concluded that it is not a matter of why the social sciences are not more like the natural sciences, but, whether the natural sciences rather more like the social sciences than we had all been led to believe.

The seminal work in this debate was Kuhn's (1962). Kuhn argued, in a similar way to Garfinkel (1967; see Part 2), that we should not look at what professionals say they do but study what they actually do. The professionals in this context are the 'white-coated' scientific researchers, who are as much members of a (scientific) community as any other professional groups. Thus, if we all became more sociologically minded when we considered what it is actually like to be a member of a scientific community, we might begin to understand how 'real' science takes place. Most young scientists are recruited to engage in what Kuhn calls 'normal science' – science which involves puzzle solving within an already accepted scientific paradigm, i.e. the science proceeds by posing problems within a wider 'taken for granted' framework of understanding and methodology. For example, if we accept that the universe contains black holes and that the subatomic world is particle-like it enables us to suspend our disbelief in these notions and attempt to solve puzzles within these frameworks. Note also (which is why I chose these examples) the extent to which observing these things as things is also problematical – are they not equally as conceptual as any social scientific 'things'?

Kuhn's more sociological approach to natural science gave rise to an enormous literature focusing on the 'real' nature of scientific work (Lakatos and Musgrave 1970; Feyerabend 1975; Zukav 1980). The nature of these changes and their implications will be the focus of most of the rest of this chapter. For the purpose of clarity there seem to be at least three different emerging themes:

- The increasing recognition that natural science is very similar to social science.
- A burgeoning postmodern sensibility and the abandonment of the search for 'the truth'.
- An increasing sense that questions of epistemological validity should be replaced by calls to justify and be reflexive about research methodology.

One of the conclusions of Kuhn's work was the argument that science does not make progress in the ordinary sense of that word, i.e. that research gradually leads to a clearer explanation of natural phenomena; rather it is much more like the upheaval brought about in times of social revolution. It is only when significant people offer the prospect of a new regime that change is brought about. The obvious example is the 'paradigm shift' that Einstein was able to engender in the scientific community when he offered the seemingly incredible proposition that Newton's laws of motion break down when objects approximate the speed of light.

The notion of a paradigm shift is doubly interesting for it offers the prospect that two different paradigms might be able to offer competing explanations of the same phenomena simultaneously – both correct from within their own frameworks of understanding. Those who believe that there must be one correct explanation behind this competition will obviously be extremely irritated by this lack of desire to find the truth, but what Kuhn and his followers are alerting us to is that paradigms act as pre-operational guiding mechanisms, which help to make sense of phenomena, i.e. we do not simply rely on experimental observations when we undertake scientific work. Lakatos and Musgrave refer to this as science's 'heuristic' devices, i.e. the need to be able to ignore countervailing tendencies in order to produce insight:

> The positive heuristic of the programme saves the scientist from becoming confused by the ocean of anomalies. The positive heuristic sets out a programme which lists a chain of ever more complicated *models* simulating reality: the scientist's attention is riveted on building his models following instructions which are laid down in the positive part of his programme. He ignores the *actual* counterexamples, the available '*data*'.
>
> (Lakatos and Musgrave 1970: 135)

To some, this clearly moves us beyond the ability of science to see the world as it really is; for others it is simply the recognition that seeing involves a lot more than mere sight. The complications that this has brought about in the philosophy of science have been discussed in popular accounts of the new physics (i.e. the theoretical physics associated with quantum theory)

(Capra 1975; Zukav 1980). These books look at how 'natural' objects are affected by the presence of measuring devices; that the attempt to focus on one aspect of natural phenomena puts other aspects out of focus (the uncertainty principle); that it is perfectly feasible for the same observed phenomena to be explained by different theoretical frameworks; and, perhaps most startling, that the whole study of the movement of subatomic particles, is itself, premised on the view (not observation) that they are, indeed, particles, i.e. the language of subatomic particles is an important pre-operational 'paradigmatic' element. Putting it crudely, treat something as particle-like and it will act particle-like. On reflection, it could be argued that the whole history of science is littered with examples of this paradigmatic influence on observation. For example, what exactly did Galileo 'see' through his telescope? Rings around Saturn and the earth orbiting the sun? In the first case, we might suggest that 'rings' *made sense* and, in the second, it was the logical *inference* that, if there is observational evidence of planets in orbit elsewhere in the universe, then this could be said to be the case with earth and the sun (see Horizon (1988) *Science . . . Fiction?* BBC2).

Discussion point

To what extent would you share the view that our problematical relationship with 'reality' could still be resolved by decisive observational evidence?

It is often claimed that Einstein did not like the developments he saw in quantum mechanics (the study of subatomic particles) and preferred to believe that 'God didn't play dice', i.e. there must be a definitive explanation for natural phenomena. What seems to have emerged in the philosophy of science during the 1980s is a much clearer sense that there are important options here for researchers to consider when they undertake research:

- Do I believe when I undertake research that I am, slowly but surely, uncovering the truth? That is, the world, 'reality', exists independently of me, and through the careful use of a combination of reasoned argument and experimental data I will explain it (forms of 'realism').
- Do I believe that the world exists independently of me, but explanations of it do not? That is, I recognize that explanations are based on my own conceptual understandings and these are applied to reality; some will be better than others and thus there can still be a sense of progress towards understanding 'reality'.
- Do I believe that the world can only be understood through my conceptual understanding? That is, there is no sense in referring to another world; we are not representing reality through language and concepts but constituting the world through language and concepts.

The first position is the positivistic tradition, which continues today through versions of philosophical 'realism'. The second tradition, the one

probably favoured by Einstein, is the recognition that conceptual understandings can have extraordinary explanatory power, but they will always
have a tentative existence:

> Physical connections are free creations of the human mind, and are
> not, however it may seem, uniquely determined by the external
> world. In our endeavour to understand reality we are somewhat
> like a man trying to understand the mechanism of a closed watch.
> He sees the face and the moving hands, even hears its ticking, but
> he has no way of opening the case. If he is ingenious he may form
> some picture of a mechanism which could be responsible for all
> the things he observes, but he may never be quite sure his picture
> is the only one which could explain his observations. He will
> never be able to compare his picture with the real mechanism
> and he cannot even imagine the possibility of the meaning of such a
> comparison.
>
> (Einstein, in Zukav 1980: 35)

Postmodern science

The third tradition above is clearly part of the burgeoning postmodern
sensibility which, on the one hand, harks back to forms of philosophical
idealism, and on the other, celebrates the denigration of all notions of
progress, pointing to the ironies and contradictions which all scientific
knowledge produces. In this conception we lose the sense that we can even
approximate a 'real' truth for reality is constituted by our own conceptions.
This problematical relationship we have with 'reality' is neatly summarized
by Rorty (1989):

> The world is out there, but descriptions of the world are not.

With research communities clearly divided on forms of realism, it could
be argued that, collectively, we seem to have made something of a mess of
the research process. Indeed, it is not uncommon to see some philosophers
proudly proclaiming that, at last, 'anything goes!' (Feyerabend 1975), but
equally, there are others claiming that they are appalled by what they see
as forms of intellectual laziness. To judge between these extremes is very
difficult. One way to do so is to ask yourself the extent to which each
position makes sense from within either a 'modern' perspective or a 'postmodern' perspective. For example, Feyerabend's claim that 'anything goes'
does not literally mean that: only that the positivistic tradition has been
forced to come down from the pedestal on which it had placed itself, and
sit, more equitably, with other methodological approaches and forms of
knowledge. The more you embrace a postmodern sensibility the more you
are likely to see the 'sense' in this argument, i.e. if science simply comprises
our descriptions of the world then there is no reason why other forms of
knowledge should not compete equally with it.

Discussion point

How far are you willing to go in accepting that many forms of knowledge might offer insights into the nature of (educational) reality and that they should compete more equally?

Alternatively, it could be argued that what these arguments have all been about is moving us beyond the sense that epistemological questions are about justifying the validity of our truth claims – that some give more insight into the nature of (educational) reality – but are now much more about asking researchers to recognize the foundations upon which their research knowledge rests. This is often referred to as becoming reflexive about knowledge, i.e. reflecting on the basis upon which a statement has been made. A classic example of this could be said to be when theoretical physicists came to question the basis upon which their knowledge of the particle world was formed:

> We act as if there really were such a thing as an electric current (or a particle) because, if we forbade all physicists to speak of electric current (or particles) they could no longer express their thoughts.
>
> (Heisenberg, in Zukav 1980: 220)

In other words, we are being asked to think about not just how the research tools we use influence our research, but also how our thoughts and language fashion the ways in which we come to conceive of the reality we are researching. Postmodern theorists take this one step further by asking us to consider the extent to which, when we speak, we are actually 'spoken', i.e. we are as much produced by conceptual language as producers of it. This brings us close to the notion of reflexivity where knowledge is said to have a form of prophecy written into it, i.e. once we begin to see the world in a particular way not only does the world come to resemble its description but people under the influence of this description might further fashion the world through this description.

Theory

Background

The question of theory is at one and the same time perhaps the least and the most important consideration in the research process. It is unimportant for at least two reasons. First, if the main aim of research is either to uncover the social facts or to document the ways that people make sense of the world, surely the question of theory is largely irrelevant. Second, if we have a more lofty aim for our research, perhaps to make the world a better place, theory will either contribute to this or it will not. However, there is one overriding reason why the question of theory is always considered to be important in the research process and I have been alluding to this throughout this chapter: the extent to which all research could be said to be theory-laden. This final section of the chapter considers these questions and concludes with a discussion of the rise of action research in educational settings over the past 25 years.

One of the most common criticisms levelled at teachers by students is that lessons contain too much theory. This could be heightened where there is a professional development focus on the programme of study with questions and comments such as: 'What's all this theory got to do with practice?'; 'If these theorists had to actually do the job they'd tell a different story'; and so on. Indeed, there was a time when governments seemed to wish that there was no such thing as educational theory, and that the training of teachers concentrated on classroom skills and the observation thereof (Elliot 1993). Of course, this might have had much more to do with wresting control of the curriculum away from professional educators rather than any serious concern for the status of theory (see Part 2). But is it possible to imagine a world without theory? This is precisely the question posed by Eagleton in his book on literary theory:

> A long time ago . . . people used simply to drop things from time to time. But nowadays we have physicists to inform us of the laws of gravity by which objects fall; philosophers to doubt whether there are really any discrete objects to be dropped at all; sociologists to explain how all this dropping is really the consequence of urban pressures; psychologists to suggest that we are really trying to drop our parents; poets to write about how all this dropping is symbolic of death; and critics to argue that it is a sign of the poet's castration anxiety. Now dropping can never be the same again. We can never return to the happy garden where we simply wandered around dropping things all day without a care in the world.
>
> (Eagleton 1989: 26–7)

What has happened is that theory has entered the scene. Picking up on what I said about reflexivity we might now say that not only will our understanding of dropping never be the same again, but also future acts of dropping might never be the same because the theories are now attached to the behaviour. However, what I particularly like about this quotation is the way it challenges us to reconsider whether we ever, seriously, walk around without having theories about things. It is almost as if without theory things simply would not make much sense. Philosophically we might say that sense data accords us the raw experiential evidence as to the nature of the world but this is not enough to make sense of it all, i.e. making sense of the world is an action of mind and the mind is a factory for concepts and theories. Furthermore, we might say that sense data provides us with information but any real insights can only come with a conceptual framework and this is the work of the mind not the data. Hopefully these comments can be seen to flow naturally from what was said above.

Theory as hypothesis

Philosophers of science, such as Popper (1959, 1963), have produced convincing accounts arguing that we really do not need to be too worried about theory. So long as we can put theory to the reality test it does not matter where it comes from, or what its pre-experimental status is. Popper's 'falsificationism', although criticized and refined (Lakatos and Musgrave 1970), has become a tried and trusted formula for dealing with theory. For example, if I have a theory that every time I close my office door it rains, clearly I am positing the existence of a significant causal chain. All I need to do is turn this theory into a testable hypothesis and conclude that either the theory holds (survives the test) or it is falsified. Popper's use of language is careful here, for he wants to challenge the view that scientific experiments can 'verify' the truth of experimental statements. Rather, scientific experiments can only tell us what is not true. If I conduct a simple experiment and my hypothesis survives the test this does not mean that 'every time I open my office door it rains', it simply means that it has not been falsified. However, one observation of it not raining when I open my door would falsify the statement. Popper is indicating that science does permit of progress, but progress is based on what we know to be untrue; all non-falsifiable statements simply have the status of 'not falsified'. On the face of it this would appear to be a very sensible way of dealing with theory.

Unfortunately, things are rarely that simple. Not only have we already seen Kuhn rejecting the idea of a linear progress model of science (albeit one based on falsification rather than verification), claiming that we should always see science revolving around the notion of a community of scholars and the ways that these scholars are socialized into their research practices, but we should also consider carefully whether a model of falsificationism could actually bring about, by itself, the refutation of theories. To be fair to Popper, he was clearly aware of some of these problems, but they are problems nonetheless. First, what happens if our theory under consideration is not open to 'testable hypothesis', such as the statement: 'There is a God'? For a test to be administered, empirical data needs to be collected. The problem with this theory is that it is likely to be uttered from within an epistemological framework where 'faith' is a cornerstone. We all know the story of 'doubting Thomas' – he may lay claim to wanting to conduct the first Popperian test of falsification but his real fame lies in his inability to swap empirical data for faith as his epistemological foundation. Popper simply dismissed these untestable hypotheses as 'non-science', but of course, they still exist as knowledge claims.

What is perhaps more worrying is where theories are much more overarching, i.e. they contain a range of concepts within a much larger logical framework (perhaps a meta-narrative to use a postmodern phrase). I am thinking here, for example, of Marxism or Freudianism. Just as most of us would not expect Christians to accept the results of a series of Popperian tests on Christianity, why should Freudians or Marxists? After all, there is a lot at stake should the theories be falsified. This brings us to a thorny issue when dealing with theory and something which exercised Popper's own mind (Popper 1957). This is sometimes referred to as 'ad hoc theoretizing', i.e. the inbuilt survival mechanisms which theories contain, or perhaps better, their defenders invent to protect theories from refutation. For example, if Marxism is partly predicated on the belief that capitalism will collapse and the proletariat will rise up to produce a socialist revolution, then surely it should not be too difficult to construct some testable hypothesis for this (Popper 1957). However, it is not that simple, for if 'the law of the tendency of the rate of profit to fall' (Marx) is not operating to push capitalism to the brink of collapse, there must simply be some countervailing tendencies at work. Similarly, if the working class is not revolting, then either there must be an outbreak of false class consciousness or, again, there must be some countervailing tendencies – powerful ideological state apparatuses, maybe (Althusser 1971).

Similarly with Freudianism: if every young boy secretly harbours the desire to kill his father and sleep with his mother (the Oedipus complex), then he either recognizes this or he is said to be suffering from a form of repression – either way the theory is always right and will always survive any test constructed to refute the proposition. Philosophically minded readers will recognize these problems as part of the analytic–synthetic debate, i.e. the inability to find statements that are not simply logically coherent and require reference to an empirical reality to support them.

Research as theory-impregnated

Questions of theory are difficult questions partly because theories act like 'domain assumptions' (Gouldner 1971), i.e. they are often more implicit than explicit and contain deeply held assumptions. They often act as underpinning structures, like Kuhnian paradigms, which set the ground rules for research but are never (or rarely) questioned, or they have the effect of making it impossible for empirical research to refute them. Also, at a more fundamental level, they might be seen as part of the conceptual apparatus that we all (often unwittingly) use in order to make sense of sense data (our observations). In this sense we might speak of observations as always being theory-impregnated.

There is a also a sense in which theory is associated with bias, i.e. a sense that if you have taken a theoretical standpoint in your research your account of reality is somehow tainted by this stance. This is a difficult notion for it might be felt that if we took the theoretical interpretation away we would be able to see what lay behind it, like peeling off wallpaper. However, if the wall can only be conceived with some theoretical insight, to remove the wallpaper would actually remove the wall. Bias is another word that has undergone something of a transformation over the past 25 years. There was a time when we spoke of eliminating bias by the careful use of our research methods. However, increasingly, in reflexive times, we are now encouraged to see it as more like a position, i.e. so long as we take steps to articulate the position that we are speaking from, or promoting, bias might be celebrated rather than denigrated:

To do the work involved in creating Black women's studies requires not only intellectual intensity, but the deepest courage. Ideally, this is passionate and committed research, writing, and teaching whose purpose is to question everything. Coldly, 'objective' scholarship that changes nothing is not what we strive for. 'Objectivity' is itself an example of the reification of white-male thought. What could be less objective than the totally white-male studies which are still considered 'knowledge'? Everything that human beings participate in is ultimately subjective and biased, and there is nothing inherently wrong with that. The bias that Black women's studies must consider as primary is the knowledge that will save Black women's lives.

(Hull and Smith 1982, in Humm 1992)

Discussion point

Do you feel comfortable with research which avowedly supports a political position?

There was a time when we spoke of value-free research – that research should search for the facts and not promote the values of the researcher or a political or theoretical position. However, increasingly with a postmodern sensibility, this argument is being undermined: how could one speak from no position; surely everybody is located in some way and promotes (perhaps unwittingly) some vested interest? It is perhaps worth remembering the sociologist Becker's avowed support for 'the underdog' as a prime motivator when he was conducting research on society's 'outsiders' (Becker 1970). In this context the most worrying type of research is perhaps the research that promotes the idea that it is detached from values when it is clearly commissioned in some way:

More and more we see the career trajectories of scholars, especially of scientists rise and fall not in relation to their intellectually-judged peer standing, but rather in relation to their skill at selling themselves to those, especially in the biomedical field, who have large sums of money to spend on a well-marketed promise of commercial viability.

(Michaelson, in Rampton and Stauber 2001: 214)

Of course, for many researchers these issues are largely unproblematical for there will always be the reality test: if the world really does exist independently of our understanding of it, we should always be able to measure and judge our understandings (and those of others) with this in mind. This is clearly more complicated for those who take an Einstein 'unopened watch' view of interpretation, and is clearly impossible for postmodern theorists who cannot conceive of a world outside of the language in which it is constituted. In the latter case, all research must be seen as promoting a position. Our job as readers is to consider what this position is and whether we agree with it.

Grounded theory and action research

There is another sense in which theory might be important to us and this is the sense in which it is possible to conceive of 'grounding' it in some way. It could be argued that one way out of the problems I have been discussing is to attempt to conduct research 'from the ground up', i.e. always start from patient and consistent direct observations and statements from research respondents and slowly build a conceptual understanding only on this foundation. Not surprisingly, this is often referred to as 'grounded theory' and it does have a carefully worked out framework for aspiring practitioners (see Bartlett and Payne, in McKenzie *et al.* 1997).

Another form of grounding has emerged from the ideas that surrounded the publication of Schon's seminal work (Schon 1983). Variously referred to within educational circles as 'practical educational science' or simply 'teachers as researchers', it produced a coherent rationale for understanding that not only should practitioners (rather than professional researchers) be undertaking research, but also that within professional reflective practice lays a form of grounded theory (Elliot 1993). Directly related to the concern to study what professionals actually do rather than what they say they do (see Part 2), Schon skilfully distinguished between the 'modern' bureaucratic conception of the professional, concerned with following the agreed rules and procedures laid down for the effective achievement of (educational) ends, and his preferred (more postmodern) conception of reflection-in-action, centred on the professional's ability to make judgements, often recognized as overtly moral in nature, and the rationalizing skills required to operate in this way:

> When someone reflects-in-action, he becomes a researcher in the practice context. He is not dependent on the categories of established theory and technique, but constructs a new theory of the unique case. His inquiry is not limited to a deliberation about means which depends on a prior agreement about ends. He does not keep means and ends separate, but defines them interactively as he frames a problematic situation. He does not separate thinking from doing, ratiocinating his way to a decision which he must later convert to action. Because his experimenting is a kind of action, implementation is built into his inquiry. Thus reflection-in-action can proceed, even in situations of uncertainty or uniqueness, because it is not bound by the dichotomies of Technical Rationality.
>
> (Schon 1983: 68–9)

This is often taken as an emerging model of research for it suggests that (teacher) effectiveness is not a technical-rational matter of honing skills, but is a professional matter of developing critical awareness, and that this might be best facilitated through the recognition that professional development is, in essence, a research activity.

> **Discussion point**
>
> To what extent do you believe that continuous professional development should be reconceptualized as a research activity?

This brings us to what is perhaps the biggest movement in educational research over the past 25 years, the growth of action research. Hopefully the previous discussions will help you to see why this movement might be said to be 'of its time'. First, its growth has corresponded with the disenchantment with models of research that focus on the idea that the aim should be the discovery of (educational) truths. And, second, it has coincided with (indeed it might be said to be an outgrowth of) a widespread celebration of the Schon notion of 'the reflective practitioner'. However, in order to agree or disagree with this assessment we need to be clear about what exactly action research is.

Action research is often described as research conducted by practitioners, for practitioners. This might not sound very earth-shattering, but contained within this statement are two fundamental points. First, it is not research carried out by professional researchers. For some this already breaks a canon of research procedure – that there should be a sense of detachment, established by the researcher, from the research 'object'. Second, its overarching aim is the improvement of practice; again, for some, this breaks a research canon – that research should be more 'pure' and focused on the pursuit of truth. Let us look at these points in more detail.

> Action research is carried out by practitioners seeking to improve their understanding of events, situations and problems so as to increase the effectiveness of their practice.
>
> (McKernan 1996: 4)

Although action research is not a uniquely education-centred activity, it does lend itself well to educational contexts. This is largely due to the fact that teaching clearly comes under the Schon (1983) definition of 'the professional' as the person who recognizes the need to engage in 'reflection-in-action'. McKernan (1996: 3), again, makes the point very succinctly: 'teaching is not one activity and inquiring into it another'.

To some extent this might be taken as a rallying cry, i.e. teachers should see their own professional contexts as ready-made research fields, they should not wait for others (professional researchers) to come in and frame these fields for them. One reason why this is extremely important is because the professional researcher is likely to frame the field in such a way as to pose questions that will not have improvements in practice as the main outcome. Of course, this might also have the effect of grounding theory in practice, rather than having theory imposed on practice. Another way of looking at this might be to consider the extent to which more traditional educational research was likely to find its way into educational journals, which would be read only by other professional researchers and not teacher practitioners.

Discussion point

How often would you consider looking in educational journals when you are not either studying for a course or engaged in some form of traditional research activity? Is this a problem?

It could be argued that most of these points follow naturally from the notion of the reflective practitioner and they clearly go some way towards explaining what might be meant by 'practical educational science'. There seem to be two important points here. First, that action research could be one of the ways in which the intuitive, uninvestigated knowledge which professional practitioners use on a daily basis might become the source for an examined, documented professional life. Second, action research could be an important means by which professional life might become internally accountable for itself, i.e. it could form the basis for a challenge to the view that external, public accountability is the only valid form of accountability.

The practice of action research

Most models of action research depict a cycle (or series of cycles) to encourage the view that the process involves reflection and evaluation at each stage and is ongoing. McNiff describes the Whitehead approach thus:

i) I experience a problem when some of my educational values are denied in practice (for example, my pupils [sic] do not seem to be taking as active a part in my sessions as I would want them to).

ii) I imagine a solution to the problem through discussion, reading etc. (Should I organise my lessons so that my pupils have to ask questions? Shall I try group work, or structured exercises?)

iii) I implement the imagined solution. (I try group work as from Tuesday's lesson, and I introduce structured worksheets that lead my pupils to ask and answer questions without my constant supervision.)

iv) I evaluate the outcome of my actions. (Yes, my pupils are certainly participating more, but they are making too much noise. Also, they are still depending on me in the form of worksheets.)

v) I re-formulate my problem in the light of my evaluation. (I must find a way of persuading them to be involved but less noisy. I must find a way to make them more independent of me in their own educational development.)

(McNiff 1992: 38)

This action research cycle, or variations of it, is now a tried and trusted formula for practitioners to use in their own professional context as the basis for research. It exists in stark contrast to those who would prefer to see research returned to its more 'pure' form. These cycles are avowedly instrumental in their aim: they do not constitute an attempt to search for educational truths; they are primarily concerned with looking for improvements in professional practice. It is for this reason that the research takes on a postmodern form: the knowledge it produces parades itself as transient and as fulfilling a vested professional need. In this sense it has no lofty aspirations and makes a virtue out of what more traditional researchers might see as a sin. Also, it often sees research respondents as collaborators and includes them in the 'experiments' at the level of design and implementation, rather than seeing them as people who are being experimented on. Canons of, particularly, positivistic research are clearly being ignored in these procedures.

There is an interesting ethical dimension contained in these issues, and this concerns the role of those being researched. Traditionally, respondents within the research process might be compared to laboratory rats – they were being experimented on for the greater good, i.e. the insights that the research would bring. Action research raises the question of whether the research collaborators could be said to have rights, i.e. the right to be consulted and considered when aims and results are being discussed. It is normal when conducting any social research to respect the confidentiality of the respondents by allowing them to remain anonymous, but this feature of action research would seem to require us to look again at the notion of anonymity. Researchers using qualitative methods have always had to consider whether even to tell respondents that they are part of a social experiment. Whilst this has often been considered to be a means to limit Hawthorne effects, it also has an ethical dimension, again now given an interesting new angle within the context of action research.

It is not uncommon to see action researchers using qualitative methods in their work and, based on what has just been said, it is easy to see why. However, it would be a mistake to think that quantitative methods have no place in action research. It is perfectly feasible to envisage collecting quantitative data at any stage in an action research cycle. This could simply be a source of information or used when engaged in a form of triangulation. The real difference between the positivist and the action researcher would be seen when we come to consider purpose. The positivist will be using the data within a paradigmatic confine, using the research methods as the means to uncover social facts. The action researcher, however, will be using the methods solely to gain some insight into the means by which improvements in his/her own effectiveness might be enhanced. On occasion the two purposes could conceivably come together. However, we should not forget that the same means could equally serve different ends.

It is an intriguing thought that we might envisage PCET practitioners coming to work each day, all at various points on an action research cycle. And, furthermore that these cycles might be built into appraisal systems. However, given the current pressures on time, this is unlikely to happen. In higher education, where the pressure to engage in research is a very real one, it might be thought that action research could easily establish itself as a norm in professional life. However, action research is often not considered to be real research – it is simply too instrumental in its aim; too narrowly focused in its scope; and will not score highly in the RAE. In this context, action research could be viewed as professional 'navel gazing' and unlikely to contribute to the award of 5* for the institution. In further education, where there is not the pressure to engage in research it could also be seen as something of a distraction from the main purpose of the organization – achieving learning targets. Of course, it could also be argued that as contact teaching hours have crept up over the past ten years, this is precisely not the period in educational history to be seen to be promoting this form of reflective practice.

However, if action research is seen as a 'movement', it could easily become one of the ways in which professionals in PCET seek to enhance their practice. This could, in part, be achieved through the simple restatement that teaching is not a technical exercise but contains a fundamental ethical base – requiring reflection in and on practice. Also, it could be an important means by which the call for more public accountability could be promoted from within the profession rather than being imposed on it.

Conclusion

Conducting social research in educational settings requires us to consider a number of issues, chief amongst them seems to be: recognition of the uses and limitations of various research methods; awareness of the epistemological debates concerning the validity of the knowledge we produce; and a clear sense that we understand the purposes behind why we are conducting the research. In this context, all educational researchers need to have a clear sense of whether they are conducting research in order to uncover social facts or whether, by documenting the meanings that people attach to their lives, they are content to see research as a form of storytelling.

Furthermore, researchers need to ask themselves whether they have a strong epistemological commitment to certain types of educational knowledge or whether they will permit themselves to engage in epistemological border crossing for the purposes of triangulation and thus be able to use the full range of research methods. Although you may not feel particularly epistemologically committed yourself, we all need to be mindful of the implications of being naive in these matters, for we leave ourselves open to the wolves who take these matters very seriously if we do not.

If things have changed in the past 25 years concerning research matters we might list these as being: an increase in the use of qualitative data in educational research and a confidence about its appropriateness; an increasing sense that we should no longer be concerned to make the social sciences look more like the natural sciences but consider how similar all sciences are to each other; and an increasing awareness that more instrumental purposes for conducting research are not only acceptable but are also more valid than 'pure' research.

However, we should not be encouraged to rest easy with these developments. As I have tried to point out, it would be unwise to jettison quantitative data from educational research – it is clearly appropriate in order to address certain questions. Furthermore, in pointing out that all research contains social processes it becomes incumbent on all researchers to develop reflexive skills – requiring that we all accept the fact that we are 'positioned' in our research work and that we can articulate an understanding of this when we conduct and write up our research. Finally, in accepting that instrumental purposes are perfectly valid in research settings we may be forced to stop looking for bias in research work and accept that all research is politically motivated in some way.

These conclusions will be unsettling for some. Those who are particularly committed to educational research focusing on qualitative data may look upon any resurrection of quantitative data as the unwelcome return of a ghost that refuses to be laid to rest. In this context, not only might qualitative data collection be seen as more 'sexy' – participant observation particularly has a long history of being seen as exciting undercover detective work – but it could also be undertaken by people who cannot add up.

Furthermore, our other two developments might be rather too close to the postmodern bone for some. Becoming reflexive might be fine in some circles but in others it might be perceived as intellectual laziness where questions of research validity simply become justifications for why you did what did in your research. Finally, although some might celebrate the fact that the Enlightenment project has finally come to an end, others might bemoan this as the acceptance that all forms of knowledge are now equally valid, which in its extreme form would mean that my mother's off-hand comments on educational matters were now as valid as any professional researcher's who had painstakingly produced and analysed data collected over a three-year period – as slippery a slope to a 'modern' theorist as you could find.

Those who adopt a thoroughgoing postmodern position are keen to have us see not just ethnographic work as storytelling but all educational research. In this context any call to objectivity or authority through the use of certain privileged research methods is simply pretence – it is the veil that is placed over the research in order to hide the same social processes, which are avowedly accepted as being at work by the postmodern researcher:

> making knowledge claims is not just a matter of appealing to universal truths of validity, since claims are justified within collectively held conceptions about the world, and how to relate to it: in other words . . . producing knowledge claims is a social practice. It is the social conceptions that are embodied in an epistemology, the most powerful of which is the conception that holds up the methods and procedures of the natural sciences as the model for producing valid knowledge claims.
>
> (Scott and Usher 1999: 12)

The key research concern here is the increasing difficulty we now all have in claiming that there is a Mount Olympus from which we can observe educational reality. The idea that it was possible to be a neutral observer, seeing things as they really were, always had an appealing logic and it lay at the heart of the positivistic tradition. However, developments in the philosophy of science have come to question the notion of direct observation and the impossibility of observation divorced from conceptual frameworks and theoretical insights. And with the rise of a more thoroughgoing postmodern sensibility, with its celebration of the partial and the transient, and the acceptance of the impossibility of seeing oneself as a speaker rather than as 'spoken', it is now all too easy to hammer metaphorical nails into a 'realist' coffin.

Finally, although we might view the recognition of the limitations of using particular research methods as a technical exercise, i.e. the more adept we become in the use of the methods the more we might be able to overcome the limitations, we might also want to reconsider that perhaps the real message is the recognition that all social research is social. That is, the phrase 'social research' does not just mean that the objects of study are social objects, but that the process of undertaking research is always social as well, i.e. choice of study, choice and use of method, interpretation of data – all involve social processes. In this context the adept researcher is one who recognizes the social context in which the research has been undertaken and that this is the real limitation on all research.

If you are about to engage in educational research for the first time you may now be somewhat daunted by all this philosophical talk about the nature of reality. My advice is to be clear about what it is you want to know, understand the uses and the limitations of the research methods, be mindful of the epistemologically committed who may trip you up, display confidence about why you are conducting the research (who and what it is for), and develop the ability to stand back from the context in which you have conducted the research. If you operate with these points in mind and consider them in this order you should gradually develop your own understanding of the purpose to which research might be put and why there is more to educational reality than simply that which meets the eye.

Further reading

Bell, J. (1999) *Doing Your Research Project*. Buckingham: Open University Press.

Chalmers, A.F. (1999) *What Is This Thing Called Science?* (3rd edition). Buckingham: Open University Press.

Cohen, L. and Manion, L. (1994) *Research Methods in Education* (4th edition). London: Routledge.

Elliot, J. (ed.) (1993) *Reconstructing Teacher Education*. London: Falmer Press.

Gomm, R. and Woods, P. (1993) *Educational Research in Action*. London: Paul Chapman.

Hitchcock, G. and Hughes, D. (1995) *Research and the Teacher* (2nd edition). London: Routledge.

McKenzie, G., Powell, J. and Usher, R. (eds) (1997) *Understanding Social Research*. London: Falmer Press.

McKernan, J. (1996) *Curriculum Action Research*. London: Kogan Page.

McNiff, J. (1988) *Action Research: Principles and Practice*. London: Routledge.

Schon, D.A. (1983) *The Reflective Practitioner*. London: Arena.

Scott, D. and Usher, R. (1999) *Researching Education*. London: Continuum.

Shipman, M.D. (1997) *The Limitations of Social Research* (4th edition). London: Longman.

Part 3 exercises

1 Using research methods

Compare and contrast two research methods commonly used in educational research. Use the following as a guide:

(a) Focus on the uses and limitations of the methods.

(b) How appropriate will each method be to studying a topic in education which is of interest to you?

(c) Discuss whether you think the methods might be complementary.

(d) Identify pieces of educational research where the methods have been used.

2 Conducting action research

Identify a problem that you are grappling with in your professional context. Produce an action research cycle as a means to explore solutions to this problem. Use the following popular websites to investigate current developments in PCET:

www.ali.gov.uk

www.bbc.co.uk/education/fe

www.dfes.gov.uk
www.escalate.ac.uk
www.fento.co.uk
www.ilt.ac.uk
www.lifelonglearning.co.uk
www.lsda.org.uk
www.lsc.gov.uk
www.oecd.org
www.qaa.ac.uk
www.qca.org.uk
www.ucas.co.uk

In the first of the following two polemical pieces, Sharon Markless champions the cause of action research. She celebrates not only the ways in which action research is aimed at improving professional practice, but also how it has helped us to reconceptualize what it means to be involved in research work. By contrast, in Chapter 9 Dennis Hayes reminds us that research is a serious business and how movements like action research are encouraging us to fall down a slippery slope of postmodern relativism. This is tantamount to arguing that there is no such thing as educational reality, and he challenges us to consider what might be the consequences of such beliefs.

QUESTION TO THINK ABOUT

After having read the two polemical pieces contained in this section how far would you want to argue that more instrumental attitudes to research are inevitable in a postmodern age?

Chapter 8

THE CASE FOR ACTION RESEARCH

Sharon Markless

A small group of professionals (a school teacher, school librarians, FE lecturers and a college librarian) who had recently completed their MAs in Education were discussing how they could continue to develop their practice. They wanted to keep up the momentum gathered during their Masters studies. The group felt that attending short staff development courses would not do: these tended to be too superficial. Reading might be interesting but would not necessarily galvanize them into activity or provide the links between theory and practice that they wanted. They decided to set up an informal action research group and asked their MA tutor to facilitate termly meetings. A year later, individuals in the group have: enhanced the after-hours support that they provide; developed approaches to extended reading for adults with learning difficulties; collaborated with colleagues to integrate the teaching of 'learning strategies' into subject courses; and enhanced the handling of differentiated groupwork in the college library. The group meetings are held on Saturdays and attendance levels have always been high. Group members are clear that the improvements in educational practice that they have initiated in their institutions are due to their adoption of action research strategies.

Group members have been enabled to investigate aspects of their practice in a carefully structured and focused way; they have read relevant research but have been supported whilst they question its relevance to their own contexts and develop their own ideas about what they have read. They have used a variety of data-gathering techniques both in their initial investigations and when evaluating the impact of their changed practices. Group members have openly reported their difficulties and have held up their own development and their emerging ideas to critical scrutiny.

Despite working in difficult contexts, faced with increasing demands on their time and, in some cases, with decreasing budgets, engagement in the action research process has prevented group members from feeling powerless and deprofessionalized. They have been able to enhance the quality of their work in areas that they care about and in ways that accord with their educational values.

Action research provided these practitioners with an effective tool for their own professional development and a way of improving the quality of education within their institutions. But what is action research? McKernan claimed that

> Action research is carried out by practitioners seeking to improve their understanding of events, situations and problems so as to increase the effectiveness of their practice. Such research does not have the writing of research reports and other publications as a primary goal.
>
> Action research aims at feeding the practical judgement of actors in problematic situations. The validity of the concepts, models and results it generates depends not so much on scientific tests of truth as on their utility in helping practitioners to act more effectively, skilfully and intelligently. Theories are not validated independently of practice and then applied to curriculum; rather they are validated through practice. Action research is thus grounded curriculum theory.
>
> (McKernan 1991: 4)

In other words, action research should be an important and serious activity. Yet too many academics and professionals persist in viewing action research as second rate. It is often designated as nothing more than good professional practice, not a source of important knowledge and theory. The form of research that 'enables teachers to develop their own understandings of their own practice, and to turn their practice into a form of research' (McNiff 1992: 15) is portrayed as much less important than research undertaken by researchers who 'propose certain hypotheses which are then implemented by others within practical situations. Theory comes before practice. The form of theory is propositional' (1992: 14).

Many approaches to the professional development of teachers seem to rest on the supposition that there is a body of accumulated knowledge, developed by academics, that teachers are required to accept and may draw on as and when they need, to improve their practice. In this view of teacher education and development, knowledge is often used to control practice – it presents the norms or prescribes acceptable approaches. There is a fundamental issue here about the extent to which knowledge derived from traditional research is actually, or indeed can be, applied in practice. (The current, often heated debates about evidence-based medicine, make this point well. Many doctors and medical researchers admit that as much as 70 per cent of the practice of medicine is based on individual professional judgement arising from experience. Rules, procedures and treatment protocols can only be used effectively in a small proportion of cases.) Action research offers an alternative approach to professional development in which practitioners are empowered to engage with the fundamental problems arising in their work.

Action research is based on the view that knowledge is socially constructed by individuals or by groups. It emphasizes the importance of personal knowledge and the ongoing creation of meaning by individuals committed to extending their understanding of the situations in which they operate. Personal enquiry leads to the generation of explanations of actions and reactions, then to the formulation of personal theories of education. These theories are discussed, critiqued by peers and tentatively accepted as knowledge about education. Action research 'challenges the view that legitimate knowledge rests in the academy or in the literature and is not generally viewed as the creation of individual teachers' (McNiff 1992: 49). It rejects the notion of teachers as, at best, passive consumers of the research literature (implicit in the traditional forms of research dissemination through the scholarly article and synthesized treatise). Instead of moving from theory to practice, action research moves from practice into theory.

What, then, is the status of the knowledge produced by teachers engaged in action research? Some people question whether small-scale investigations by practitioners in one setting can lead to genuinely new insights. They want research that leads to 'grand theory' and certain knowledge that is transferable across a number of settings. However, 'grand theory' and 'generalization' often present problems to practitioners trying to understand their own work situations. Many theorists contradict each other (think about the different learning theories or about views on how to teach reading); and if practitioners are legitimately to base their practice on 'grand theory' the quality of the research on which it is based should be beyond reproach – but how is the practitioner as recipient of the researchers' judgements expected to judge their worth? Moreover, at least at the current stage of educational research knowledge, the available 'grand theory' has hardly begun to make inroads into the processes of helping individuals enhance their practice – it does not explain enough to support individual professional development.

In his book with the challenging title *The Courage to Teach*, Preston Palmer (1998) recounts how he asked a group of university lecturers to describe their most effective and influential teachers. The approaches adopted by these teachers differed enormously: some lectured almost continuously, others said little; some used active group exercises, others quietly stretched the imagination; some challenged, others supported. The only generalization that could be made was that all the teachers described were able to connect with their students. This piece of knowledge would hardly support professional development. In a similar vein, ex-Ofsted inspector and popular author Gervaise Phinn enlivened a talk to a group of teachers and school librarians by describing his visit to a school to observe some lessons. The Ofsted framework is supposedly drawn from research into effective teaching and cites such elements as clear objectives, careful planning, and time on task as important to quality. The teacher being observed was clearly living in a different universe: 'What was I to say to this teacher?

His classroom was a tip, his lesson plans were scrappy, his planning virtually non-existent and yet ... the children were getting a broad and balanced education, they were being challenged and stretched ... he had just given one of the best lessons I had ever seen.' One size does *not* fit all. Action research resists the temptation to oversimplify cases by applying a high level of theoretical abstraction.

In education, a high degree of uncertainty exists in most situations – the same approach can be tried and will have different results in different contexts. The provisional nature of knowledge is paramount; individuals can never be *sure* that they will 'get it right'. This means that the routine application of generally established 'rules' arising out of more traditional research is problematical. Elliott writes about the need for practitioners to be continually judging the relationship between educational process and product afresh, in order to choose the best course of action in particular circumstances to reflect one's values (Elliott 1991).

Certain knowledge can be very comforting and therefore attractive to stressed teachers (it certainly is to policy makers and politicians). However, the self-conscious systematic analysis of situations is more likely to provide practitioners with the detailed insights they need to make sense of what is happening and to find solutions to their complex problems. It is also more likely to open up neglected possibilities and to challenge existing views. Altrichter and colleagues summed up this approach in three 'assumptions' that they believe to be the basis of action research:

- Complex practical problems demand specific solutions
- These solutions can only be developed inside the context in which the problem arises ...
- The solutions cannot be successfully applied to other contexts but they can be made accessible to other practitioners as hypotheses to be tested.
                                                                (Altrichter *et al.* 1993)

This last point brings us onto the thorny issue of generalizability. It is a mistake to assume that the knowledge produced by teachers engaged in action research is of no use beyond the particular context in which it is generated. Although, according to Patton (1987) 'generalising from qualitative findings is an impossibility', he argues that what he calls 'reasonable extrapolation' is possible. He describes extrapolation as 'modest speculations on the likely applicability of findings to other situations under similar, but not identical, conditions'. The ideas emerging from action research projects are not expected to be reproducible in all contexts but it is reasonable to expect that they will resonate with other practitioners (striking chords and offering insights into problems that they have also encountered).

I have worked with numerous professionals who have found inspiration in the descriptions of their work provided by fellow practitioners. These descriptions seem to fuel enthusiasm and a desire to work on current problems that rarely result from reading more theoretical accounts. This is not to say that theory is absent from the action research process. Theories drawn from a range of published sources should be explored when an individual is reflecting on ideas for action. More importantly, 'the construction of [research] knowledge is integral with the development of action . . . action research is not merely a practical model for the professional development of practitioners; it also makes an essential contribution to the further development of educational theory' (Altrichter *et al.* 1993: 207). Elliott (1991) is equally clear that theorizing is an essential element of action research.

All forms of education research rely on testing ideas in practice to establish whether they are valid. In action research, the gap between constructing knowledge, theorizing and testing (action) is very small. 'The rigour of action research is that practitioner-researchers must live with the mistakes of their theorising' (Altrichter *et al.* 1993: 208). When practitioners believe that their theories stand up in practice, they are then in a position to share them with colleagues. This is a vital step: action research is collaborative and involves public activities. The act of sharing opens up an individual's theories and knowledge to the critical scrutiny necessary in any rigorous process. It also enables reflection on the values embodied both in the theory and in the actions tried out in the classroom.

Many years ago, Stenhouse argued for the creation of the 'teacher researcher', believing that effective curriculum development depended upon the capacity of teachers to take a research stance to their own teaching. He was concerned to ensure that teachers took action to better understand their own classrooms; that they became self-conscious and self-critical and continually tested assumption and habit. 'A research tradition which . . . feeds teaching must be created if education is to be significantly improved' (Stenhouse 1975). I would argue that 'traditional' research has failed to feed teaching. Time and again, academics have bemoaned the problems of research take-up and use (see for example Elliott 1990). In the 1980s, millions of dollars were spent in the US in trying to encourage 'knowledge utilization', that is, the take-up of research findings by schools and teachers (Paisley and Butler 1983). The projects had some success – this is not surprising given the level of funding – but in the longer term the problem of take-up remained. This problem of take-up has more recently been addressed by the UK government, which has set up centres for evidence-informed education and has held seminars to generate strategies for increasing the use of research (tacit acknowledgement that the various approaches already used by the research community have failed to achieve these ends). All this activity sustains the passive approach to knowledge acquisition referred to earlier in this paper: in this view, knowledge is externally generated and handed over to teachers for them to accept and implement.

Again, action research offers a different perspective in which research used by practitioners flows from their active engagement, based on real interest in the issues under review. If we want to improve the quality of education and see research as a useful tool in this process, the action research approach may well turn out to be a more productive and effective route to take and one which is more likely to 'feed teaching' in the way that Stenhouse envisaged. Perhaps it is not unreasonable to expect that teachers who adopt a research stance to their own practice will be also be more open to other forms of research and to the knowledge that they generate.

Action research demands a lot from busy professionals. It not only takes time (usually in short supply), but also necessitates a critical approach to one's own practice (often very uncomfortable) and is based on the use of high quality research skills. At this point some external support may be useful. Action research supported by HE institutions has been a feature of the professional development scene for some time. In my experience, teachers may need help when initially engaging in data collection. They may not be aware of the wide range of options available, how to involve colleagues, and how to be systematic in their approach. They may become concerned about objectivity. However, it is important to realize that

> To undertake action research does not require participants to be professional researchers. It is a developmental process, one of learning by doing. Participants develop researcher skills and knowledge by being reflective practitioners and active and reflective team members . . . at times we have found teachers initially reluctant to be involved in action research because they feel they do not have a sound knowledge of statistics and research methodologies . . . we have needed to put energies into breaking down these perceptions.
>
> (Todd 1997)

With effective and timely support, practitioners quickly focus on what might constitute 'good' data to stimulate reflection on and analysis of their practice. They then find appropriate ways to collect and analyse this data. Practitioners can also be reassured that their involvement in the situation that they are studying is a strength rather than a weakness. All researchers bring 'filters' to their work arising out of their individual attitudes, perceptions and conceptual frameworks. Data is filtered through the light of their experience. One of the strengths of action research (shared with other qualitative research approaches) is that it recognizes the subjectivity of the researcher and celebrates this as a valid and essential feature. Systematic and rigorous approaches to data are substituted for the search for the illusion of objectivity. Action research is based on the view that naturalistic settings are best studied and researched by participants who are experiencing the problems within them: however, 'considering alternative perspectives is an important criterion in judging the quality of the action research process' (Altrichter *et al.* 1993). Action research is essentially collaborative and seeks to use the perceptions of all those involved in the situation (such as pupils and colleagues) to inform reflection on action. Attention to different perspectives helps to ensure research rigour and the validity of any reinterpretations.

In summarizing the overall impact of an ambitious action research project initiated in a large number of schools in Australia, Todd (1997: 32) wrote:

We dared to dream, at the same time being realistic about the enormous and long-term challenge that confronted us. We saw action research as an essential part of this process for a number of important reasons. Action research is immediate, local, and change-oriented. It intervenes, initiates, investigates, and improves. It investigates aspects of practice in a systematic way in order to improve that practice and the current situation.

Todd cited with approval Kemmis (1993), who views action research as emancipatory, 'always connected to social action ... a concrete and practical expression of the aspiration to change the social (or educational) world for the better for improving shared social practices' (Kemmis 1993: 2). Again, in Todd's view,

> action research is undertaken to investigate real concerns, to take action to solve real-life problems, and at the same time contribute to the knowledge base of the profession. It is grounded in the reality of the organisation, its mission, its structure, and its processes. It is involved with the situation, rather than being detached from it. It aims at increased understanding of a particular situation or problem and provides a basis for making decisions, establishing directions, and taking actions to make improvements. At the same time, it is research-oriented – systematic and planned in its approach, with clear goals and data collection methods, to be documented and shared in the wider educational community.

Whether or not the action researcher is able to live up to all of Todd's aspirations, the approach provides a useful antidote to the centralist, controlling and often sterile prescriptions concocted by academic researchers. More importantly, action research offers practitioners a way of combating the sense of disempowerment currently pervading teaching by opening up new possibilities for growth and continuing professional development in keeping with teachers' own educational values.

Chapter 9

THE TRUTHS ABOUT EDUCATIONAL RESEARCH

Dennis Hayes

Academics and researchers need to be serious about educational research. They also need to be more intolerant of 'alternative' or 'different' approaches to educational research. In saying this, I am drawing attention to the fact that all researchers should seek to advance knowledge (and truth), whatever their particular field of study, and that this means they have to oppose all forms of relativism. Relativism, for our purposes, is the set of ideas that results in the easy acceptance of alternative 'knowledges' or 'truths'. This is no longer purely a matter of concern to professional philosophers. To understand the generality of contemporary relativism, consider it as what lies behind the virtue of 'openness' to all viewpoints that is now demanded by, and of, students and teachers (Bloom 1987: 26). Or consider the moral outrage that often occurs when some 'dogmatic' person defends their views as being 'right'. This relativistic morality leads to an odd psychological state in which people reverse the normal conditions of knowledge and think of any belief they have that it might not be true. This ubiquitous ethical relativism helps undermine the basis on which we undertake or, really value, research. We do research because we want to know *what is the case* in any particular situation, subject or field. The result of research is knowledge, and what we know as *states of affairs or propositions* (Anderson 1962a: 32). Academics advance this knowledge, and that is the proper basis of their authority. It allows academics to be troublemakers in the realm of ideas and to say: '*We* are the experts here; we can tell you (the Law, the State) what has force, what *runs*, in this department of social activity' (Anderson 1980: 220).

Discussions of educational research raise some of the most difficult issues in philosophy (Pring 2000: 6–7). In this brief chapter, I am concerned with the contemporary state of research mostly in relation to what it says about the *knowability of reality*.

There are few academic educational researchers who defend value-free, objective social research in the interest of pursuing the truth, wherever it leads (Hammersley 2000, 2001). If they do, they receive strongly worded criticisms from those who believe that research should be partisan in political or ethical ways (Delamont *et al.* 2001). The phrase 'value-free enquiry', of course, is a misnomer as it is strictly not value-free, in the sense that the pursuit of 'knowledge' and 'truth' is a value of overriding importance. This was what Socrates meant in the *Apology* (38a), when he says, that life without 'this sort of examination is not worth living', and when Aristotle says in *Ethics* (10.7) that 'the life of the intellect is best and pleasantest for man, for the intellect more than anything else *is* the man. Thus it will be the happiest life as well.'

Recently there have been alliances, and the 'Lone Rangers' who defended research as the value-free pursuit of truth have been supported by post-Popperians, new realists and some research bodies (Swann and Pratt 1999; BERA 2000: 1; Phillips and Burbules 2000: 3–4). These groups all defend the view that all educational research has a common purpose in providing 'warranted' knowledge and, although the qualification given by 'warranted' is clearly a concession to the critics, this is not a popular or even an acceptable view.[1] A much more typical view is provided by John Elliott in a keynote address to the European Educational Research Association (EERA):

> There was a time when we could all *live under the illusion* that we were practitioners of a value-free science, generating knowledge about education that mirrored an objective reality, which existed independently of the observer and the data-gathering and analytic instruments s(he) employs. It is increasingly difficult to do so.
>
> (Elliott 1998: 17, my italics)

In a single sentence, Elliott declares that objectivity, scientific method and knowledge of reality are *illusions*. This chapter discusses why academics have, for the most part, come to accept and promote such views, and will go some way to defending these 'illusions'. They are not only worth defending they are defensible.

My intention is not to offer such a defence *per se* – the work of Susan Haack (1995) can be referred to for an outstanding attempt at the reconstruction of traditional epistemology – but to explain the contemporary socio-political context of cynical and incoherent attacks on the possibility of knowing any truths (see Haack 1995: 191–4). In any case, a small number of educationalists in the UK have already begun to challenge the postmodern and relativist assumptions of educational thought (Bailey 2001; Willmott 2002). My arguments in this chapter, likewise assume that the knowability of reality is a concept that is indispensable in thinking, and that the rejection of this concept undermines educational research.

For the most part, I will concentrate in what follows on 'internal', rather than 'external', constraints on educational research. This is because it is the internal threats that I consider more damaging. It is the *attitudes of academics* to knowledge, and educational research, that is at the heart of the current bout of 'collective uncertainty about the status and identity of educational research' (Rudduck 1998: 1), rather than obvious problems such as the lack of funding. If all the funding needed for every project were available, the research would not get any better.

There is an educational research culture in FE only in a very special sense (Truth 1)

One clear difference between further education and higher education is that higher education is research-focused. Even this is a somewhat functional description, and it is important to stress that research in a university should be the work of a *community of scholars*, and not merely of paid professional researchers working on short-term contracts. The consequence of this difference is that in FE the focus is on the delivery of (existing) knowledge, whereas HE is concerned with the advancement of knowledge. As with all such distinctions, there are qualifications to be made. Some of the new universities and higher education institutions undertake little research and function, by this definition, as FE institutions. In a very few FE colleges, some practical R&D development is undertaken, and some academic research and writing go on, but this is insignificant. It could be argued that this is an accidental state of affairs and that there could be a research culture in FE institutions. This argument would simply make them into universities and this is not possible. There could be a situation that is said to exist in the American Community College system, where there is, it is said, a 'research culture' of a sort (Eade 1998). This is a highly contestable point, and in any case, there is an important social role for FE. Like schools, FE institutions can have a critical approach to education and the imparting of knowledge. In case this is misunderstood as a negative approach, it is worth remembering that there is nothing second rate in what Matthew Arnold called the 'disinterested endeavour to learn and propagate the best that is known and thought in the world' (Arnold [1864] 1906: 23). Attempts to blur the distinction at the present time are much more likely to be aimed at undermining educational research in 'ivory towers' than doing anything to build a different culture in FE. This distinction between FE and HE is, however, not really a matter of contention, and it is helpful to keep it in mind.

This lack of a research focus explains, at least in part, why the impact of Thatcherite 'market' mechanisms into FE, which culminated in the incorporation of those colleges in 1992 was so successful. It was easy to adapt a consumerist, customer-focused orientation to the efficient delivery of a pre-existing or 'underpinning' knowledge, that could be measured, controlled and, in terms of learning outcomes, was entirely predictable. Things are entirely unpredictable when your aim is the development of knowledge, and the consumerist orientation is not only resisted by academics but is entirely illogical in HE. There are, of course, other criticisms of the 'market'-oriented and 'new managerialist' approaches to FE, in terms of the impact on staff and their general inappropriateness to that sector. Although I discuss these criticisms elsewhere in this book, they are simply irrelevant as far as this argument goes. There are, nevertheless, continual attempts to define and to seek to introduce a 'research culture' into FE.

In 1996 a conference entitled 'A Research Network for FE?' was organized by the Further Education Development Agency (FEDA), a body that subsequently became the Learning and Skills Development Agency (LSDA). As a result of that conference, what became the Learning and Skills Research Network (LSRN) was established. The debate about the nature of research in FE or the 'learning and skills' sector has gone on inside that organization and its journal ever since. The general direction of LSRN thinking, it seems, is that research in FE is of a corporate nature and models itself not on the R&D that takes place in industry but on the marketing department. Having said this, it must be said that R&D in industry is often oriented towards capturing an increased market share, rather than on product innovation. This would complement what is normally held to be 'research' in FE:

> An FE college must adopt a broad definition of research. It must not attempt to mirror research carried out in universities. Its outcomes must not be driven by publications or the award of higher degrees. Its primary purpose is to add value to FE and its own characteristic mission. Since incorporation, it is incumbent on colleges to broaden their definition of research to include the range of activities normally associated with a corporate body.
>
> (Evans 1998: 17)

The corporate orientation of 'research' is not the whole story, and there is much discussion of other forms of research, such as 'evidence-based' research and 'action research', and their applicability to FE. These research methods, however, are entirely practical, focusing on the improvement of the management and delivery of courses and the development of teaching skills (A. Morris 2001: 33–4). This it not an error, but is grounded in an important, if unarticulated, understanding of the nature of FE. Because FE is the site for the delivery of pre-existing knowledge, lecturers and teacher trainers working in the sector will naturally look to improving the management of courses and the development of their teaching in relation to the delivery of knowledge. The drift to 'edutainment' or the 'McDonaldization' of FE is, therefore, a constant but unrecognized problem. Through the blurring of distinctions, this drift also affects HE, particularly through the introduction of teacher training courses for academics.

The focus of the debate about educational research in FE remains its 'usefulness', even if the crude corporate orientation has gone. Major recent developments show that this is the case. The generosity of spirit that wishes to see more research involving FE as the 'users' in the way that the Economic and Social Research Council's (ESRC) Teaching and Learning Research Programme (TLRP) does, merely redefines what is educational research and makes it practical and concerned with projects that are judged on the basis of concepts such as 'value added'. Money that could have gone into researching the 'unthinkable' now is restricted to researching for the evidence to back up lists of pre-stated 'outcomes'. The truth is that research, other than that concerned with application of knowledge and 'adding value' has no role in FE and attempts to introduce a 'research culture', sow confusion and allow the redirection of funding away from the advancement of knowledge in the universities.

Educational research is generally not valued and is often despised (Truth 2)

The conjunction of the publication of the results of the 1996 Research Assessment Exercise and the demand for evidence-based research (EBR) by the government in the same year, started an anxious discussion about the nature of academic research that continued during the run up to the 2001 RAE and beyond. It is this debate, and the inability of academics to defend research as a way of knowing reality, that has brought research into disrepute, rather than the derision poured on theoretical or 'blue skies' research by the government.

The RAE assesses the quality of research in universities and colleges every five years or so and rates it on a scale from 1 to 5* depending on how much of the research in an institution is held to be of national or international quality. Almost £5 billion of funding is allocated on the basis of this rating, with lower-rated colleges receiving nothing. It has resulted in a huge leap in the quantity of books and journal articles produced by academics. Getting published to get a high grade, rather than because lecturers have anything to say, has become the norm in HE. Book and journal mountains, unread and unreadable, are the result.

The demand for EBR was made in 1996 in a lecture by David Hargreaves, which was sponsored by the Teacher Training Agency (TTA) entitled 'Teaching as a Research-based Profession: Possibilities and Prospects.' Hargreaves makes two basic criticisms of educational research. First, that it makes no 'serious contribution to fundamental theory or knowledge' and, second, that it is 'irrelevant to practice' (1996: 7). His conclusion is that we should 'move as soon as possible to an evidence-based teaching profession' (1996: 8). Hargreaves's proposals would not only make all research practical and subject to fashionable whims, but would also place it in the hands of policy makers. As Hammersley commented, the funders, who back practical and evidence-based research, assume too much about the contribution research could make towards practice. The result is, 'disappointment, recrimination and a negative attitude towards research' (Hammersley 1997: 149). We could add that research need not have or seek any practical outcomes. Clarity of thought is what academics and teachers need. They need to know what is the case, not just 'what works' (Hargreaves 1997: 414). Hargreaves has a point when he says that a practical aim is taken for granted by organizations such as BERA, and possibly by Hammersley himself (pp. 415–16), but we need not accept an orientation towards the practical here.

Hargreaves was providing an academic defence of EBR in an address sponsored by a government body and we can be forgiven for the suspicion that EBR is just about providing evidence that what the government wants to work, works.

The government shares Hargreaves's concerns. David Blunkett, when he was Secretary of State for Education and Employment, was scathing about research in a speech to the Economic and Social Research Council (ESRC):

> There is a widespread perception, both within and beyond government, that too much social science research is inward looking, too piecemeal rather than helping to build knowledge in a cumulative way, and that issues for research are too 'supplier driven' rather than focusing on the key issues of concern to policy makers, practitioners and the public at large, especially parents
>
> (Blunkett 2000: s19)

This section of his speech echoes Hargreaves's criticism about research not leading to cumulative knowledge, which may be true, but this state of affairs is a government creation, it supports only piecemeal funding for 'research', rather than providing adequate funding for the *community of scholars* that the university could be. Having 'key issues' set or influenced by non-academics would also not improve research. It would become whimsical or political. Although, in relation to what has been said about the RAE, Blunkett seems to be right when he asks: 'What is the point of research which becomes narrower and narrower, with small groups of people responding to each other's writing in esoteric journals, read only by themselves and relevant only to themselves? This is a dangerous turning which we must try and address' (s21). Once more, it is important to note that it was a government quango, the HEFCE, that brought about this sterile focus through the introduction of the RAE, which put emphasis on publication in refereed journals.

It is because academics are compliant and complicit in the government's agenda to make educational research practical, or to produce papers for the RAE, that research has become despised as out of touch. Real educational research, undertaken by academic researchers (or teachers in that role), is no longer felt to be of any practical value. Academics should have the confidence to say: 'Why should research be of any practical value? Isn't the advancement of educational knowledge good enough?' They may feel that they have to be accountable, but their accountability is to the academic community not to the philistines.

Much of what is called 'educational research' today is not really research (Truth 3)

When I said at the outset that we should be intolerant of alternative approaches to educational research, I deliberately did not say intolerant of 'alternative methodologies', as many of the approaches to research that I discuss in this chapter cannot be described as methodologies, unless we succumb to nominalism. In arguing that you need to be both *serious* and *intolerant*, I imply a criticism of 'postmodern' views of educational research, as well as many other so-called 'methodologies'.

The main criticism I will make of these methodologies is that they are all relativistic and, therefore, false. They present a false way of looking at the world that presents us with false conclusions. Relativism is common in ordinary thinking and in H.E. holds back developments in all subjects but particularly in education where it is celebrated almost as much as in 'cultural studies', which is the host to contemporary academic relativism. To understand relativism we should think of it as the argument that knowing something is not explained by the state of affairs we know but is dependent on knowledge on a third thing. Rather like the familiar 'triangulation' exercises where two people talk and a third person tells them what they have been saying. A simple and typical example from philosophy may help in identifying how three things are involved in relativistic errors. If I know that 'this is a tree', it is sometimes claimed that I know it through my having an *idea* of that tree. The three things involved in knowing this proposition are, the knower, what is known and the idea of what is known. However, we do not have to interpose 'ideas', 'sense data' or anything else to explain that we know something to be the case. The logical problem with any interposition is that we may then need another 'idea' interposed between ourselves and the first 'idea' to show how we know that first idea. An infinite regress soon opens up. All this is familiar from traditional criticisms of Platonic and some empiricist explanations of how we understand the real world (Anderson 1962a,b,c).

Relativism is encountered most frequently and simplistically in instances when it is asserted that whenever someone claims that something is the case, this belief is explained by reference to their being a man, or white, or western, or middle class, or all these, and having the 'ideas' associated with being that sort of person. There is clearly an abusive *ad hominem* fallacy at work in these instances, and we could just say that, but relativism runs deeper and more needs to be said.

When I, a white, middle-class male, say that I know that something is the case, my knowing it has nothing to do with what is known. The two are distinct but are in a relation:

> Knowledge being taken as a relation, it is thus asserted that, when I know this paper, 'I know' in no way constitutes this paper, nor does 'know this paper' in any way constitute me, nor does 'know' in any way constitute either me or this paper.
>
> (Anderson 1962a: 27)

To assume otherwise is to say that they are not different (or that the difference was merely relative), but this would be absurd. The statement 'I know this paper' is a statement about a particular instance of knowing what is the case. That in any statement of this sort there is a 'subject' and an 'object' is just another way of saying that in the statement 'I know this paper' there are two terms. Furthermore

> Those who argue that the knower and the known are in some way identical because they are in a *certain* relation, have also to maintain that any two different things are in some way identical, since any difference is a certain difference or since 'A is different from B' is a certain state of affairs. So that when we say A is not B, we are also saying that A is B and B is A. On this basis discourse would be impossible.
>
> (Anderson 1962a: 28)

This criticism, taken from John Anderson, seems to me to *apply to all relativistic thought*. Cultural relativism can be our example here. If it is argued that our 'cultural' identity ('maleness' or 'westerness') in some way constitutes what is known, then discourse becomes impossible. It is the case that some relativists accept this logical conclusion. This should have the benefit that we do not have to argue with them. Unfortunately, as we shall see, inconsistency and self-contradictoriness is never a problem for this category of illogical thinkers.

Problems for relativistic positions arise with respect to the idea of truth. Take the statements 'all knowledge is relative' and 'there are no absolute truths'. The first statement is a universal affirmative proposition that is either true or false. If it is false then there are non-relative truths. If it is true, then there is at least one non-relative truth. In either case relativism is false. The second statement is a universal negative proposition, and the same line of reasoning shows that relativism is false. This critique first appears in Plato's *Theaetetus* (ss170–1) over 2000 years ago. Relativism is clearly self-contradictory if formulated in propositional form. David Bridges has examined the writings of postmodernists and shown that they constantly and consistently use propositional language and the language of reason, evidence and argument. His argument is a telling one. He uses the common definition of knowledge as 'justified true belief' and shows that, despite difficulties in defining truth in traditional terms through 'correspondence', 'coherence', 'consensus' or 'pragmatic' theories there is an acceptable alternative and he proposes Dewey's notion of truth as 'warranted belief' (Bridges 1999: 607). Having done this, he shows that relativists and postmodernists talk *truth talk*: they assert propositions like 'there is no universal truth to which our construction is a more or less good approximation' (see pp.610, 614). This seems enough to do away with relativism. If there is propositional or *truth* talk, and statements about belief, and argument about evidence, then these statements about there being no truth are self-contradictory. This is the case even if we, like Bridges, are sensitive to the difficulties they recall of giving an epistemological account of the foundations of our knowledge. Of course, postmodernists can be playful and need not make any statements and may just ask questions. This is difficult to do consistently and is also uninteresting, which is why they revert to making truth claims.

Standpoint research

'Standpoint research' refers to the 'standpoint' of a group that claims to hold a privileged access to reality and truth. Some feminist, Marxist, anti-racist and Disabled researchers adopt this sort of position about their research. They will argue that all research is constituted so that it represents a distorted view of reality because it is 'gendered', 'classist', 'racist' or 'disablist'. In the view of these researchers, research requires a partisan approach and should adopt a standpoint (see Hammersley and Gomm 1997a; Hammersley 2001). I will take one example – Diana Leonard's *A Woman's Guide to Doctoral Studies* – as a reference point because people reading this book may be considering further study and because it is excellent in its way.

Feminist research is neither research that is relevant to women nor research into women's oppression. This is just everyday research with 'women' as the object. One assumption that is, I think, a 'straw man', is that feminist research is research that assumes that there is a women's viewpoint that is different from men's. If women do have something to say and are heard, they will in what they say appeal to objectivity and reason and accept the standard tests for validity and reliability that are appropriate in any discipline. Leonard, in her book, both recognizes this fact and ignores it. She argues that, 'in science (or professional life, or academia, or management) "masculine" "rational" values must hold sway because of the nature of the field, and therefore, here at least women must and can emulate men' (Leonard 2001: 6). This seems perfectly correct if we remove the quotation marks around *rational*. Are women not 'rational' except when they undertake academic work? Defining normal human values of objectivity and reason as masculine is an insult to women. These are just normal human values (Haack 1995: 8).

Leonard, however, considers that the academy and research is clearly 'gendered'. She says that 'academia' actively *constitutes* gender. It is a place where individuals 'construct and reconstruct' themselves in gendered relations. As a concrete example, she states that 'being an academic is gendered and classed' because the middle-class academic role is built around divisions of labour 'which actually require and use the labour of women and the lower classes' (2001: 7). This seems to be no more than a statement that the university is an institution within capitalist society and tells us nothing new. More important is the fact that the university is the place in capitalist society where knowledge is pursued in a disinterested way. That inequalities of this sort exist says nothing that undermines the disinterestedness of that project. Leonard would, of course, want to make the university interested and biased. She romanticizes a situation in the academy when, 'women fight back individually and collectively' and 'enjoy the warmth of women's support and the joys and excitement of feminist research' (p.7). She says that 'It would be nice if the book made people in higher education more generally aware that women matter' (p.8). But the real excitement in the academy for women – and men – is the epistemological one of advancing knowledge.

There are other views of what 'feminist' research is other than being 'gendered'. It is often suggested that research should stress 'feminist values' such as 'collaboration' or that it should 'ensure that the process of allowing for mutual encounter in the experience of being-in-the-world operates in a fair manner' (Romm 1997: ss6.4, 6.5). All this amounts to is an appeal to be nice to one another when doing research or evaluating research. But one of the tests of the objectivity, validity and reliability of research findings is that they are subject to the most rigorous possible examination by one's professional peers. The heat in the research kitchen is intense and if you can't stand it there is a well-known solution.

The relativism in standpoint research is obvious. It is, once again, the claim that a third thing, something in the character or nature of the knower, determines what is known.

Postmodern research

Postmodern researchers are often said to adopt the view that 'anything goes'. I think this is true, despite sophisticated claims that this is not the case. Denying the Enlightenment values of reason, objectivity and truth as well as the 'grand narrative' of progress it is difficult to see what they could restrict or proscribe. Indeed postmodernists assert that, in their view, 'Instead of only one truth, there are many' (Scott and Usher 1999: 3). This is not a serious approach to research that could be held outside the field of cultural studies. Imagine it applied in medicine and then reflect on your next visit one of its consequences, the postmodern dental surgery: 'The horror! The horror!'

More 'sophisticated' postmodern views such as those popularized in educational writings by Scott and Usher and others, really do not amount to more that celebrating a relativism with a radical edge. They adopt a language of being 'transgressive', which means no more than that they adopt a lumpen-scepticism about all methodologies of research in addition to the Enlightenment values they denounce. This transgressive approach is held to be an 'ethical' activity by contrast with 'performativity', which is an approach to research in which professional 'researchers' just undertake whatever research their clients require in a technically efficient way. However, Scott and Usher interpose a notion of 'power' between the knower and the known:

The place of ethics as immanent rather than purely procedural also provides a different way of understanding the research process – a way which foregrounds the need to be aware of the relationship between researchers, knowledge and power where an emphasis on reflexivity is not simply another technique but a reminder that research is never a purely technical process.

(Scott and Usher 1999: 155–6)

Thus again, postmoderism provides us with an example of relativism, by reminding us that a third thing is present that explains the 'reality' pictured. This time it is a power relation.

Postmodernists, including Lyotard (1999: 64–7), use the notion of variety and of 'language games' to question the dominance of science. This is fair enough as an attack on scientism, but it in no way undermines science or the knowledge it produces. Even taking the Wittgensteinian metaphor at face value, the language game of science is still one that provides us with secure knowledge. Knowledge has not been made insecure. The belief that it has produces statements like this:

When knowledge is delegitimated, when it is no longer so closely bounded and patrolled by the epistemological police, what takes its place is an 'un-ruliness' of knowledge which even perfomativity cannot halt – which indeed performativity by its boundary-breaking and disregard for the traditional canons of research actually helps to bring about . . . It is the very 'unrul-iness' which it stimulates that provides the scope of resistant practices of research – even against itself.

(Scott and Usher 1999: 161).

This comes towards the end of Scott and Usher's book and amounts to nothing more than the statement that in postmodern research, anything does go, as long as it is on the side of the angels.

Action research

Is action research really research? This is said, quite correctly, to be a perennial question (Scott and Usher 1999: 3). Another way of putting it is: is action research just common sense? It is not to be denied that action research may be inspiring, it may move professionals on in their thinking, and it may even be informed by research, but it is *not* research. It is a form, not of common sense, but of quite ordinary professional investigation into practice. This sort of practical investigation has no academic pretensions. It is not theoretical or scientific although it might, by throwing up problems, be something that could lead to serious academic study. In this sense alone it might be seen as a bridge between research and practice.

Yet, once investigation acquires the label 'action research', it appeals to the practical philistine. The spurious scientific methodology that is then attached to it, such as descriptions and diagrams of the 'action research spiral', gives it a false objectivity. This amounts to no more than a formalization of the informal, and is unworthy of serious academic concern. It is the stuff of business textbooks that provide easily digestible 'theories' for hard-pressed businesspeople, like Handy's shamrock model for organizing your business (Handy 1990).

For our purposes, the essential feature of both 'action research' and much of 'reflective practice' is that it is described in a way that reinforces relativism. The origins of these approaches and their most extensive subsequent application are in the area of curriculum development:

> I began . . . by arguing that effective curriculum development of the highest quality depends upon the capacity of teachers to take a research stance to their own teaching. By a research stance I mean a disposition to examine one's own practice critically and systematically . . .
>
> It is important to make the point that the teacher in this situation is concerned to understand better his own classroom. Consequently, he is not faced with the problems of generalizing beyond his experience. In this context, theory is simply a systematic structuring of his understanding of his work . . .
>
> Accordingly we are concerned with the development of a sensitive and self-critical subjective perspective and not with an aspiration towards an unattainable objectivity.
>
> (Stenhouse 1975: 156–7)

Stenhouse's definition is relativistic. It emphasizes an individual's subjective structuring of experience. This is held to be unique and non-generalizable. Another way of looking at his notion of 'theory' in this context, is to say that experiential truths, suitably structured, are true for the individuals who have those experiences. This is the commonest and crudest relativism that says, yet again, that a third thing, our subjective structuring of experience, determines what counts as knowledge. The consequence of popularizing this notion of practitioner research is to promote vulgar relativism, even if it was not Stenhouse's intention.

Real educational research requires a realist approach and methodology (Truth 4)

Although the relativists may claim that knowledge and truth have been made 'problematic' or are 'discredited', 'undermined' or 'challenged', these claims are empty (Siegel 1998: 30–1). Saying that they are undermined does not mean that they are undermined. These claims are often supported by talk of a rejection of the notions of 'absolute' or 'universal' truth or of 'foundationalism' in the form of some 'Archimedian point' that can provide a neutral starting point outside of human history on the basis of which we can make knowledge claims.

Taking these points in turn, what does it mean to say that any truth is not 'absolute' (or 'universal')? We hold what we hold to be true as absolute, until it is disproved. To say that any truth is 'fallible' does not make it insecure. To do that, an alternative must be suggested and, hopefully, *proved*. The claim that there is an alternative to any particular truth is rarely substantiated and what we are offered is merely the assertion of statements like, 'Instead of one truth, there are many'. This is an absolute for relativists and provides an objective foundation for relativistic educational research. This also gives us the nearest example we have of the 'Archimedian point'. It is not foundationalists but relativists that believe in an 'Archimedian point'. It is the view that there are many truths. Against this, all statements, arguments, hypotheses and theories must be judged. The arguments of the relativists are unconvincing and contradictory.

This contradictoriness is evident, as we have said, in the relativists' use of propositional or truth talk. Knowledge and truth have not been undermined. Propositional language cannot be avoided because it is the way in which we talk about the world. That the relativist attack on knowledge and truth fails because it is incoherent, is evidence that we need to adopt a realist philosophy and a realist approach to educational research.

However, defenders of relativistic approaches to research make out that their particular form of relativism, acknowledged or not, is a strength rather than a weakness. Using arguments derived from John Anderson's defence of realism, I have indicated that if they are consistently adhered to, normal discourse becomes impossible. Practical, political or partisan approaches to educational and other research imply a relativism that is logically incoherent and, therefore, *false*. There should be nothing more to be said about them, but they will not go away because they reflect the mood of the times.

The search for truth has been abandoned (Truth 5)

The purpose of undertaking what David Blunkett called 'blues skies' research is to think the unthinkable and say the unsayable:

> If we are to encourage a more open debate of ideas there must also be a place for the fundamental 'blue-skies' research which thinks the unthinkable. We need researchers who can challenge fundamental assumptions and orthodoxies and this may well have big policy effects much further down the road. Civil servants, politicians, journalists and others do not have time for this kind of work. If academics do not address it, then it is difficult to think of anyone else who will. We must recognise its importance.
>
> (Blunkett 2000: s59)

The government's concern with 'blues skies' research must be understood in a political context. It needs experts because it lacks any big ideas of 'blue skies' thinking of its own. Having abandoned politics in the form of welfare state 'socialism' (the first way), and being unhappy with the Thatcherite reliance on the 'market' (the second way), all that is left is what works, or rather anything that might work (the Third Way). But although the government needs those who are willing to think the unthinkable, it lacks the confidence truly to allow such academic freedom and fears new ideas:

> It is vital that we overcome a culture in which ideas are unwelcome. It is the lifeblood of politics and the foundation for continuing progress by any radical Government that they embrace ideas at every level and allow debate to take place. But this needs to be within very clear parameters, so that misinterpretations and half truths are not half way round the world before the real facts have got their boots on. We need to be careful to distinguish between an ill-conceived speculation which damages Government, and a fear of ideas which damages the potential for critical thought.
>
> (Blunkett 2000: s38)

The government has really nothing to fear, as academics and educational researchers have abandoned the Enlightenment ideals of science, reason and progress. They are more likely to declare the 'end of knowledge' and argue that the academic's role is to help us live with the uncertainty that is the result (Barnett and Griffin 1999; Barnett 2000a). It is academics themselves who hold back the sort of research that may advance educational knowledge, because of what is nothing more than a general lack of confidence. Promoting forms of relativism is one way in which this lack of confidence manifests itself. Adopting the 'precautionary principle' in research, particularly in scientific research, is another manifestation of a loss of confidence in humanity's ability to develop our knowledge and understanding and take control of our lives.

This is why it is wrong for teachers and educational researchers to think that 'Research is a way of giving control back to teachers' (Rudduck 2001: 4). Teacher research gives the illusion of control while detracting attention from objective educational research which could provide the knowledge that would give teachers real control. Once again, the undermining of educational research comes from within the profession.

There is something ironic in arguing that educational and other research is being undermined by a lack of political and professional confidence when daily papers and news bulletins regularly carry accounts of new research. This concern with the findings of research, and the obsession with getting 'sound bite' interviews with academic 'experts', is the reflection in the media of the lack of political debate and the depoliticized times we live in. This search for someone with something new to say is entirely whimsical and arbitrary. Academic research cannot substitute for a political vision, and because much of what is reported is not really understood, it merely sows public confusion – the pseudo-scientific discussion of MMR being a case in point – and brings all research into contempt. It helps to create a dangerous public cynicism.

Nevertheless, the political crisis of confidence opens up the possibility that academic researchers, and particularly educational researchers, could regain a public role. This would mean having the confidence to make ideas accessible. This would mean rejecting the RAE. This would also mean having the confidence not to write to the latest policy dictates from the TTA or Ofsted or to go on producing the practical textbooks and manuals that their dictates require. More than this, it would require the confidence to abandon fashionable political and partisan approaches to research, and to set about the development of a realist philosophy of educational research.

Note

1. It is far from clear why Dewey's 'warranted knowledge' has been adopted as the aim of educational research by all of these groups (see Dewey [1938] 1966: 104). Outside of epistemology the concern to express the recognition of knowledge as 'warranted' or 'fallible' is hostage to fortune being both an unnecessary and defensive qualification and can only undermine people's belief that anyone can know anything about reality. The fallibilistic tone of contemporary educational writers in this context has political consequences (see truth 5). We need to sound more confident than we feel (cf. Haack 1995: 7).

BIBLIOGRAPHY

Abbs, P. (1986) The poisoning of the socratic ideal, *Guardian*, 13 January.

Abbs, P. (1994) *The Educational Imperative*. London: Falmer Press.

Adam, K., Johanson, M. and Gravesen, I. (1995) Service productivity: a vision or a search for a new outlook. Paper presented at the Ninth World Productivity Congress, Istanbul, 4–7 June.

Ainley, P. (1990) *Vocational Education and Training*. London: Cassell.

Ainley, P. (1993) *Class and Skill*. London: Cassell.

Ainley, P. and Bailey, B. (1997) *The Business of Learning*. London: Cassell.

Althusser, L. (1971) *Lenin and Other Philosophical Essays*. London: NLB.

Altrichter, H. and Elliot, J. (eds) (2000) *Images of Education Change*. Buckingham: Open University Press.

Altrichter, H., Posch, P. and Somekh, H. (1993) *Teachers Investigate their Work*. London: Routledge.

Anderson, J. (1962a) The knower and the known, *Studies in Empirical Philosophy*, pp. 27–40. Sydney: Angus & Robertson.

Anderson, J. (1962b) Realism and some of its critics, *Studies in Empirical Philosophy*, pp. 41–59. Sydney: Angus & Robertson.

Anderson, J. (1962c) Realism versus relativism in ethics, *Studies in Empirical Philosophy*, pp. 238–47. Sydney: Angus & Robertson.

Anderson, J. (1980) The place of the academic in modern society, *Education and Inquiry*, pp. 214–21. Oxford: Basil Blackwell.

AQA (Assessment and Qualifications Alliance) (1999) *GCE A/AS English Language and Literature Specification A*. Guildford: AQA.

Armitage, A., Bryant, R., Dunnill, R. *et al. (1999) Teaching and Training in Post-Compulsory Education*. Buckingham: Open University Press.

Armitage, A., Bryant, R., Dunnill, R. *et al.* (2003) *Teaching and Training in Post-Compulsory Education* (2nd edition). Buckingham: Open University Press.

Arnold, M. ([1864] 1906) The function of criticism at the present time, *Essays Literary and Critical*, pp. 1–25. London: J.M. Dent.

Austin, J.L. (1962) *How To Do Things with Words*. Oxford: Oxford University Press.

Avis, J. (1996) Learner identity: vocationalism and global relations, *British Journal of Education and Work*, 9(3).

Avis, J., Bloomer, M., Esland, G., Gleeson, D. and Hodkinson, P. (1996) *Knowledge and Nationhood: Education, Politics and Work*. London: Cassell.

Bailey, C. (1984) *Beyond the Present and the Particular*. London: Routledge.

Bailey, R. (2001) Overcoming veriphobia – learning how to love truth again, *British Journal of Educational Studies*, 49(2): 159–72.

Barnett, R. (1994) *The Limits of Competence*. Buckingham: SRHE/Open University Press.

Barnett, R. (1997) *Higher Education: A Critical Business*. Buckingham: SRHE/Open University Press.

Barnett, R. (2000a) *Realizing the University in an age of supercomplexity*. Buckingham: SRHE/Open University Press.

Barnett, R. (2000b) Supercomplexity and the curriculum, *Studies in Higher Education*, 25(3): 255–65.

Barnett, R. and Griffin, A. (eds) (1999) *The End of Knowledge in Higher Education*. London: Cassell.

Barrow, R. and Woods, R. (1988) *An Introduction to Philosophy of Education* (3rd edition). London: Routledge.

Barton, L. (ed.) (1996) *Disability and Society*. London: Longman.

Bates, I., Clarke, J., Cohen, P. *et al.* (1984) *Schooling for the Dole?* London: Macmillan.

Bates, I., Bloomer, M., Hodkinson, P. and Yeomans, D. (1998) Progressivism and the GNVQ: context, ideology and practice, *Journal of Education and Work*, 11(2).

Becher, T. (1989) *Academic Tribes and Territories*. Buckingham: SRHE/Open University Press.

Becher, T. (1999) Quality in the professions, *Studies in Higher Education*, 24(2): 225–35.

Beck, U. (1992) *Risk Society. Towards a New Modernity*. London: Sage.

Beck, U. (2000) *The Brave New World of Work*. Cambridge: Polity Press.

Becker, H. (1963) *Outsiders*. New York: Free Press.

Becker, H. (1970) *Sociological Work*. New Brunswick: Transaction Books.

Ben-Ami, D. (2001) *Cowardly Capitalism: The Myth of the Global Financial Casino*. Chichester: John Wiley.

Benn, C. and Fairley, J. (eds) (1986) *Challenging the MSC on Jobs, Training and Education*. London: Pluto Press.

Bentley, T., Jupp, B. and Steadman Jones, D. (2000) *Getting to Grips with Depoliticisation*. London: Demos Briefing Paper.

BERA (2000) *Good Practice In Educational Research Writing*. Southwell: BERA.

Berger, P. and Luckman, T. (1966) *The Social Construction of Reality*. New York: Doubleday.

Bett (1999) *Independent Review of Higher Education Pay and Conditions*. London: The Stationery Office.

Blair, T. (1998) *The Third Way: New Politics for the New Century*. London: Fabian Society.

Bloom, A. (1987) *The Closing of the American Mind: How Higher Education has Failed Democracy and Impoverished the Souls of Today's Students*. Harmondsworth: Penguin.

Blunkett, D. (2000) Influence or irrelevance: can social science improve government? Speech to the ESRC on 2 February. Reprinted in *Research Intelligence*, No.71. BERA Newsletter.

Bottomore, T. and Nisbett, R. (eds) (1978) *A History of Sociological Analysis*. London: Heinemann.

Bourdieu, P. (1998) Job insecurity is everywhere now, *Acts of Resistance. Against the New Myths of Our Time*, pp. 81–7. Cambridge: Polity Press.

Bradley, H., Ericson, M., Stephenson, C. and Williams, S. (2000) *Myths at Work*. Cambridge: Polity Press.

Braverman, H. (1974) *Labor and Monopoly*. Capital, NY: Monthly Review Press.

Bridges, D. (1999) Educational research: pursuit of truth or flight into fancy? *British Educational Research Journal*, 25(5): 597–616.

Bruner, J. (1960) *The Process of Education*. New York: Vintage Books.

Burgoyne, J. (1995) in C. Cassell and G. Symon (eds) *Qualitative Research Methods in Organisational Research*. London: Sage.

Burrage, M. and Torstendahl, R. (1990) *Professions in Theory and History*. London: Sage.

Bush, T. (1995) *Theories of Educational Management* (2nd edition). London: Paul Chapman.

Capra, F. (1975) *The Tao of Physics*. Berkeley, CA: Shambhala.

Carnall, C. (1999) *Managing Change in Organisations*. Hemel Hempstead: Prentice Hall.

Carr, D. (1998) *Education, Knowledge and Truth*. London: Routlege.

Carter, B. (1997) The restructuring of teaching and the restructuring of class, *British Journal of Sociology of Education*, 18(2).

CAST (Center for Applied Special Technology) (2002) http://www.cast.org/

CBI (1998) *Innovation Trends Survey*. London: CBI.

Centre for Research into Quality (2000) *The 2000 Report on the Experience of Postgraduate Research Students at the University of Central England*. Birmingham: University of Central England.

Centre for Research into Quality (2001) Integrating feedback, *Update – Newsletter of the Centre for Research into Quality*. Birmingham: University of Central England.

Chadwick, P. (1995) Academic quality in TQM: issues in teaching and learning. *Quality Assurance in Education*, 3(2): 19–23.

Clarke, J. and Willis, P. (1984) Introduction, in I. Bates *et al.* (eds) *Schooling for the Dole*. London: Macmillan.

Clayton, M. (1995) Encouraging the Kaizen approach to quality in a university, *Total Quality Management*, 6(5/6): 593–603.

Cohen, P. (1984) Against the new vocationalism, in I. Bates *et al.* (eds) *Schooling for the Dole*. London: Macmillan.

Cohen, L. and Manion, L. (1994) *Research Methods in Education* (4th edition). London: Routledge.

Cohen, L., Manion, L. and Marrison, K. (2000) *Research Methods in Education*. London: Routledge.

Comte, A. (1842) *Course in Positive Philosophy*.

Corbett, J. and Barton, L. (1992) *A Struggle for Choice*. London: Routledge.

Cox, C.B. and Boyson, R. (eds) (1977) *The Black Paper*. London: Temple-Smith.

Croham, Lord. (1987) *Review of the University Grants Committee*, Cmnd 81. London: HMSO.

Cully, M., Woodland, S., O'Reilly, A. and Dix, G. (1999) *Britain At Work. As Depicted by the 1998 Workplace Employee Relations Survey*. London: Routledge.

Curran, J. *et al.* (1988) Loony tunes, *Open Space*. BBC 2.

Dearing, R. (1996) *Review of Qualifications for 16–19 Year Olds*. Hayes: SCAA.

Dearing, R. (1997) *Higher Education in the Learning Society: Report of the National Committee of Inquiry into Higher Education*. London: HMSO.

Delamont, S. (ed.) (1984) *Readings on Interaction in the Classroom*. London: Methuen.

Delamont, S., Oliver, M. and Connolly, P. (2001) Review symposium: taking sides in social research: essays on partisanship and bias, *British Journal of Sociology of Education*, 22(1): 157–69.

Delanty, G. (2001) *Challenging Knowledge: The University in the Knowledge Society.* Buckingham: Open University Press.

Derrida, J. (1967) *Of Grammatology* (tr. G.C. Spivak). Baltimore: Johns Hopkins University Press.

DETR (Department of the Environment, Transport and the Regions) (1999) *Modernising Local Government: Improving Services through Best Value.* London: HMSO.

Dewey, J. ([1916] 1966) *Democracy and Education.* New York: Macmillan/Free Press.

Dewey, J. ([1936] 1963) *Experience and Education.* London: Collier-Macmillan.

Dewey, J. ([1938] 1966) *Logic: The Theory of Inquiry.* New York: Holt, Rinehart & Winston.

DfEE (1997) *Qualifying for Success.* London: DfEE.

DfEE (1999) *Learning to Succeed.* London: DfEE.

DfES (2002) *14–19: Extending Opportunities, Raising Standards.* London: The Stationery Office.

Docking, J. (ed.) (2000) *New Labour's Policies for Schools – Raising the Standard?* London: David Fulton Publishers.

Doherty, G. (1995) ISO 9000 series 1987 and education – do they fit and is it worth it? *Quality Assurance in Education*, 3(3): 3–9.

Dopson, S. and McNay, I. (1996) Organisational culture, in D. Warner and D. Palfreyman (eds) *Higher Education Management.* Buckingham: Open University Press.

Duke, C. (1992) *The Learning University: Towards a New Paradigm?* Buckingham: SRHE/Open University Press.

Durkheim, E. (1895) *The Rules of Sociological Method.*

Eade, D. (1998) Towards a research culture, *College Research*, 2(1): 20–1.

Eagleton, T. (1989) *The Significance of Theory.* Oxford: Blackwell.

Edwards, R. (1997) *Changing Places: Flexibility, Lifelong Learning and a Learning Society.* London: Routledge.

Elliot, J. (ed.) (1993) *Reconstructing Teacher Education.* London: Falmer Press.

Elliott, J. (1990) *How to Achieve Research-based Action: A Problem of Disseminating Research Knowledge or of Utilisation?* Norwich: University of East Anglia.

Elliott, J. (1991) *Action Research for Educational Change.* Buckingham: Open University Press.

Elliott, J. (1998) Living with Ambiguity and Contradiction: The Challenges for Educational Research in Positioning Itself for the 21st Century. Keynote address: European Conference for Educational Research (ECER), Ljubljana, September.

Etzioni, M. (2000) *The Third Way to a Good Society.* London: Demos.

Evans, R.G. (1998) Establishing a culture of college research, *College Research*, 2(1): 16–19.

Evans, J.M., Lippoldt, D.C. and Marianna, P. (2001) Trends in working hours in OECD countries, *Labour Market and Social Policy*, Occasional Paper No. 45. Paris: OECD.

Farmer, T. (1999) In my opinion, *Management Today*, July, p. 12.

Feldman, R.S. (ed.) (1992) *The Social Psychology of Education.* Cambridge: Cambridge University Press.

Feyerabend, P. (1975) *Against Method.* London: Verso.

Feyerabend, P. (1978) *Science in a Free Society.* London: NLB.

Fielden, J. (1990) The shifting culture of higher education, in P. Wright (ed.) *Industry and Higher Education*. Buckingham: SRHE/Open University Press.

Finn, D. (1987) *Training without Jobs: New Deals and Broken Promises*. London: Macmillan.

Florian, L. (1997) Inclusive education: the reform initiative of the Tomlinson Committee, *British Journal of Special Education*, 24(1).

Foucault, M. (1974) *The Archaeology of Knowledge*. London: Tavistock.

Freud, S. ([1900] 1976) *The Interpretation of Dreams*. London: Pelican.

Friedman, M. and Friedman, R. (1979) *Free to Choose*. London: Penguin.

Fullan, M.G. (1991) *The New Meaning of Educational Change*. London: Cassell.

Furedi, F. (2002) *Culture of Fear* (2nd edition). London: Continuum.

Gallie, D., White, M., Cheng, Y. and Tomlinson, M. (1998) *Restructuring the Employment Relationship*. Oxford: Oxford University Press.

Gardner, H. (1983) *Frames of Mind*. London: Fontana.

Gardner, H. (1993) *Multiple Intelligences*. New York: Basic Books.

Garfinkel, H. (1967) Good organisational reasons for bad clinical records, in H. Garfinkel, *Studies in Ethnomethodology*. London: Penguin.

Gibbs, G. (1988) *Learning by Doing*. London: FEU/Longmans.

Gibbs, G. (1992) *Improving the Quality of Student Learning*. Bristol: Technical and Educational Services.

Gibbs, P. (2001) Higher education as a market: a problem or solution, *Studies in Higher Education*, 26(1) 85–94.

Giddens, A. (1991) *Modernity and Self-identity*. Cambridge: Polity Press.

Giddens, A. (1998) *The Third Way: The Renewal of Social Democracy*. Cambridge: Polity Press.

Giddens, A. (2000) *The Third Way and its Critics*. Cambridge: Polity Press.

Giroux, H. (1983) *The Theory of Resistance: A Pedagogy for the Opposition*. London: Heinemann.

Goleman, D. (1995) *Emotional Intelligence*. London: Bloomsbury.

Gouldner, A. (1971) *The Coming Crisis of Western Sociology*. London: Heinemann.

Gray, D.E. and Griffin, C. (eds) (2000) *Post Compulsory Education and the New Millennium*. London: Jessica Kingsley.

Guest, D. (1987) Human resource management and industrial relations, *Journal of Management Studies*, 24(5): 503–21.

Haack, S. (1995) *Evidence and Inquiry: Towards Reconstruction in Epistemology*. Oxford: Blackwell.

Habermas, J. (1986) *The Theory of Communicative Action. Reason and the Rationalization of Society*. Cambridge: Polity Press.

Hammer, M. (1997) *Beyond Re-engineering*. London: HarperCollins.

Hammersley, M. (1997) Educational research and teaching: a response to David Hargreaves' TTA lecture, *British Educational Research Journal*, 23(2): 141–61.

Hammersley, M. (2000) *Taking Sides in Social Research: Essays on Partisanship and Bias*. London: Routledge.

Hammersley, M. (2001) A reply to partisan reviewers, *British Journal of Sociology of Education*, 22(3): 417–21.

Hammersley, M. and Gomm, R. (1997a) Bias in social research, *Sociological Research Online*, 2(4). http:/www.socresonline.org.uk/2/4/7.html

Hammersley, M. and Gomm, R. (1997b) A response to Romm, *Sociological Research Online*, 2(1). http:/www.socresonline.org.uk/2/1/3.html

Handy, C. (1990) *The Age of Unreason*. London: Arrow.

Handy, C. (1993) *Understanding Organizations* (4th edition). London: Penguin.

Handy, C. (1995) *The Empty Raincoat: Making Sense of the Future*. London: Arrow.

Haralambos, M. and Holborn, M. (1995) *Sociology: Themes and Perspectives*. London: Collins International.

Hargreaves, A. (1994) *Changing Teachers, Changing Times*. London: Cassell.

Hargreaves, D.H. (1996) Teaching as a research-based profession: possibilities and prospects, *Teacher Training Agency Annual Lecture 1996*. London: Teacher Training Agency.

Hargreaves, D.H. (1997) In defence of research for evidence-based teaching: a rejoinder to Martyn Hammersley, *British Educational Research Journal*, 23(4): 405–19.

Harkin, J., Turner, G. and Dawn, T. (2001) *Teaching Young Adults. A Handbook for Teachers in Post-compulsory Education*. London: Routledge/Falmer.

Hart, C. and Shoolbred, M. (1993) Organisational culture, rewards and quality in higher education, *Quality Assurance in Education*, 1(2): 22–9.

Harvey, D. (1989) *The Condition of Post Modernity*. London: Blackwell.

Harvey, L. (1999) Engagement is key, *Times Higher Educational Supplement*, 19 November, p. 15.

Harvey, L. and Green, D. (1993) Defining quality, *Assessment and Evaluation in Higher Education*, 18(1): 9–34.

Harvey, L. and Knight, P. (1996) *Transforming Higher Education*. Buckingham: Open University Press.

Hayes, D. (2001) Too embarrassed to vote, *Public Management and Policy Association Review*, 15 (November): 12–13.

Hayes, D. (2002a) Taking the hemlock: the new sophistry of teacher training for higher education, in D. Hayes and R. Wynyard (eds) *The McDonaldization of Higher Education*, pp. 143–57. Westport, CT: Bergin & Garvey.

Hayes, D. (2002b) New Labour: New Professionalism. Paper presented at the Discourse, Power and Resistance in Post-compulsory Education and Training Conference, Plymouth University, 12–14 April.

Hayes, D. (2003 forthcoming) *The Rise of Therapeutic Education*.

Hayes, D. and Hudson, A. (2001) *Basildon: The Mood of the Nation*. London: Demos.

Hayes, D. and Hudson, A. (2003) *Attitudes to Work*. London: Education and Work Research Group.

Hayton, A. (ed.) (1999) *Tackling Disaffection and Social Exclusion*. London: Kogan Page.

HEFCE (1997) *Conduct of the Exercise: RAE Manager's Report*. Bistol: HEFCE.

HEFCE (2002) *Final Report of the Task Group – Information on Quality and Standards in Higher Education*. Bristol: HEFCE.

Heller, R. (1997) *In Search of European Excellence*. London: HarperCollins Business.

Henkel, M. (1997) Academic values and the university as corporate enterprise. *Higher Education Quarterly*, 51(2): 134–43.

Hirst, P.H. (1974) *Knowledge and the Curriculum*. London: Routledge & Kegan Paul.

Hirst, P.H. (1993) Education, knowledge and practices, in R. Barrow and P. White (eds), *Beyond Liberal Education: Essays in Honour of Paul H. Hirst*, pp. 184–99. London: Routledge.

Hitchcock, G. and Hughes, D. (1995) *Research and the Teacher* (2nd edition). London: Routledge.

Hobrough, J. and Bates, R. (1998) Progression of skills and competencies through university to employment: with reference to SME's within the European labour market, *Industry and Higher Education*, 12(5): 290–6.

Hodgson, A. and Spours, K. (eds) (1999) *New Labour's Educational Agenda. Issues and Policies for Education and Training from 14+*. London: Kogan Page.

Hodgson, A. and Spours, K. (2001) *Evaluating Stage 1 of the Hargreaves Review of Curriculum 2000*. London: Institute of Education, University of London.

Hodkinson, P. (1998) They tell you what to do and then they let you get on with it, *Journal of Education and Work*, 11(2): 167–86.

Hodkinson, P. and Issitt, M. (eds) (1995) *The Challenge of Competence: Professionalism through Vocational Education and Training*. London: Cassell.

Hoggett, P. (1996) New modes of control in the public service, *Public Administration*, 69 (Spring): 3–19.

Holmes, G. (1993) Quality assurance in further and higher education, *Quality Assurance in Education*, 1(1): 4–8.

Honey, P. and Mumford, A. (1992) *Manual of Learning* (3rd edition). Maidenhead: P. Honey.

Horizon (1988) *Science . . . Fiction?* BBC2.

Howell, P. (1975) Once again on productive and unproductive labour, *Revolutionary Communist*, 3/4. London: RCG Publications.

Hudson, A., Hayes, D. and Andrew, T. (1996) *Working Lives in the 1990s: The Provisional Findings of the Attitudes to Work Survey*. London: Global Futures.

Hume, D. ([1739] 1973) *A Treatise of Human Nature*, edited by L.A. Selby-Bigge. Oxford: Clarendon Press.

Humm, M. (ed.) (1992) *Feminisms*. London: Harvester.

Hyland, T. (1990) Education, vocationalism and competence, *Forum*, 33(1).

Hyland, T. (1994a) *Competence, Education and NVQs: Dissenting Voices*. London: Cassell.

Hyland, T. (1994b) Silk purses and sows' ears: NVQ's, GNVQ's and experiential learning, *Cambridge Journal of Education*, 24(2): 233–43.

Hyland, T. (1996) Professionalism, ethics and work-based learning, *British Journal of Educational Studies*, 44(2): 168–80.

Jacobs, M. (2001) The environment, modernity and the Third Way, in A. Giddens (ed.) *The Global Third Way Debate*, pp. 317–39. Cambridge: Polity Press.

Jarratt, A. (1985) *Report of the Steering Committee for Efficiency Studies*. London: CVCP.

Jarvis, P. (1995) *Adult and Continuing Education* (2nd edition). London: Routledge.

Jessop, T.E. (1970) Some misunderstandings of Hume, in V.C. Chappell (ed.) *Hume*, pp. 35–52. Basingstoke: Macmillan.

Jessup, G. (1991) *Outcomes: NVQ's as the Emerging Model of Education and Training*. London: Falmer Press.

Kanji, G. and Tambi, A. (1999) Total quality management in UK higher education institutions, *Total Quality Management*, 10(1): 129–53.

Kant, I. ([1787]1929) *Critique of Pure Reason* (tr. N. Kemp Smith). London: Macmillan.

Kavanagh, J. (2001) New Labour, new millennium, new premiership, in A. Seldon (ed.), *The Blair Effect*, pp. 3–18. London: Little Brown.

Kemmis, S. (1993) Action research and social movement: a challenge for policy research, *Education Policy Analysis Archives*, 1(1).

Kennedy, H. (1997) *Learning Works: Widening Participation in FE*. Coventry: FEFC.

Kinnes, S. (2001a) Go home – please. *Guardian*, 6 August.

Kinnes, S. (2001b) *Presenteeism: For Goodness Sake Go . . .* http://www.stressbusting.co.uk./news present.htm (accessed 24 June 2002)

Kirschenbaum, H. (ed.) (1990) *The Carl Rogers Reader*. London: Constable.

Kiwi, M. (1989) With prejudice, *Times Educational Supplement*, 13 January, p. 24.

Knight, P. and Trowler, P. (2000) Department-level cultures and the improvement of learning and teaching, *Studies in Higher Education*, 25(1): 69–82.

Knowles, M. (1984) *The Adult Learner, a Neglected Species* (3rd edition). Houston, TX: Gulf Publishing Company.

Kolb, D.A. (1984) *Experiential Learning*. Englewood Cliffs, NJ: Prentice Hall.

Kuhn, T. (1962) *The Structure of Scientific Revolutions*. Chicago: University of Chicago Press.

Lakatos, I. and Musgrave, A. (eds) (1970) *Criticism and the Growth of Knowledge.* Cambridge: Cambridge University Press.

Lash, S. and Urry, J. (1987) *The End of Organised Capitalism.* Cambridge: Polity Press.

Lave, J. and Wenger, E. (1991) *Situated Learning: Legitimate Peripheral Participation.* Cambridge: Cambridge University Press.

Lawes, S. (2003) The end of theory? A comparative study of the decline of educational theory and professional knowledge in modern foreign languages teacher education in Britain and France. Unpublished PhD thesis. Institute of Education, University of London.

Leonard, D. (2001) *A Woman's Guide to Doctoral Studies.* Buckingham: Open University Press.

Lewin, K. (1951) *Field Theory in Social Sciences.* New York: Harper & Row.

Lomas, L. (2002) Does the development of mass education necessarily mean the end of quality? *Quality in Higher Education,* 8(1): 71–9.

Lomas, L. and Tomlinson, K. (2000) Standards: the varying perceptions of senior staff in higher education institutions, *Quality Assurance in Education,* 8(3): 131–8.

Lovelock, C. (2001) *Services Marketing: People, Technology, Strategy* (4th edition). Englewood Cliffs, NJ: Prentice Hall.

Lyotard, J.F. (1999) *The Postmodern Condition: A Report on Knowledge.* Manchester: Manchester University Press.

MacDonald, K. (1997) *The Sociology of the Professions.* London: Sage.

MacDonald, R. (ed.) (1997) *Youth, the 'Underclass' and Social Exclusion.* London: Routledge.

Marcousé, I., Gillespie, A., Martin, B., Surridge, M. and Wall, N. (1999) *Business Studies.* Abingdon: Hodder & Stoughton.

Mayo, E. (1933) *The Human Problems of an Industrial Civilisation.* New York: Macmillan.

Mayo, M. and Thompson, J. (eds) (1995) *Adult Learning: Critical Intelligence and Social Change.* Leicester: NIACE.

McClure, S. (1988) *Education Reformed: A Guide to the Education Reform Act 1988.* London: Hodder & Stoughton.

McGinty, J. and Fish, J. (1993) *Further Education in the Market Place.* London: Routledge.

McKenzie, J., Powell, J. and Usher, R. (eds) (1997) *Understanding Social Research.* London: Falmer Press.

McKernan, J. (1991) *Curriculum Action Research: A Handbook of Methods and Resources for the Reflective Practitioner.* London: Kogan Page.

McKernan, J. (1996) *Curriculum Action Research.* London: Kogan Page.

McNiff, J. (1988) *Action Research: Principles and Practice.* London: Routledge.

McNiff, J. (1992) *Teaching as Learning: An Action Research Approach.* London: Routledge.

Mintzberg, H. (1983) *Structure in Fives: Designing Effective Organisations.* London: Prentice Hall.

Mishel, L., Bernstain, J. and Schmitt, J. (2001) *The State of Working America 2000–2001.* Ithaca, NY: Cornell University Press.

Moore, A. (1996) Masking the fissures: some thoughts on competencies, reflection and closure in initial teacher education, *British Journal of Educational Studies,* 44(2): 200–11.

Morgan, G. (1996) *Understanding Organizations* (2nd edition). London: Sage

Morley, L. (1997) Change and equity in higher education, *British Journal of Sociology of Education,* 18(2): 231–42.

Morris, A. (2001) Making use of research, *College Research,* 4(2): 33–4.

Morris, E. (2001) *Professionalism and Trust: The Future of Teachers and Teaching. A Speech by the Rt Hon Estelle Morris MP Secretary of State for Education and Skills to the Social Market Foundation, November 2001*. London: DfES.

Mullan, P. (2000) The Remodelling of Work. Paper presented at the Institute of Ideas Conference, Mind The Gap: Education and the Restructuring of Work, Canterbury Christ Church University College, 17 June.

NATFHE (National Association of Teachers in Further and Higher Education) (1992) *A Question of Quality*, Discussion paper. London: NATFHE.

National Statistics (2001) *Business Enterprise Research and Development 2000*. London: National Statistics.

National Statistics (2002) *Gross Domestic Expenditure on Research and Development 2000*. London: National Statistics.

Nolan, J.L. (1998) *The Therapeutic State: Justifying Government at Century's End*. New York: New York University Press.

Noon, M. and Blyton, P. (1997) *The Realities of Work*. London: Macmillan.

O'Conner, J. and Seymour, J. (1990) *Introducing NLP*. London: Routledge.

Overell, S. (2002) The workplace revolution that never happened, *Financial Times*, 27 May.

Paisley, W.J. and Butler, M. (eds) (1983) *Knowledge Utilization Systems in Education: Dissemination, Technical Assistance, Networking*. Newbury Park, CA: Sage.

Palmer, P.J. (1998) *The Courage to Teach*. San Francisco: Jossey-Bass.

Parasuraman, A., Zeithaml, V. and Berry, L. (1991) Refinement of expectations as a comparison standard in measuring service quality: implications for further research, *Journal of Retailing*, 67(4): 420–50.

Patrick, J. (1973) *A Glasgow Street Gang Observed*. London: Methuen.

Patton, M.Q. (1987) *How to Use Qualitative Methods in Evaluation*. Newbury Park, CA: Sage.

Phillips, D.C. and Burbules, N.C. (2000) *Postpositivism and Educational Research*. Lanham, MD: Rowman & Littlefield.

Piaget, J. (1971) *Psychology and Epistemology*. Harmondsworth: Penguin.

Popper, K. (1957) *The Poverty of Historicism*. London: Routledge & Kegan Paul.

Popper, K. (1959) *The Logic of Scientific Discovery*. London: Hutchinson.

Popper, K. (1963) *Conjectures and Refutations*. London: Routledge & Kegan Paul.

Poynter, G. (2000) *Restructuring in the Service Industries*. London: Mansell.

Prais, S.J. (1991) Vocational qualifications in Britain and Europe: theory and practice, *National Institute Economic Review*, May: 86–92.

Pring, R. (1976) *Knowledge and Schooling*. London: Open Books.

Pring, R. (1995) *Closing the Gap: Liberal Education and Vocational Preparation*. London: Hodder & Stoughton.

Pring, R. (2000) *Philosophy of Educational Research*. London: Continuum.

Pupius, M. (2001) Quality – The End or Just the Beginning? The End of Quality? Paper presented at the Society for Research in Higher Education Conference, Birmingham, May.

QAA (2002) *QAA External Review Process for Higher Education in England*, QA 019 03/02. Gloucester: Quality Assurance Agency for Higher Education.

QCA (Qualifications and Curriculum Authority) (2001a) *Review of Curriculum 2000: Report on Phase 1*. London: QCA.

QCA (Qualifications and Curriculum Authority) (2001b) *Review of Curriculum 2000: Report on Phase 2*. London: QCA.

Quine, W.V.O. (1953) *From A Logical Point of View*. New York: Harper & Row.

Raggatt, P. (1994) Implementing NVQ's in colleges: progress, perceptions and issues, *Journal of Further and Higher Education*, 18(1): 59–74.

Raggatt, P., Edwards, R. and Small, N. (eds) (1996) *The Learning Society: Challenges and Trends*. Buckingham: Open University Press.

Rampton, S. and Stauber, J. (2001) *Trust Us, We're Experts*. New York: Penguin Putnam.

Randle, K. and Brady, N. (1997) Managerialism and professionalism in the 'Cinderella service', *Journal of Vocational Education and Training*, 49(1): 121–39.

Rifkin, J. (2000) *The End of Work. The Decline of the Global Workforce and the Dawn of the Post-Market Era*. Harmondsworth: Penguin.

Ritzer, G. (1996) McUniversity in the post-modern consumer society, *Quality in Higher Education*, 2(3): 185–99.

Ritzer, G. (1998) *The McDonaldization Thesis*. London: Sage.

Ritzer, G. (2000) *The McDonaldization of Society*. Boston: Pine Forge.

Rogers, R. (1983) *Freedom to Choose for the 80s*. Columbus, OH: Merrill.

Romm, N. (1997) Becoming more accountable: a comment on Hammersley and Gomm, *Sociological Research Online*, 2(3). http:/www.socresonline.org.uk/2/3/2.htm

Rorty, R. (1989) *Contingency, Irony and Solidarity*. Cambridge: Cambridge University Press.

Rowley, J. (1997) Beyond service quality dimensions in higher education and towards a service contract, *Quality Assurance in Education*, 5(1): 7–14.

Rudduck, J. (1998) Educational research: the prospect of change . . ., in J. Rudduck and D. McIntyre (eds) *Challenges for Educational Research*, New BERA Dialogues. London: Sage.

Rudduck, J. (2001) Teachers as Researchers: The Quiet Revolution. Address to the DfEE and TTA Conference, Using Research and Evidence to Improve Teaching and Learning, London, March.

Rust, C. (1997) Teaching and Learning in Times of Change. Paper presented at the Staff Conference, Canterbury Christ Church College, 7 January.

Rustin, M. (1994) Incomplete modernity: Ulrich Beck's risk society, *Radical Philosophy*, 67 (Summer): 3–12.

Ryle, G. (1973) *The Concept of Mind*. Harmondsworth: Penguin.

Schon, D.A. (1983) *The Reflective Practitioner*. London: Arena.

Schutz, T. (1932) *The Phenomenology of the Social World*. London: Heinemann.

Scott, P. (1998) Massification, internationalisation and globalisation, in P. Scott (ed.) *The Globalisation of Higher Education*. Buckingham: SRHE/Open University Press.

Scott, D. and Usher, R. (1999) *Researching Education: Data, Methods and Theory in Educational Enquiry*. London: Continuum.

Seddon, J. (2000) *The Case Against ISO 9000* (2nd edition). Dublin: Oak Tree Press.

Seldon, A. (2001) The net Blair effect, in A. Seldon (ed) *The Blair Effect*, pp. 593–600. London: Little Brown.

Sennett, R. ([1977] 1993) *The Fall of Public Man*. London: Faber & Faber.

Sennett, R. (1998) *The Corrosion of Character*. New York: Norton.

SEU (Social Exclusion Unit) (2002) *Reducing Re-offending by Ex-Prisoners*. London: SEU.

Sharp, S. (1995) The quality of teaching and learning in higher education: evaluating the evidence, *Higher Education Quarterly*, 49(4): 301–15.

Shore, C. and Roberts, S. (1995) Higher education and the panopticon paradigm: quality assessment as disciplinary technology, *Higher Education Review*, 27(3): 17.

Siegel, H. (1998) Knowledge, truth and education, in D. Carr (ed.) *Education, Knowledge and Truth*, pp. 19–36. London: Routledge.

Siegrist, H. (1994) The professions, state and government in theory and history, in T. Becher (ed.) *Governments and Professional Education*. Buckingham: Open University Press.

Simmons, J. and Iles, P. (2001) Performance appraisals in knowledge-based organisations: implications for management education, *International Journal of Management Education*, 2(1): 3–18.

Skeggs, B. (1988) Gender reproduction and further education: domestic apprenticeships, *British Journal of Sociology of Education*, 9(2).

Skilbeck, M. *et al.* (1994) *The Vocational Quest*. London: Routledge.

Smith, J. (1998) Beyond the rhetoric: are GNVQ's doing students any good? *Journal of Vocational Education and Training*: *The Vocational Aspect of Education*, 50(4): 537–48.

Smithers, A. (1993) *All Our Futures*. London: Channel 4 Television.

Smithers, A. (2001) Education policy, in A. Seldon (ed.) *The Blair Effect*, pp. 405–26. London: Little Brown.

Smithers, A. and Robinson, P. (eds) (2000) *Further Education Reformed*. London: Falmer Press.

Squires, G. (1990) *First Degree*. Buckingham: Open University Press.

Stenhouse, L. (1975) *An Introduction to Curriculum Research and Development*. London: Heinemann.

Swann, J. and Pratt, J. (1999) *Improving Education: Realist Approaches to Method and Research*. London: Cassell.

Tarrant, J. (2000) What's wrong with competence? *Journal of Further and Higher Education*, 24(1): 77–84.

The Lecturer (2002) NATFE demands pay boost, *The Lecturer*, June: 1.

Therborn, G. (1978) The Frankfurt School, in New Left Review (ed.) *Western Marxism: A Critical Reader*, pp. 83–139. London: Verso.

THES (2002) 135% rise in student numbers, *Times Higher Education Supplement*, 8 March: 2.

Thomas, L. (2001) *Widening Access and Participation in Post Compulsory Education*. London: Continuum.

Thorne, M. and Cuthbert, R. (1996) Autonomy, bureaucracy and competition: the ABC of control in higher education, in R. Cuthbert (ed.) *Working in Higher Education*. Buckingham: Open University Press.

Todd, R.J. (1997) Teacher librarians and information literacy: getting into action, *School Libraries Worldwide*, 3(2).

Toffler, A. (1971) *Future Shock*. London: Bantam Books.

Toffler, A. (1981) *The Third Wave*. London: Bantam Books.

Toffler, A. (1990) *Powershift: Knowledge, Wealth, and Violence at the Edge of the 21st Century*. London: Bantam Books.

Tomlinson, J. (1996) *Inclusive Learning: Report of the Learning Difficulties and/or Disabilities Committee*. Coventry: FEFC.

Townley, B. (1992) In the eye of the gaze: the constitutive role of performance appraisal, in P. Barrar and C. Cooper (eds) *Managing Organisations*. London: Routledge.

Trowler, P. (1995) *Investigating Education and Training*. London: Collins Educational.

Trowler, P. (1998) *Academics Responding to Change: New Higher Education Frameworks and Academic Cultures*. Buckingham: SRHE/Open University Press.

Tuxworth, E. (1989) Competence-based education: background and origins, in J.W. Burke, (ed.) *Competence Based Education and Training*. Lewes: Falmer Press.

Usher, R. and Edwards, R. (1994) *Postmodernism and Education*. London: Routledge.

Weick, K. (1988) Educational organisations as loosely coupled systems, in

A. Westoby (ed.) *Culture and Power in Educational Organisations*. Buckingham: SRHE/Open University Press.

Whyte, W. (1955) *Street Corner Society*. Chicago: University of Chicago Press.

Wilkinson, A., Redman, T., Snape, E. and Marchington, M. (1998) *Managing with Total Quality Management: Theory and Practice*. London: Macmillan Business.

Williams, G. (1997) The market route to mass higher education: British experience 1979–1996, *Higher Education Policy*, 10(3/4): 275–89.

Williams, S. (2000) The paradox of assessment: the effectiveness of the GNVQ as a preparation for higher education, *Journal of Education and Work*, 13(3): 349–65.

Williams, J., Dunning, E. and Murphy, P. (1984) *Hooligans Abroad*. London: Routledge & Kegan Paul.

Willis, P. (1977) *Learning to Labour*. Farnborough: Saxon House.

Willmott, R. (2002) Reclaiming metaphysical truth for educational research, *British Journal of Educational Studies*, 50(3): 339–62.

Winch, P. (1990) *The Idea of a Social Science*. London: Routledge.

Winch, C. (2002) The economic aims of education, *Journal of Philosophy of Education*, 36(1): 101–8.

Wittgenstein, L. (1953) *Philosophical Investigations*. Oxford: Basil Blackwell/Mott.

Wolf, A. (1995) *Competence-based Assessment*. Buckingham: Open University Press.

Woudhuysen, J. (1999) *CULT IT*. London: ICA.

Woudhuysen, J. (2000) Work Place as Play Pen. Paper presented at the Institute of Ideas Conference, Mind The Gap: Education and the Restructuring of Work, Canterbury Christ Church University College, 17 June.

Wright Mills, C. (2000) *The Sociological Imagination*, Fortieth anniversary edition. Oxford: Oxford University Press.

Yaffe, D. ([1976] 1998) *The State and the Capitalist Crisis*. http://www.rcgfrfi.easynet.co.uk/marxism/articles/

Young, M.F.D. (1971) *Knowledge and Control*. London: Macmillan.

Zeithaml, V. (1987) Defining and relating price, perceived quality and perceived value, *Request*, no. 87–101. Cambridge, MA: Marketing Science Institute.

Zukav, G. (1980) *The Dancing Wu Li Masters*. London: Fontana.

INDEX